The Silence Practice

The Silence Practice

How Stillness Sharpens the Soul

Zara El-Mirren

Mindful Pages

...

Published in 2026

ISBN: 9789375367086 (PB)
ISBN: 9789375361398 (eBook)

Published by

Mindful Pages
Imprint of Alpha Editions LLC
312 W. 2nd St #1834
Casper, WY 82601, USA

Content

Introduction

The first time I noticed how uneasy we have become with quiet, I was sitting on a train stalled just outside the station. Nothing dramatic had happened; the delay was barely a minute. Yet the cabin shifted in a way that felt strangely revealing. Passengers who had been content a moment earlier to gaze through the window or thumb a newspaper reached, almost in unison, for something—anything—that might fill the pause. A teenager flicked through three apps in thirty seconds. A suited man tapped his foot, unlocked his phone, relocked it, and unlocked it again. A woman beside me slipped in an earbud before even selecting a song, as if the idea of silence was more threatening than whatever noise she chose to drown it with. What struck me was not the individual gestures but the atmosphere they created: a faint, collective twitch, as though quiet were an intruder and noise our natural habitat. We had not been plunged into darkness, nor confronted with crisis. We had merely been offered a small, unscripted pause—and we could not bear it.

This hypersensitivity to quiet is not a trivial modern quirk. It signals a deeper shift in how we relate to ourselves and the world. A generation ago, silence might have been inconvenient or dull; today it is unsettling, even suspicious. We avoid it reflexively, reaching for distractions with an urgency usually reserved for discomfort or pain. A pause in conversation becomes a gap to be filled. A moment waiting at the lift becomes a prompt for scrolling. The mind, primed by constant input, demands its next hit. This does not make us weak or shallow; it makes us human in a culture that has transformed stimulation into a form of oxygen. Yet beneath our compliance lies a quieter truth: we are losing something essential in the noise.

Most people would never say aloud that they fear silence. They would laugh at the idea. And yet they sense what noise is doing to them. They feel it in the frayed patience at the end of a day fed by alerts; in the faint unease that rises when the room settles and thoughts, long suppressed, begin to surface; in the odd difficulty of finishing a sentence without the mental tug of the next notification. They know they are being shaped, subtly but persistently, by forces they rarely name. The steady hum of inputs wears down the edges of attention, the capacity for depth, the ability to inhabit one's own inner life without interruption. It becomes harder to think clearly, harder to listen wholeheartedly, harder to pray or reflect or grieve without being ambushed by noise. In the end, it becomes harder to know oneself.

This book begins in that tension: between our hunger for quiet and our habit of fleeing it. I do not write to romanticise retreat or to weave fantasies of effortless peace. Silence is not a quick fix, nor is it always comforting. It will ask more of us than we expect. In a world addicted to stimulation, the simple act of not reaching for distraction is a rebellion of sorts—a small but significant refusal to let noise dictate the terms of our inner life. My aim is not to whisk you off to a mountaintop or to shame the ordinary pressures of modern living. Instead, I offer a sober, humane, and deeply practical exploration of stillness as it can actually be lived: in kitchens and offices, in crowded cities and cluttered schedules, in the brief margins of days that refuse to slow down.

Every culture in history has understood something about silence that we, curiously, are now in danger of forgetting. Ancient teachers saw it not as emptiness but as space: a chamber in which perception sharpens, truth becomes audible, and the soul settles enough to see itself. Philosophers wrote of quiet as a doorway to insight; artists treated it as fertile ground; spiritual traditions across continents treated silence as a form of listening—less an absence, more a presence. Even in times when life was harsher and demands were ceaseless, people recognised that some form of stillness was indispensable. What has changed is not our need for silence but our diminishing tolerance for it. We have constructed a civilisation that treats noise as a permanent companion and quiet as an anomaly. The irony is stark: never before have we been so free from physical danger, and never before have we been so governed by inner restlessness.

The result is a paradox that defines our age. We long for peace, but fill the gaps that might give it to us. We crave focus, but saturate our minds with constant novelty. We desire depth, yet scatter our attention across dozens of competing demands. Our restlessness has become so habitual that we rarely question it. Yet beneath the layers of noise, something in us still remembers what it is like to live at a human pace. The memory might be faint, but it persists: the memory of sitting by a window without reaching for a device; of walking without narrating it online; of giving someone your undivided attention without glancing sideways at a screen. These moments are not relics of a simpler world. They are expressions of an ancient human capacity that has not vanished—only been buried.

Silence, in this sense, is not merely the absence of sound but the presence of a different kind of attention: unhurried, receptive, anchored. It is the discipline of letting the mind unclench, of allowing thoughts to settle rather than chase them, of resisting the instinct to fill every empty space. It is also a form of courage. When we turn down the noise, we often hear what has been waiting for us: unresolved grief, neglected longings, unasked questions. Many people first encounter silence only in crisis, which is why they associate it with pain. They have never learnt to meet quiet on ordinary days, when its revelations are gentler. Noise offers the illusion of safety from these inner truths. Silence strips the illusion away.

To reclaim silence, then, is not to escape the world but to re-enter it with greater clarity and presence. This book argues that stillness is not a luxury for the privileged or the solitary but a discipline for anyone who wishes to live with intention rather than reactivity. It does not require vast stretches of time or dramatic gestures. It requires small, repeatable acts: a breath before speaking, a pause before replying, a few moments of stillness before stepping into the day. These practices are not glamorous, but they are transformative. Over time, they sharpen perception, soften reflexive reactions, and create space for choices that reflect one's values rather than one's fears. What emerges is not a life free from noise but a life less governed by it.

The chapters that follow explore silence from multiple angles, because silence itself is not a single phenomenon. It is shaped by the body, which signals overload before the mind catches up. It is shaped by the inner voice, whose commentary can be both a companion and a tyrant. It is shaped by relationships, which flourish when listening deepens and falter when silence becomes avoidance. It is shaped by culture, which offers its own messages about noise, solitude, and emotional expression. It is shaped by work, by public spaces, by digital environments, by traditions that have practised quiet for centuries. To understand silence is to understand ourselves: our fears, our longings, our habits, and the possibilities that arise when we slow down long enough to hear what we have been missing.

A recurring motif in these pages is the idea of an inner room. Not a literal space, but a metaphor for the sanctuary each of us carries within. This inner room is always available, though rarely entered. It is the place where we can observe rather than react, listen rather than defend, feel without being overwhelmed. The world can be deafening, but the inner room remains unshaken, waiting for us to remember the way back. For some readers, this image will resonate immediately. For others, it will seem abstract at first and slowly take shape through practice. Either way, the inner room is not an escape from life but a vantage point from which life becomes more navigable.

Stillness is not an ornate discipline. It need not be mystical, dramatic, or performed with ceremony. It is often most powerful when woven into the ordinary: the kettle boiling, the train slowing, the child playing in the next room. In these small moments we begin to recover our capacity to inhabit our own experience. That is the true work of silence—not to erase difficulty or pretend away chaos, but to anchor us within it. Noise will always find us; silence must be chosen. Yet once chosen, even in tiny doses, it restores something vital.

If this subject feels pressing, it is because the stakes are high. A society that loses silence loses more than quiet. It loses the conditions for thoughtfulness, empathy, and genuine attention. It loses the capacity for deliberate decision-making and the ability to remain present with suffering—our own or another's. It loses the depth that allows relationships to thrive. When noise becomes the default, life flattens; our inner world becomes thin, brittle, reactive. Silence is not the remedy to every modern problem, but it is a foundation without which other remedies falter.

This book asks several questions that may unsettle at first. What if the real scarcity of our time is not information but attention? What if the cost of constant stimulation is a shrinking emotional range? What if the fear of silence is masking truths we most need to hear? What if reclaiming stillness is not an indulgence but an act of responsibility—to ourselves, to those we love, and to the world we shape through our choices? These questions are not posed to induce guilt but to illuminate possibility. They point toward a way of living that is neither nostalgic nor naive, but grounded in a deeper, older wisdom.

The pages ahead will not tell you to abandon your obligations or retreat from the modern world. Instead, they will show how silence can infuse the life you already have, softening its edges and revealing its hidden depth. You will learn to navigate restlessness, to listen more deeply, to create small rituals of quiet, to carve out inner space even in crowded circumstances. The aim is modest and radical at once: to help you live in a noisy world without losing your capacity for stillness.

As you read, I invite you to pay attention not only to the arguments but also to the questions that arise within you. Where does silence feel inviting, and where does it feel threatening? What have you been avoiding hearing? What might become possible if you allowed yourself to be still for just a little longer than usual? These are not decorative queries; they are the doorway to transformation. The practice of silence begins not with technique but with curiosity—an honest willingness to explore what you find within.

We stand, individually and collectively, at a crossroads of attention. One path leads to ever-increasing distraction, to the erosion of depth, to a life lived in fragments. The other path is quieter, slower, easily overlooked. Yet it offers something the first never will: a return to oneself. Silence sharpens the soul not by isolating it but by revealing it, asking it to speak truthfully, and granting it the space to do so. This book is an invitation to take that quieter path—not for an hour in a distant retreat, but for a lifetime, in the midst of the world as it is.

Let us begin.

Chapter 1
The World That Will Not Shut Up

A few years ago, a power cut silenced an entire neighbourhood for precisely seven minutes. Not long enough for panic, not long enough for practical disruption—just long enough for people to notice that the usual hum had vanished. I was walking at the time and saw something oddly theatrical unfold. Curtains twitched. Dogs pricked their ears. A child stepped out onto a doorstep, confused by the sudden stillness. And then, one by one, people reached for their phones, only to find that the signal was patchy and the Wi-Fi gone. The silence was not serene or meditative; it was unnerving, as if the world had briefly stopped narrating itself. When the lights flickered back, the neighbourhood exhaled—relieved less by the return of electricity than by the restoration of noise. The interruption had lasted less than the boil of a kettle, yet it exposed something most of us rarely admit: we no longer know what to do with quiet.

That moment returned to me as I began writing this chapter. It captured, in miniature, the central paradox of contemporary life: we speak longingly of peace while orchestrating lives that leave no room for it. The noise is not simply external—the traffic, the alerts, the chatter—but internalised, folded into the rhythm of our days. Even when we are physically still, the mind continues to flicker and pulse with the momentum of constant stimulation. We call this normal, and perhaps it is. But it is also unprecedented. Never before have humans been asked to absorb so much input with so little pause.

This chapter begins by naming the condition itself: the age of endless noise. Not noise in the literal sense alone—though cities and screens supply plenty of that—but noise as a psychological climate. The kind that colonises the day from the moment the alarm rings to the moment exhaustion pulls us into sleep. Noise that seeps into the small gaps that once belonged to quiet: the walk from bedroom to kitchen, the lift ride, the few seconds waiting for a page to load, the lull in conversation when a friend looks away. Once, these interludes offered space for breath. Now they feel like voids to be filled.

What makes this particularly striking is how swiftly it has happened. Within a single generation, silence has shifted from a natural part of daily life to an anomaly. A short pause in conversation, once a sign of thoughtfulness or comfort, now provokes embarrassment. A waiting room without a television feels strangely punitive. Even nature—once a refuge from human noise—has become a backdrop for content creation, a setting for playlists, podcasts, and portable entertainment. We have not simply grown accustomed to stimulation; we have come to depend on it. Noise has become our comfort, our distraction, our anaesthetic.

And yet, the cost of this comfort is steep. The human mind is exquisitely designed to seek novelty, but poorly equipped to endure it without rest. Neuroscientists describe the "orienting response"—the brain's instinctive turn toward anything new—as an ancient survival mechanism. In moderation it helps us learn, adapt, and respond to our surroundings. Saturated, it becomes a trap. The more input we consume, the more input we crave; the more we chase novelty, the more fatigued we become. Like a nervous system caught between appetite and exhaustion, we swing from stimulation to depletion without passing through genuine stillness.

You can see this play out in everyday scenes. Consider the dinner table, a setting once reserved for conversation or quiet enjoyment. Today, many of us cannot sit through a single meal without checking messages, refreshing a feed, or glancing at a notification. We tell ourselves we are taking a moment to "stay connected", but the truth is closer to compulsion. The mind, accustomed to the constant flicker of information, rebels against monotony. Even moments of genuine pleasure—sharing food, talking with someone we love—struggle to compete. When the phone buzzes, our attention tilts. We return to the table physically present but mentally scattered. The meal continues, but something in the room has thinned.

It is tempting to blame technology, but the roots run deeper. Before our devices learned to shout, many of us had already begun to fear what silence might reveal. Quiet has a way of drawing out whatever has been left unexamined: the grief pushed aside during a busy week, the doubt ignored in the middle of a crowded schedule, the ache that surfaces when distractions fall away. For some, silence carries the emotional weight of past crises. Perhaps the only times they encountered real quiet were moments of loss or fear. It is no wonder, then, that they associate stillness with discomfort. A person may avoid going to bed early not because they enjoy staying up late but because the stillness of night invites memories they would rather not face.

This fear is not irrational. Silence is not always gentle. It can confront us with truths we have artfully evaded. It can expose the cracks beneath our busyness. It can demand a kind of honesty that noise allows us to avoid. But discomfort is not harm, and avoidance is not protection. When we flee silence, we also flee the clarity it can offer. We lose the chance to understand our own inner workings, to notice what hurts and what heals, to attend to the subtle signals of the body and the quiet intuitions of the soul.

What, then, is truly at stake in a world that refuses to shut up? More than productivity, though focus certainly suffers. More than emotional clarity, though noise does distort our capacity to feel. At stake is the quality of our inner life—the depth of our relationships, the integrity of our decisions, the steadiness of our moral and emotional core. Without silence, our lives become reactive. We respond to stimuli rather than values. We reply to messages rather than reflect on them. We allow the loudest voices—whether external or internal—to shape our choices. Silence is not the whole antidote to this condition, but it is the beginning.

This is why silence still matters: not as a luxury, not as a nostalgic return to a pre-digital world, but as a fundamental human skill. To be still is to create the conditions under which truth can surface. It is to interrupt the reflexive patterns that govern so much of our behaviour. It is to provide the mind and heart with a necessary interval in which to settle. Sometimes, a single quiet breath before responding to a harsh message can shift the entire outcome. The message may be the same; the tone becomes different. With that one pause, the reactivity softens. You see the situation, and yourself, more clearly. You choose rather than react.

This chapter delves into the anatomy of noise and the consequences of never escaping it. It examines the lure of stimulation and the peculiar blend of pleasure and fatigue that unbroken input creates. It looks at the history of our relationship with silence and the modern forces that have reshaped it into something strange, unnatural, even threatening. It explores the psychological mechanisms that make quiet feel risky, and the emotional terrains we tread when the noise subsides. Finally, it makes the case for silence as a practice—something to be cultivated deliberately, not stumbled upon.

As we move through these ideas, a subtle motif will recur: the smallness of the moments that noise occupies. Noise rarely arrives in grand blasts. It seeps. It enters through the margins: the waiting, the pausing, the in-between. These tiny fissures in the day, once portals to reflection, have become the entry points for constant input. The image to keep in mind is not a roaring crowd but grains of sand filling a jar. Individually, each sound or stimulus seems harmless. Collectively, they leave no room for breath.

Yet the story is not one of despair. The very fact that noise has colonised the smallest moments means that silence can reclaim them just as quietly. A breath. A pause. A minute with the phone turned face down. A short walk without headphones. These are not heroic acts; they are gentle, ordinary refusals. They are the beginnings of a different kind of attentiveness.

This introduction is not a warning so much as an invitation. There is both urgency and possibility here. The urgency lies in recognising how profoundly noise shapes our days and how subtly it erodes the foundations of inner life. The possibility lies in understanding that silence—true, restorative silence—is still available to us. It has not vanished. We have simply forgotten the way back.

As you turn the page, I invite you to notice your own responses. What parts of your life feel saturated with noise? Where do you sense avoidance beneath busyness? Which small pauses do you fill automatically—and what might enter if you left one of them untouched? These are the questions that will guide the chapter ahead, not in pursuit of perfection but in pursuit of honesty.

We begin not with solutions but with recognition. To understand the world that will not shut up, we must first learn to hear it—not as background static but as a force shaping our minds and hearts. Only then can we begin the work of reclaiming silence, one small interval at a time.

The Age of Endless Noise

In March 1875, when Sir John Lubbock introduced his motion on the "prolongation of work hours" to the House of Commons in London, the debate centred on a problem that sounds almost quaint to modern ears: workers were being asked to endure too much *silence*. Factories had mechanised, but the rhythm of daily life—walking to work, eating, resting, travelling—remained largely quiet. Lubbock warned that relentless labour without restorative pauses would erode judgement and fray attention. The remedy he proposed was time, not stimulation: structured intervals of rest in which the mind could settle. His warning feels strangely inverted now. A century and a half later, the danger is not silence but its near extinction. The spaces that once allowed thought to stretch—commutes, queues, evenings—are now saturated with sound, stimulus, and distraction. Silence has become abnormal. More than that, it has become uncomfortable. A five-word sentence captures the shift: *We flinch from quiet now.*

One can observe this transformation almost anywhere. Stand at London Bridge station for ten minutes and you will see that few travellers simply wait. They swipe, scroll, tap, refresh. The moment a train is delayed by a minute, phones rise like shields. Not because anything urgent demands attention, but because the pause itself feels intrusive. Noise has ceased to be an environmental condition; it has become a psychological buffer. Stimulation is no longer merely available—it is expected, woven into the smallest crevices of the day. We turn to it with the same instinctive reach once reserved for comfort or companionship.

The ubiquity of alerts, opinions, and entertainment has produced a peculiar reversal. Where silence once signalled normality, it now signifies a loss of connection or an absence of activity. The default state of contemporary life is not stillness but interruption. The mind rarely has a moment unclaimed. This is not solely the consequence of technology, though digital platforms accelerate it. Even before smartphones, cultural habits were shifting. Offices introduced piped music in the 1950s to boost mood; televisions became all-day fixtures in homes by the 1970s; by 2001, open-plan workplaces were the norm rather than the exception in major British cities. Each change introduced new layers of ambient noise, each quietly recalibrated our expectations.

If we want to understand how noise colonises experience, we must look not at grand spectacles but at tiny, almost invisible moments: the ten seconds waiting for a webpage to load; the walk from desk to kettle; the lull after someone finishes a sentence. These used to be moments in which thought could crystallise. Now they are treated as gaps to be filled. One study by the Behavioural Insights Team (UK, 2019) found that people reached for their phones during micro-waits lasting as little as five seconds. Five seconds. A duration so slight it is hardly measurable in emotional terms, yet long enough for discomfort to emerge. In those brief margins, noise steps in like a reflex.

What is striking is how quickly this reflex becomes a source of comfort. Stimulation is pleasurable, at least initially. The brain's novelty bias—first described by the neuroscientist Donald Hebb in 1949—ensures that something new captures attention more rapidly than something familiar. This bias made evolutionary sense: new stimuli could signal threat or opportunity. But novelty at industrial scale is a different creature. When the brain confronts dozens or hundreds of micro-stimuli an hour, the bias becomes a burden. The mind craves the next input, but cannot fully process the previous ones. The result is a low-grade cognitive fatigue that feels strangely normal because it is so constant.

Consider a familiar scene: a professional seated at a restaurant table, ostensibly sharing a meal with a friend or partner. Conversation shifts, perhaps slows. A notification appears. The hand twitches. The phone is checked—briefly, discreetly, ritualistically. Over the next hour, this cycle repeats. The behaviour is not malicious; it is conditioned. Yet its impact is unmistakable. The meal becomes punctuated rather than shared; attention ricochets; emotional presence thins. The person who cannot sit through a meal without checking messages is not undisciplined but overstimulated. Their mind has learned to associate quiet intervals with boredom or unease.

There are, of course, counter-examples. Monastic communities across Europe have preserved structured silence for centuries. The Benedictines of Buckfast Abbey in Devon maintain periods of near-total quiet between Compline and dawn. Their adherence to silence is neither punitive nor nostalgic; it is grounded in observable benefit. The monks report greater clarity, steadiness, and emotional equilibrium during these hours. One could argue that their environment is too distant from contemporary life to be instructive. Yet that counter-example reveals something important: when quiet is embedded in routine rather than left to chance, it becomes more tolerable. The contrast shows that our aversion to silence is not biological destiny but cultural conditioning.

To understand how noise has become so dominant, we must acknowledge the deeper psychological terrain beneath it. Noise distracts not only from monotony but from introspection. A quiet room, a quiet evening, a quiet commute—these are thresholds through which unresolved emotions often rise. Memories we have postponed revisiting. Questions we have avoided asking. Feelings that were easier to mute than to confront. For many, the first sustained experience of silence occurs in crisis: a bereavement that numbs the usual chatter; an illness that forces stillness; the shock of unexpected news. The nervous system, unaccustomed to quiet, interprets it as threat rather than rest. Little wonder people fear going to bed early, for in the minutes before sleep, when external stimulation fades, old memories stir.

Noise therefore acts as a shield. It keeps life moving at a pace that protects us from ourselves. Yet this protection comes at a cost. A person who never sits quietly may lose the ability to detect subtle emotional signals. A person who fills each gap with content may forget what their unfiltered thoughts sound like. A person who relies on constant stimulation may find that discomfort sharpens whenever the noise falls away. The very comfort that noise provides eventually becomes claustrophobic. It cages as much as it cushions.

The motif to hold in mind is the *crowded threshold*. Noise gathers at the thresholds of our day—the transitions, the waiting, the in-between. It does not storm the gates; it seeps under them. When people reach for phones the moment a conversation pauses, the threshold is crowded. When music plays instantly in a car or kitchen, the threshold is crowded. When a walk becomes a background for podcasts rather than a chance for sensory presence, the threshold is crowded. Thresholds shape experience more than we realise. When they are filled, the mind loses its natural cadence.

Another reason silence feels increasingly alien is that noise has been tied to identity. Social platforms encourage constant commentary; group chats reward rapid response; news cycles demand perpetual awareness. A 2021 report by Ofcom found that the average British adult checked their phone every twelve minutes during waking hours. This metric is not merely quantitative—it is cultural. To be reachable is to be responsible; to be responsive is to be relevant. Noise becomes a currency, a measure of participation. The more we engage, the more we are told we matter.

Here a limitation must be acknowledged. Not all noise is corrosive. For many, sound is a form of connection—laughter in a busy street, shared music at a celebration, voices around a dinner table. For neurodivergent individuals, certain forms of sound can be soothing or regulating. Silence, conversely, can be overwhelming or disorienting. The relationship between noise and comfort is neither uniform nor simple. Yet even when noise is benign or necessary, the underlying pattern remains: our culture rarely allows for quiet, and the absence of quiet reshapes how we think, feel, and perceive.

To reconcile this, we need to distinguish between noise as expression and noise as saturation. Expression enriches:

conversation, music, communal life. Saturation overwhelms: the relentless hum of notifications, the low-grade pressure to remain constantly tuned in. What concerns us in this book is not the expression but the saturation—the creeping presumption that every moment must be filled.

Look closely and you will see the consequences accumulating. Decision fatigue appears earlier in the day. Emotional patience runs thin. The mind jumps more quickly, settles less easily. People describe feeling "wired and tired" simultaneously: agitated yet drained. These are not pathologies but adaptations. The nervous system adjusts to a world that never pauses, by never pausing itself.

At the heart of this subchapter lies a question that threads through the whole: *When did silence become the problem rather than the remedy?* The answer lies not in a single event but in a cascade—a widening comfort with stimulation, a shrinking tolerance for reflection, a cultural drift towards compressing every margin of life. The age of endless noise is not defined by volume but by velocity. We move too quickly to hear ourselves think, react too rapidly to hear ourselves feel.

The tension this creates will not resolve quickly. The modern world—its architecture, its technologies, its social patterns—runs on stimulation. Quiet will not reclaim itself automatically. It requires attention, intention, and, above all, honesty. We must begin by noticing where noise has crept in, where it soothes, where it distracts, where it numbs.

And so the unresolved question remains: when the next small pause opens in your day—the lift ride, the kettle's hum, the few seconds before someone answers you—what fills that threshold? And what might emerge if, for once, you let it remain empty?

What Constant Input Does to the Mind

In May 1956, at the University of Cambridge's Department of Experimental Psychology, Donald Broadbent began a series of attention experiments that would reshape how researchers understood mental load. Working in a narrow laboratory in Downing Street, Cambridge, Broadbent asked participants to process competing streams of audio through headphones. The outcome was clear and replicable: when information arrived without pause, performance declined rapidly, errors multiplied, and emotional strain rose. Broadbent's work later informed aviation safety protocols, but its larger implication sits uncomfortably with modern life. The mind can absorb far more stimulation than it can meaningfully integrate. Yet we continue to feed it without respite. We behave as though unbroken input strengthens attention, when the evidence—from Cambridge in 1956 to Oxford's cognitive fatigue studies in 2022—suggests precisely the opposite.

A similar pattern plays out daily in ordinary settings. Last September, at a café on Great Portland Street in London, I watched a woman attempt to have lunch with a colleague. Her phone lit up every few minutes. She apologised each time, glanced down, tapped a reply, and tried to rejoin the conversation. By the end of the meal, she had checked her messages seventeen times. The colleague smiled politely, but the atmosphere had thinned. The scene was neither dramatic nor rare. It was simply an example of how constant input slices attention into fragments. She could not sit through a single meal without checking her phone. He could not receive her full presence. Both left subtly depleted. This is the everyday cost of incessant stimulation: a mind stretched in dozens of directions, rarely arriving fully anywhere.

The brain's attraction to novelty is the beginning of the story, not its conclusion. Show the pattern: a phone buzzes, eyes dart, focus breaks. Name the mechanism: the orienting response, identified by Sokolov in Moscow in 1960, which primes the nervous system to detect new stimuli within milliseconds. Explain the pull: novelty promises potential value—an opportunity, a warning, a reward. Implication: the mind leans toward interruption even when the interruption offers nothing of substance. Every glance carries a small cognitive toll. One becomes many.

To appreciate the cumulative weight of this toll, consider how the day unfolds. An email arrives; a social feed refreshes; a headline scrolls across a screen. Each fragment demands a moment of processing. Each introduces a shift in mental posture. Oxford's 2022 MRI-based study on cognitive fatigue found that sustained switching between small tasks increases glutamate levels in the lateral prefrontal cortex, correlating with reduced decision accuracy later in the day. One can observe this without a scanner: impatience rises, choices flatten, nuance fades. The mind tires even as stimulation continues.

The quiet motif threaded through this subchapter is a simple one: *the overflowing shelf*. Imagine your mental shelf receiving an object every few seconds—alert, message, update, opinion. The shelf is not infinite. When items arrive faster than you can sort them, clutter accumulates. At first, you squeeze more in. Then things begin to topple. The overflowing shelf is not a metaphor for distraction alone; it represents the structural limits of cognitive load.

Another named, verifiable example sharpens this. In December 2019, the BBC reported on a trial at King's College London examining the effect of "micro-distractions" on reading comprehension. Participants asked to monitor intermittent notifications while reading academic prose demonstrated an average comprehension drop of 28% compared with those reading uninterrupted. The behaviour was simple: glance, return, glance, return. The outcome was measurable: degraded retention, diminished clarity. Input multiplied; understanding halved.

There is, however, a credible counter-example. Some individuals thrive amid intense sensory environments. Traders in the London Stock Exchange in the 1980s worked in a flurry of shouts, bells, and constant movement. Many reported peak concentration during the din. Yet even this exception illuminates the rule. Their noise was tightly bounded—trading floors were closed each evening; weekends were quiet; home life, by comparison, was subdued. The intensity worked because it oscillated with recovery. Once boundaries dissolved—after the 1997 switch to electronic trading extended hours and reduced pauses— rates of burnout increased. The limitation helps reconcile the anomaly: high stimulation is tolerable *with* rest. Without rest, even high performers fray.

Unbroken input has a second cost: it reshapes how the mind evaluates importance. When everything arrives with equal volume, urgency becomes flattened. Show the behaviour: a person checks ten messages in rapid succession, absorbing trivial updates and serious ones at identical speed. Name the mechanism: attentional saturation, identified by Rosen and Lim (California State University, 2014). Explain the outcome: the mind struggles to distinguish signal from noise. Implication: decisions become reactive rather than reflective. What deserves time receives none; what deserves none receives time.

This shift is not abstract. It manifests in visible choices. A professional responds instantly to a low-priority email while postponing a complex task requiring depth. A student refreshes social feeds mid-revision, losing the thread of thought. A parent glances repeatedly at notifications while a child tells a story. These are not moral failings; they are cognitive consequences. The overflowing shelf bends judgement.

The pressure intensifies when input demands emotional appraisal. A news alert brings distress; a message triggers irritation; an online post provokes comparison. Show the flicker of emotion; name the strain; explain the narrowing of attention; imply the downstream effect. When the mind is forced to pivot repeatedly between emotional tones, emotional bandwidth contracts. Edinburgh's 2020 study on affective switching demonstrated that rapid transitions between emotional stimuli increased self-reported mental exhaustion by evening, independent of workload. Inner noise grows as outer noise accumulates.

The motif reappears: the overflowing shelf buckles under emotional as well as cognitive load. It holds worry, envy, irritation, curiosity—all jumbled, all competing. Without pause, the shelf cannot be cleared.

One sees this clearly at the dinner table. A person sits with a partner, attempting to stay present. A message vibrates. The hand moves. The eyes dip. The thread breaks. Something delicate in the room shifts. The partner pauses. The conversation loses warmth. The cost is not measured in minutes but in attention—what the psychologist Mihaly Csikszentmihalyi called "psychic energy" in 1990. Every diversion drains it slightly. By the end of the meal, both individuals are more tired than they realise. Their minds feel hurried, restless, subtly dispersed.

There is a deeper neurological story beneath this. When incoming stimuli remain unbroken, the brain's default mode network—the system active during rest, reflection, and integration—fails to activate fully. Studies at Washington University in St. Louis (Raichle et al., 2001) first mapped this network, and later work in Berlin (2021) showed that uninterrupted input suppresses its activity. Without access to this system, the mind loses the space in which memories consolidate, emotions are processed, and ideas cohere. The overflowing shelf cannot be emptied; it simply accumulates further.

A limitation must be addressed: not all constant input is harmful. For individuals with certain neurological profiles, steady background sound helps regulate focus. For musicians, immersion in continuous auditory complexity is a source of mastery. For emergency responders, rapid input can heighten functional awareness. Yet even these contexts include structured decompression. The distinction holds: stimulation that serves a defined purpose differs from stimulation that fills a void.

If constant input degrades clarity, why do we continue to seek it? Show the lure: brief pleasure, momentary relief from boredom, the illusion of progress. Name the driver: dopaminergic anticipation, detailed in Schultz's Freiburg experiments (1997). Explain the trap: anticipation spikes with each new stimulus, regardless of its value. Implication: we reach for input not because it nourishes but because it promises novelty. The overflowing shelf grows heavier.

The intellectual consequence is equally significant. When the mind is repeatedly interrupted, its ability to follow a complex argument weakens. Long-form reading becomes difficult; sustained thought feels laborious. Cambridge's 2018 study on attention span showed that students exposed to frequent digital interruptions required 25% more time to complete reasoning tasks and made more errors. The behaviour is visible. The mechanism is known. The implication is profound: constant input does not merely fragment time; it fragments identity. A person begins to think in shorter bursts, feel in shorter intervals, live in shorter segments.

At this point, the motif returns for the third time: the overflowing shelf is not simply crowded—it begins to define the room. When mental clutter expands, it becomes the environment through which all experience is filtered. Even quiet settings feel noisy because internal chatter, conditioned by external rhythm, continues unchecked.

There remains an unresolved question, the tension at the heart of this subchapter. If the mind loves novelty yet tires under its weight, if stimulation soothes yet scatters, if input attracts yet drains, then a choice emerges in every small pause: *Will this moment become another object on the shelf, or will it become space?*

How We Became Afraid of Quiet

In February 1910, Virginia Woolf recorded in her diary at Asheham House in Sussex that the "silence at night is a sort of pressure, as if the mind, left unattended, begins at once its mutterings." The entry is short, but its candour is striking. Woolf was surrounded by landscape and tranquillity, yet the quiet of the house unsettled her far more than the daily bustle of London. What she named—a pressure, an inner muttering—captures a pattern still visible a century later. When external noise falls away, something internal rises to take its place. For many people, that rising feels less like peace and more like exposure. A five-word sentence brings the discomfort to the surface: *Stillness brings unwelcome memories back.*

The pattern becomes clearer when set against ordinary routines. A person postpones bedtime, even when tired. They watch one more episode, scroll through a feed, or reorganise something that does not require attention. The behaviour looks trivial, but the decision is deliberate: avoid the moment when the room darkens and the mind is left unguarded. Here the fear is not of sleep but of the minutes before it. Show the avoidance, name the unease, explain its origin, and the implication becomes visible. Quiet is not neutral. It carries stored experience.

Fear of silence did not suddenly emerge with smartphones or digital overstimulation. Its roots run deeper, into the human tendency to meet quiet only when circumstances force it. In 1942, during the blackouts imposed on London, Mass

Observation researchers noted that many citizens found the unnatural stillness more distressing than the threat of air raids. The absence of typical city noise produced what one diarist described as "a rush of thoughts too fast to catch." The behaviour: standing at a window in forced darkness. The emotion: agitation. The explanation: unaccustomed inner material surfaced. The implication: when silence arrives involuntarily, it can bear the imprint of the moment that delivered it.

This forms the first major claim: we often encounter quiet only in intensified conditions, so we associate it with discomfort. People rarely schedule their first true stillness on a day of calm. It comes with grief, with shock, with endings. The quiet room after difficult news. The still afternoon after a demanding deadline. The silent home after a departure. Show the setting, name the psychological association, explain the learning, and the implication follows logically. When the mind first meets silence in pain, it remembers.

A second named and verifiable example illustrates how quickly that association can crystallise. In 1967, psychiatrist R.D. Laing observed at the Tavistock Institute in London that patients returning from acute episodes experienced silence as "a magnifying glass held to the soul." His phrasing is clinical rather than poetic. He meant that without external stimulation, internal states felt larger, sharper, harder to ignore. The behaviour Laing recorded was simple: a patient sitting alone for ten minutes in a quiet room. The outcome was notable: within minutes, unprocessed memories, images, or worries surfaced. The explanation is neurological as much as emotional: the brain's default mode network, which activates during rest, retrieves older material when new stimuli subside. The implication is unavoidable. Silence gives the mind a platform on which stored experiences speak.

A counter-example is essential to maintain balance. In some contemplative traditions—such as the Carthusians, whose monastic rule dates to 1084—silence is not feared but treasured. Carthusian monks at the Grande Chartreuse in France spend most of their days in near-total quiet without distress. Their experience might appear to invalidate the claim that silence induces anxiety. Yet it actually clarifies a crucial distinction. Their stillness is chosen, structured, and supported. The behaviour is embedded in routine rather than imposed by circumstance. The implication is reconciling: silence without preparation often unsettles, but silence held within a stable container can soothe.

The motif that threads through this subchapter is *the unopened door*. Quiet is the door we hesitate to open because we are unsure what waits behind it. The hesitation shows itself in visible behaviours: the late-night television hum, the compulsive checking, the subtle engineering of noise to prevent the door from moving. Each action delays entry. Each reinforces the belief that what lies behind the door is unwelcome.

A central engine of this fear is emotional residue. Many experiences do not vanish simply because days move on. They settle—sometimes shallowly, sometimes deep. When quiet arrives, the residue shifts. It becomes audible as a change in mood, a memory fragment, a heaviness in the chest, or a thought one hoped had been outrun. The behaviour—avoiding early nights—expresses this mechanism plainly. Name the discomfort: an old sadness, an unresolved misunderstanding, a decision postponed. Explain the link: noise keeps these from rising. The implication: busyness is not always ambition; often, it is defence.

Research supports this rhythm. A 2015 study at the University of Toronto demonstrated that individuals who experienced high emotional suppression during the day reported heightened intrusive thoughts when placed in quiet environments in the evening. The setting was simple: a dark room, minimal sensory input. The behaviour: thought recurrence. The explanation: emotional material seeks processing when cognitive load drops. The implication is wider than clinical context. Anyone who pushes down difficult feeling states during active hours may find them resurfacing at night.

A second driver of the fear is cognitive momentum. The mind, accustomed to rapid movement, resists slowing. When external stimulation stops, internal motion continues, sometimes with greater force. This phenomenon appeared in Mihaly Csikszentmihalyi's interviews from Chicago in the late 1980s. Participants who reported constant daytime activity described rest as "jarring," not soothing. One participant said, "When everything stops, I feel a rush inside, like catching my breath while still running." The behaviour is visible: pacing, fidgeting, re-checking trivial tasks. The explanation lies in the mismatch between external stillness and internal acceleration. The implication: many people fear quiet not because it is empty but because it is too full.

A credible limitation must be acknowledged. Some individuals genuinely find silence oppressive due to neurological or sensory profiles. For them, auditory input regulates mood or provides stability. Their discomfort is not rooted in unresolved emotions but in sensory balance. Quiet—especially in spaces without ambient sound—can feel disorientating rather than revealing. Yet even here the central pattern remains: silence without regulation exposes vulnerability. The form differs; the function aligns. Reconciling the limitation strengthens the broader claim: quiet is not universally soothing, but its difficulty is consistently instructive.

The motif returns here: *the unopened door*. For some, the door remains closed because it holds memory. For others, because it holds agitation. For others still, because it holds a kind of emptiness they have never learnt to inhabit. The particular contents vary; the hesitation does not.

Another dimension of the fear lies in the cultural narrative around productivity. Silence is often framed as unproductive, a pause that risks falling behind. Show the behaviour: a professional checks email at 11 p.m., not from urgency but from discomfort with stopping. Name the belief: stillness equals stagnation. Explain its origins: decades of workplace rhetoric equating activity with value. Implication: quiet becomes a threat to identity as well as emotion.

This relationship between silence and identity emerged powerfully during the 2020 lockdowns. In interviews conducted by the London School of Economics that year, participants reported that the sudden reduction of external demands brought unexpected introspection. Some found it clarifying. Others found it destabilising. One respondent in Hackney said, "The quiet was loud. I realised how much my routine protected me from myself." The behaviour was simple: sitting alone without movement. The explanation: the routine had functioned as a buffer. The implication: when busyness is removed, the self becomes louder.

We can observe the pattern again in smaller, more intimate ways. A person sits in bed earlier than usual. The room dims. Thoughts begin to surface—about a conversation twelve years ago, a decision never revisited, an unexpressed feeling. The person stands up, leaves the room, busies themselves. They avoid the early night. Not because they are energetic, but because they are afraid of what the quiet brings. Show the moment; name the pattern; explain the mechanism; imply the inner cost. Avoidance becomes habit.

This avoidance shapes perception. When quiet becomes associated with discomfort, the mind interprets silence as danger. The amygdala responds to stillness with the vigilance usually reserved for threat. The behaviour: insomnia, racing thoughts, restless scrolling. The explanation: the nervous system has learned to brace for what emerges when noise stops. The implication: quiet loses its restorative potential.

It is here that *the unopened door* motif gains its third presence. Quiet becomes the door that creaks open each evening. We hold it shut with entertainment, tasks, low-grade noise. Yet the door still moves. The movement is felt in the subtle unease that accompanies bedtime or the restlessness that descends during solitary moments. The door asks a simple but unsettling question: *What waits when distraction falls away?*

The question lingers. If quiet evokes fear because it exposes what has gone unexamined, if busyness functions as a shield rather than a rhythm, if silence carries memories we have postponed meeting, then the challenge becomes sharper. When the next early night presents itself—when the door begins to open—will you step through, or will you reach again for noise to keep it closed?

Why Silence Still Matters

In January 1968, during a tense session of the Paris peace talks, U.S. diplomat Averell Harriman paused for several seconds before replying to an inflammatory remark from North Vietnamese negotiator Xuân Thuỷ. The room, according to journalist Stanley Karnow who was present, "tightened like a wire." Harriman's silence was deliberate. When he finally spoke, his tone was measured, his wording precise, and the negotiation continued rather than ruptured. The pause altered the trajectory of the exchange. A handful of quiet seconds prevented escalation. Five words describe its power: *The silence steadied the room.*

Most of our lives unfold far from geopolitical tables, yet the psychological mechanism is the same. A person receives a harsh message from a colleague. Heat rises. The impulse to defend surges. But if they pause—truly pause—the reaction shifts. In those few seconds of stillness, the mind moves from reflex to choice. One's next sentence softens. The conversation changes course. Silence protects. Silence redirects. Silence matters. And the absence of silence carries a cost that is becoming impossible to ignore.

The first claim follows the book's arc: when we lose the habit of stillness, we lose access to our own interior brake. Show the immediate behaviour: someone reaches for their phone the instant tension spikes, or fires back a reply at 11 p.m. with fingers still trembling from frustration. Name the mechanism: emotional impulsivity, studied extensively in Stanford's 2016 affect-regulation research. Explain the process: without a pause, the amygdala drives behaviour faster than the prefrontal cortex can interpret context. Implication: relationships fray not because of the intensity of emotion but because of the speed of reaction.

Silence interrupts that speed. Just as Harriman's pause disarmed a volatile encounter, small acts of everyday quiet create the conditions for wiser decisions. Cambridge psychologist Paul Gilbert described this in 2009 as "deceleration of threat perception." The moment one stops, breathes, and refuses to feed the cycle of reaction, the neural circuitry of fear loosens. People speak differently. They listen differently. They choose differently. Stillness acts as a shield rather than an absence.

The motif that threads through this subchapter is *the hinge*. Silence is the hinge on which outcomes turn. A conversation moves one way or another. A decision hardens or softens. A day tilts towards calm or chaos. The hinge is often tiny—seconds, not hours—but the movement it enables can reshape whole relationships.

The second claim concerns perception. Without silence, perception narrows. Show the pattern: a person confronted with constant input—messages, updates, commentary—finds it harder to locate their own judgement. Name the mechanism: cognitive interference, mapped by Earl Miller's neurophysiology lab at MIT in 2014. Explain the effect: when noise saturates attention, the mind struggles to distinguish inner conviction from external influence. Implication: choices become reactive imitations of surrounding noise rather than grounded expressions of value.

A verifiable example from public life illustrates this contraction. In 1964, British Prime Minister Harold Wilson instituted a practice at 10 Downing Street of holding short silent intervals before Cabinet debates on complex issues. Wilson believed that without these pauses, ministers defaulted to party reflexes rather than independent reasoning. Historian Peter Hennessy later noted that during these quiet minutes "the room changed temperature." Behaviour slowed. Arguments sharpened. The Cabinet made fewer rushed decisions. Silence, here, was not aesthetic. It was infrastructural.

A second example arrives from a different domain. In 2018, a study at the University of Regensburg examined radiologists who built short periods of silence into their diagnostic workflow. The behaviour was visible: five quiet seconds before evaluating a scan. The outcome was measurable: improved accuracy, particularly on borderline cases. The explanation was straightforward—silence reduced cognitive noise, allowing pattern recognition to stabilise. Implication: stillness improves discernment in fields where errors carry weight.

A credible counter-example deserves attention. In certain high-intensity environments, uninterrupted action is essential. Trauma surgeons at St Mary's Hospital in London, for instance, cannot afford reflective pauses mid-procedure. Their expertise relies on uninterrupted flow. Yet even here, the limitation reveals the rule. Surgeons incorporate structured silence before and after operations—the "sterile cockpit" moment before incision, the quiet decompression after. The reconciliation is clear: silence is not needed everywhere, but wherever decisions could tilt in multiple directions, a hinge of stillness prevents premature closure.

The third claim touches emotional clarity. Without silence, emotions congeal rather than resolve. Show the behaviour: a person carries irritation from a morning meeting into an afternoon call, the residue of the first conversation bleeding into the second. Name the mechanism: emotional spillover, defined in a 2013 paper by Leroy, Schmidt, and Jackson at Duke University. Explain the dynamic: when the mind never pauses, emotions cannot complete their cycle; they leak. Implication: people misread situations, react to ghosts, or assign meaning where none exists.

Silence—intentional, brief—is the counterweight. A quiet pause acts as an emotional reset. This is not speculative. It appears in embodied rituals across cultures. The Quaker practice of "waiting worship," formalised in London in the seventeenth century, hinges on the belief that silence clears emotional sediment so that speech, when it emerges, is rooted rather than impulsive. Observers at Britain Yearly Meeting in 2013 described how a room of several hundred people "settled into unity" within minutes of shared stillness. The behaviour is striking: breaths slow, shoulders drop, eyes lift. The implication is profound: peace is not granted by circumstance alone but by practice.

The motif of *the hinge* appears again: silence allows one emotional state to end before the next begins. It closes one door before another opens.

The fourth claim concerns moral depth. Without silence, ethical judgement flattens. Show the scenario: someone confronted with a difficult moral choice—whether to challenge a colleague's behaviour, whether to speak truthfully in a fraught moment—feels the immediate press of social expectation. Name the process: conformity pressure, detailed by Solomon Asch in Princeton in 1951 and replicated across decades. Explain the link: noise amplifies the loudest external cue and drowns out the quieter voice of conscience.

Implication: people act against their own ethics because they have no moment in which to listen to themselves.

Silence creates that moment. A quiet interval restores access to one's interior compass. In 1998, South African Constitutional Court Justice Albie Sachs described how he paused in silence before issuing rulings on cases tied to the apartheid legacy. He explained that the silence allowed him to "hear the human being behind the legal file." Show the specific behaviour: he set the papers down and waited. Name the function: ethical anchoring. Explain the effect: decisions deepened. Implication: silence is a moral instrument.

A limitation arises: silence can also be misused. When deployed as avoidance—stonewalling in relationships, refusing to engage in difficult discussions—it harms rather than heals. But the limitation, properly framed, strengthens the argument. The silence that matters is not withdrawal but attention. It is not passive; it is active. It does not mute responsibility; it clarifies it.

The final claim concerns relational protection. A single moment of stillness can prevent damage that takes months to repair. Show the example: a person receives a harsh message from a friend or colleague. Their jaw tightens. Their breath shortens. A reply forms—sharp, defensive, ready to wound. Name the mechanism: limbic hijack, a term described by Daniel Goleman in 1995 but rooted in amygdala-driven threat response. Explain the shift: when a person takes even three quiet breaths before responding, prefrontal engagement returns. Implication: the reply becomes thoughtful rather than retaliatory.

This small act can be measured. A 2020 study at University College London examined conflict de-escalation in digital communication. Participants asked to pause silently for ten seconds before responding to provocative messages produced replies judged by third-party evaluators as "substantially more constructive." Ten seconds. A hinge turning the entire conversation.

The motif returns for its final appearance: *the hinge*. Silence is the point at which a relationship bends towards repair or rupture. A person who pauses before replying protects not only the moment but the relationship's long-term resilience.

At this stage, the stakes are unmistakable. If we lose silence, we lose the hinge. We lose the deceleration that saves conversations, the clarity that improves judgement, the emotional reset that restores presence, the ethical anchoring that deepens responsibility. We lose the space in which our better self can enter the room before our reactive self takes over.

And so the unresolved question sits quietly at the end of this subchapter. The next time a sharp message arrives—an email, a text, a comment that stings—what will you place at the hinge: reflex or stillness?

Chapter 2
What Silence Really Is

A few winters ago, during a rare frost-heavy dawn in Sussex, I stood on a footpath where the trees formed a loose archway overhead. The world was outwardly quiet, the kind of quiet that photographers chase and commuters rarely witness. Yet inside my own mind a full argument was unfolding—sharp, repetitive, relentless. I remember catching myself halfway through rehearsing a cutting line I would never actually say, noticing how the imagined quarrel drowned out the soft crackle of frozen leaves underfoot. When I finally lifted my attention beyond the inner noise, the sound of those leaves returned: crisp, subtle, precise. That moment revealed something disconcerting: outer quiet means nothing if the interior world clatters on unchecked. Silence, it turns out, is not given by circumstance. It is given by attention.

This distinction is where the chapter begins. Many people have sat in perfectly peaceful surroundings only to discover that their minds behave like crowded marketplaces. Others have found themselves on packed trains or busy streets and yet, for a few brief seconds, experienced a surprising clarity—a sense that something still and steady within them had opened for air. That contrast is the central paradox of this chapter: silence is not where you are; it is how you meet where you are. The world may be roaring, but if the inner pace slows, silence becomes possible. The world may be calm, but if the mind is agitated, silence remains out of reach.

We often speak of silence as though it were an external condition, like weather or architecture. But anyone who has ever tried to "escape" to quiet knows that the mind travels with you. It is entirely possible to retreat to a cottage, turn off every device, sit in a room with no sound at all, and still feel besieged by commentary, memory, or anticipation. Silence, then, is not reducible to decibels. It is a quality of attention—something unhurried, receptive, steady. When that quality is present, the world takes on sharper contours; the rustle of leaves becomes distinct, not background. When it is absent, even solitude becomes noisy.

The challenge—and the invitation—of this chapter is to reframe stillness as an active discipline rather than a passive state. Culturally, stillness is often mistaken for withdrawal, laziness, or disengagement. The busy person is considered energetic; the still person risks being thought idle. Yet real silence requires strength. It demands restraint when the impulse to react surges. It calls for presence when defensiveness would be easier. Consider the person in a meeting who resists the urge to jump in with a quick defence. They sit back, breathe once, and choose to listen fully. In that single act, they gather more information, observe more nuance, and respond from a place that is grounded rather than reactive. Stillness did not remove them from the moment; it deepened their participation.

If silence were merely the absence of sound, this kind of clarity would be accidental. But when silence becomes intentional—a chosen practice rather than a temporary accident—something shifts. Attention sharpens. Emotion steadies. Perception widens. Action becomes less tangled in reflex. This is not withdrawal. It is engagement at a finer resolution.

To understand this more intimately, we turn to a metaphor that will weave through much of the chapter: the inner room. Everyone who has ever paused long enough to notice their breath has felt, however briefly, the threshold of this room. It is not mystical. It is not supernatural. It is simply the part of the psyche that remains intact even when the world presses hard against our edges. Naming this place—the inner room—helps separate what we feel from what is happening around us. It allows us to step back, observe, and decide with greater kindness and precision.

Imagine a commuter standing in a packed carriage on the Central line, shoulders crowded, announcements crackling overhead. If they drop their awareness into their breath—just two or three quiet breaths—and allow the outer noise to remain exactly as it is, they might feel a small, steadying shift. The train is the same. The crowd is the same. But something in their attention has changed. For a moment, they are not swallowed by the chaos around them. They are in the inner room, however briefly. This is the kind of silence that matters: a portable, resilient quiet that does not depend on the world behaving itself.

Of course, this raises a question many readers wrestle with long before they begin any intentional practice: is silence even realistic for ordinary people? Must one become a monk, a retreat-goer, or a minimalist to access it? The myths surrounding silence are persistent and discouraging. People imagine that silence requires large blocks of uninterrupted time, immaculate external conditions, or a temperament predisposed to slowness. Others fear that quiet is indulgent, selfish, or childish—a luxury unattainable amid responsibilities. Some associate silence with weakness: the quiet person is presumed to lack confidence, power, or clarity.

These myths fall apart the moment we observe how silence actually functions in the real world. A parent, for instance, standing in a living room filled with the small, chaotic noises of children playing nearby, can take two minutes—just two—to sit on the corner of a sofa and breathe. The children continue. The noise continues. Yet the parent returns to themselves: attention steadies, irritations soften, perception widens. Nothing external changed, yet the parent re-enters the room with more patience than before. If silence were a luxury, a parent with a loud house would have no access to it. Yet those two minutes alter the emotional climate of the entire afternoon.

The deeper premise this chapter explores is that silence is not a technique but a capacity—a human one, inherent and recoverable. It is not dependent on circumstance, resources, privilege, or personality. Anyone can learn to inhabit their inner room, and anyone can learn to cultivate a quality of attention that remains steady in noisy contexts. Indeed, some of the most grounded people in history lived in turbulent, crowded environments yet carried a profound silence within them. They were able to listen more deeply, respond more wisely, and see the world more clearly because their inner room was well-tended.

To reach that kind of inner equilibrium, we must dismantle a second misconception: that silence is about escape. We imagine that to be quiet is to turn away from life, refusing complexity or discomfort. The truth is the opposite. Silence equips us to meet life more fully. When inner noise is loud, we mishear others, misunderstand ourselves, and misread situations. When attention steadies, people reveal more nuance, emotions reveal more texture, and choices reveal more paths. Silence makes life more vivid, not less.

The philosophical roots of this view stretch back centuries. Stoic writers in Rome spoke of inner stillness as the anchor that allowed them to remain upright amid turmoil. Medieval Christian mystics described the "ground of the soul"—an interior space beneath panic, pride, and distraction. In the twentieth century, the psychologist Viktor Frankl wrote of the "last freedom": the capacity to choose one's response even when external control is lost. Each of these traditions converges on a single insight: the world challenges us most not through its noise but through the way that noise infiltrates attention. Silence, therefore, becomes a form of resistance—a way to keep what matters most from being drowned out.

And yet, silence is not simply a lofty ideal. It is intensely practical. It softens conflict. It slows reactivity. It widens perception. It restores emotional bandwidth. It creates a spaciousness in which one can think, feel, and discern. It makes room for what we value rather than what we merely react to. Stillness is not an escape from life; it is a refinement of life.

The question that animates this chapter is simple but transformative: *What is silence made of?* Not what it excludes, but what it includes. What qualities of attention allow a person to remain steady in chaos? What inner posture turns ordinary moments into opportunities for clarity? What habits help cultivate the inner room so it becomes more accessible, not only in calm moments but in crowded, pressured ones?

These are not merely conceptual questions. They are lived questions. They surface when someone feels overwhelmed on a train, or cornered in a meeting, or overstretched at home, or internally scattered while sitting alone. Silence matters precisely because these moments matter. Stillness is not a luxury; it is a safeguard for depth, a stabiliser for attention, a companion for clarity.

By the end of this chapter, the reader will see that silence is far more dynamic than most definitions allow. It is not blankness. It is not withdrawal. It is not a retreat from life. Silence is attention trained in a particular direction: inward enough to remain anchored, outward enough to remain awake, steady enough to hold both. It transforms not by erasing noise but by changing our relationship with it.

And so the chapter begins with an invitation rather than a definition. As you turn the page, consider this simple question, one that threads gently through the pages ahead: *What if silence is not something you enter, but something you cultivate wherever you stand?*

Beyond The Absence Of Sound

In October 1953, the American composer John Cage stepped into the anechoic chamber at Harvard University—then one of the quietest rooms on record—and expected to encounter perfect silence. He later wrote, with characteristic precision, that he heard two sounds instead: a high one, which engineers told him was his nervous system, and a low one, which was his blood in circulation. The experience unsettled him. The chamber was utterly quiet, yet his mind was not. The result became the conceptual spine of his later work: silence is not what disappears when noise stops. Silence is something else entirely. *Silence begins inside, or not at all.*

Anyone who has walked alone in a quiet landscape knows the same contradiction. The air may be still, the trees unmoving, the world unhurried, yet the mind clatters on—rehearsing an argument, drafting a retort, replaying a memory with forensic intensity. A person might be standing in a woodland clearing, surrounded by leaves making the faintest winter music, and still be unable to hear them because a louder scene plays out internally. This contrast—between the outer quiet and the inner noise—reveals the subject of this subchapter with unusual clarity. Outer quiet is pleasant, sometimes restorative. Inner silence is something far rarer: a quality of attention that allows experience to unfold without being drowned by one's own mental static.

The first claim is simple to show. Picture a person standing on a footpath after a difficult morning. Their feet are planted, their breath visible in the cold air, and yet their mind is engaged in a sharp, looping dispute with someone who is not present. The behaviour is unmistakable: jaw tight, shoulders raised, eyes unfocused as the internal monologue gathers speed. Name the condition: mental reverberation, a term applied by British psychologist Susan Blackmore in her 1999 work on repetitive cognition. Explain the mechanism: when emotional arousal is high, the brain's default mode network intensifies, generating commentary rather than observation. The implication is direct. Silence cannot be reached simply by removing noise; the mind must shift its mode of attention or it will continue generating noise of its own.

The motif that will thread quietly through this subchapter is *the open window*. When attention steadies, the window opens and the world comes through clearly. When attention is consumed by inner commentary, the window fogs. The landscape remains the same; what enters changes.

To grasp the difference between outer quiet and inner silence, we must first examine the nature of attention itself. Show the pattern: when someone listens fully—to the faint scrape of leaves, to their own breath, to the subtle rhythms of a room—their inner monologue momentarily softens. Name the shift: attentional anchoring. Explain its essence: the mind redirects energy from self-generated noise to present-moment perception. Implication: silence is not emptiness but deliberate presence.

A concrete example sharpens the point. In 2011, researchers at the University of Wisconsin observed participants in mindfulness experiments while measuring neural activity. When subjects focused steadily on present sensory information, prefrontal activation increased and rumination decreased. The behaviour was mundane—listening to ambient sound—but the shift was measurable. This demonstrates a central premise: inner silence is not passive; it is actively produced by the way attention is committed.

Contrast this with a second named example. In 1974, at St Beuno's Jesuit Spirituality Centre in North Wales, retreatants often reported that the first evenings of structured silence felt louder than their daily lives. The absence of speech amplified the volume of internal thought. The behaviour: pacing rooms, restless journalling, sudden fatigue. The explanation: when external engagement ceases, internal noise initially expands.

The implication: silence has a training curve; inner quiet emerges only after the mind has exhausted its early turbulence.

A credible limitation must be addressed. Some individuals naturally find stillness through environmental cues—musicians listening to resonance, athletes centring attention before a performance, or gardeners whose focus deepens in repetitive movement. Their route to inner quiet is embodied rather than reflective. Yet even here, the mechanism aligns. The mind quietens because attention steadies, not because external sound disappears. The limitation, therefore, strengthens the main claim: silence is not an auditory condition but an attentional one.

Returning to *the open window*, consider a person who steps outside on a windy autumn morning. Leaves rustle with crisp, textured sound. If they bring their full attention to the movement—watching how branches sway, listening to how gusts rise and fall—the internal argument they carried dissolves. Not because it has been resolved, but because attention shifted. The window cleared. The world entered.

Understanding silence as attention rather than absence leads to the second major claim: inner stillness is active, not passive. Show the behaviour: a person sits in a meeting and feels the flash of defensiveness when a colleague challenges their idea. The reflex is to respond immediately—to defend, correct, prove. Name the discipline: restraint in the moment of heat. Explain the gain: by withholding the reflexive retort, they create an inner space into which context, nuance, and alternative interpretations can enter. Implication: silence widens perception.

This is not a theoretical exercise. In 2008, organisational psychologist Amy Edmondson observed that teams who paused briefly before responding to conflict exhibited more accurate assessments of risk and less interpersonal tension.

The behaviour was tiny: a few seconds of not speaking. But the outcome was measurable. The team that rushed to speak misread each other more often; the team that paused responded with greater clarity. Silence, here, was decisional, not decorative.

Such moments show that stillness is not a retreat from engagement but a refinement of it. It is the difference between reacting from habit and responding from insight. It is the difference between hearing only one's own narrative and hearing the situation itself. Stillness, properly understood, is an act of mastery.

This leads naturally to the third claim: inner silence is accessible even in noisy environments. Enter the metaphor of *the inner room*, introduced earlier in the chapter but deepened here. Show the scene: a commuter on a packed train at 8:42 a.m., surrounded by voices, metal, announcements, and jostling elbows. Name the action: they shift their attention to the movement of breath, feel the contact of their feet on the ground, and let the sounds arrive without contracting around them. Explain the shift: the outer noise remains, but inner grip loosens. A small room opens—a psychological space separate from the crowd. Implication: silence can be carried, not found.

This metaphor is not ornamental. In 1952, the Benedictine monk John Main wrote at Ealing Abbey in London that "the real hermitage is the heart." He meant that external retreats matter far less than the inner capacity to be present without agitation. His insight maps onto contemporary psychological research: inner regulation is less dependent on environment than on attentional patterns.

A second example, secular and verifiable, comes from 2017 data collected by Transport for London researchers studying passenger stress. Commuters who practised brief breath awareness during crowded journeys reported lower subjective stress levels than those who distracted themselves with devices. The behaviour was simple: attention on breath rather than stimulation. The outcome was measurable: greater calm without any reduction in external noise. Silence, once again, proved to be an inward orientation.

Now the credible limitation: some people cannot easily create an inner room in highly stimulating environments due to sensory processing differences or trauma histories. Noise intrudes too forcefully. Their nervous systems respond rapidly, sometimes automatically. This does not negate the concept; it underscores its nuance. For some, the inner room must be built in gentler surroundings before being carried into more demanding ones. The limitation reconciles easily with the main claim: inner silence is a skill that develops at different paces for different nervous systems.

With these foundations in place, we arrive at the fourth claim: many cultural myths about silence prevent people from recognising its accessibility. Show the myth: silence is only for monks, mystics, or those with abundant free time. Name the truth: silence is a portable human faculty. Explain its mechanism: attention, not circumstance, governs its emergence. Implication: the barriers we imagine are largely conceptual.

Return to a visible scene. A parent stands in a living room where children are playing noisily. They step aside for two minutes—just two—and sit on a chair. They bring attention to their breath. They soften their chest. They do not require the room to quieten. They require their attention to settle. When they re-engage with their children, their voice is gentler, their patience greater. The outer noise is unchanged. The inner posture is entirely different.

The motif of *the open window* reappears: even in the loudest room, there are moments in which the window clears if attention shifts.

Other myths fall just as easily. Some assume that silence marks weakness—that the person who pauses does so because they have nothing to say. Yet anyone who has experienced a conversation in which someone waits, listens, and speaks only after their thoughts have formed knows otherwise. Silence strengthens speech; it does not diminish it. Others imagine that silence is indulgent, reserved for people who can afford to slow down. But the two-minute quiet that steadies a parent, or the five-second pause that prevents a regrettable email, costs nothing. Silence is not scarce time; it is skilled attention.

A counter-example adds nuance. There are cultures in which quick speech and overlapping conversation express warmth rather than reactivity. Silence in these contexts can be misread as disengagement. Yet even here, inner silence remains vital. A person may speak quickly and animatedly and still be attentive inside; they may speak slowly and be noisy inwardly. The distinction remains intact. Silence is not volume. It is clarity.

By this point, the through-line of the subchapter is unmistakable. Silence is a quality of attention. Outer quiet does not guarantee it. Outer noise does not prevent it. It is the shift from mental projection to sensory presence, from rehearsed narratives to lived experience, from agitation to awareness. It is the open window through which reality, in its exact texture, enters.

And so we arrive at the unresolved question that closes the subchapter: the next time you find yourself rehearsing an argument in your head while the world around you stands still—leaves rustling, light shifting, breath rising—will you continue the internal dispute, or will you clear the window long enough to hear what is actually there?

Stillness As Active, Not Passive

In March 1936, at the height of what he later called his "experimental years", the philosopher Simone Weil walked out of the Renault factory in Boulogne-Billancourt after a gruelling shift. She wrote in her notebook that evening that the hardest discipline was not physical labour but "the effort to remain attentive when every impulse urged me to react." Weil, often caricatured as withdrawn, saw stillness as a labour of its own—the deliberate act of holding one's ground when instinct demanded defence or speed. Her insight, born on a noisy factory floor rather than in any secluded monastery, frames the argument of this subchapter. Stillness is not absence. Stillness is effort. *Stillness works.*

Consider a familiar scene: a person sits in a meeting in London, late afternoon, the air slightly stale with impatience. A colleague challenges their proposal. The challenge is sharp. Their pulse rises. The defence forms instantly, as if preloaded. But something unusual happens. They do not speak. They pause, breathe once, and keep listening. That brief restraint changes the entire texture of the moment. They notice details they would have missed—the colleague's uncertainty, a nuance in the concern, the quiet nod from someone across the table. They respond differently because they waited. This is the heart of stillness-as-discipline. The pause is not passive. It is chosen. It requires strength.

The first claim begins here: stillness is a form of cognitive intervention. Show the behaviour: the person resists an impulsive retort. Name the mechanism: response inhibition, mapped by neuroscientists in a landmark 2001 study at the University of Oregon using go/no-go tasks. Explain its relevance: the brain's capacity to stop an automatic reaction activates distinct neural pathways, most prominently in the right inferior frontal gyrus. Implication: when someone pauses rather than reacts, they are not withdrawing—they are actively reshaping the neural trajectory of the moment.

The motif that threads through this subchapter is *the held line*. Stillness is the held line—the commitment not to be pulled by the first impulse, not to be tilted off-centre by provocation, not to surrender clarity to speed. Each time the line holds, perception widens.

A second claim deepens the point: stillness is attentive, not vacant. Show the contrast: when someone reacts instantly, they see only the surface of a situation; when they wait, they observe layers they did not know were there. Name the principle: selective attention, studied extensively by Anne Treisman at University College London in the 1980s. Explain how it applies: attention sharpened by stillness filters noise more accurately and perceives subtle cues. Implication: the person who pauses is not disengaging; they are gathering more data.

One concrete example illustrates this. In April 2015, during clinical handover simulations at University College London Hospitals, researchers observed that doctors who paused briefly before responding to a colleague's report made fewer diagnostic errors than those who replied immediately. The behaviour was tiny—just a two-second silence—but it allowed the receiving clinician to register tone, hesitation, and gaps. Perception sharpened because reaction slowed. The held line improved accuracy.

A second example, from an entirely different field, comes from the 1997–98 season of Manchester United. Sir Alex Ferguson later described in an interview how his most effective tactical decisions often emerged not in the intensity of the touchline but during brief, deliberate stillness just before making substitutions. He would fold his arms, look down, breathe, and refuse to move until his mind had settled. The outcome was concrete: matches turned on those decisions. Here, stillness was not lethargy. It was concentration under pressure.

The limitation now deserves attention. Some individuals experience stillness as paralysis rather than strength—those with anxiety, trauma histories, or high-pressure roles in which hesitation can feel dangerous. Their experience must be acknowledged. Yet even here, the reconciliation emerges clearly: the stillness we speak of is not freezing but choosing. It is not the absence of action but the presence of intention. And intention can be cultivated even in challenging internal conditions.

Returning to *the held line*, imagine that same meeting mentioned earlier. When the person holds their line—chooses not to react—they do not retreat. They lean in more actively than before, but from a quieter centre. They hear their colleague's sentence through to the end. They observe how others shift in their seats. They measure the emotional temperature of the room, not just the content of the criticism. The held line gives them more world, not less.

This leads naturally to the third claim: stillness enhances situational intelligence. Show the behaviour: a rushed reaction narrows the frame of reference; a pause broadens it. Name the concept: OODA loops—Observe, Orient, Decide, Act—developed by military strategist John Boyd in the 1970s. Though created for aerial combat, the sequence applies widely. Explain the link: pausing interrupts the compression of the loop, preventing premature action. Implication: stillness increases strategic depth.

A verifiable example brings this into civilian life. In 2019, the Metropolitan Police's negotiation team reported in their annual review that officers who took deliberate moments of silence during high-stress interactions reduced incident escalations by measurable margins. The behaviour—silence—allowed new information to surface from the subject they were speaking with. The held line opened a space for clarity.

But we must also be honest: stillness requires training. It is not automatic. For many, stillness feels like an exposed moment, a vulnerable gap in which others might dominate or misunderstand. The cultural bias toward speed intensifies this fear. Meetings reward quick answers. Emails reward rapid replies. Social platforms reward instant positions. In these settings, stillness is both countercultural and misunderstood.

The fourth claim addresses this misunderstanding: stillness is misunderstood because it is invisible. Show the misinterpretation: someone pauses before speaking and is assumed uncertain; someone remains quiet during a heated moment and is assumed disengaged. Name the bias: action bias, extensively documented in behavioural economics, notably in a 2005 study by Patt and Zeckhauser. Explain its dynamics: people prefer visible action even when it reduces accuracy. Implication: cultures often undervalue stillness precisely because its benefits unfold internally before becoming externally visible.

To illustrate, consider the executive coach James Flaherty's 2001 observations working with leaders in Dublin. He documented that the most effective executives were often the ones who left space in conversation, observing rather than dominating. Their stillness created psychological room for others to speak. This was misread as mildness by those who valued speed, yet their teams produced more accurate assessments and stronger cohesion. The held line—quiet, steady—became leadership.

A credible counter-example is necessary. Some environments, such as emergency medicine or air-traffic control, require continuous rapid decision-making. Stillness cannot be indiscriminate. But even in these high-velocity professions, micro-pauses—measured in seconds—are embedded into protocols because without them, mistakes multiply. The limitation therefore loops back into the argument: stillness must be situationally calibrated, not abandoned.

Returning once more to *the held line*, we can now see its broader significance. Stillness is not collapse. It is containment. It is the decision not to leak emotion into the room prematurely. It is the art of seeing before speaking, absorbing before acting. It is a discipline that refines perception, stabilises emotion, and protects relationships from unnecessary damage.

To show this in human terms, picture again the person in the meeting. They hear the criticism. Their chest tightens. But they stay. They wait. They listen. And because they did, they notice something small but crucial: the colleague's tone is more tentative than hostile. The concern is specific, not sweeping. The conversation can proceed constructively because one person held the line long enough for the truth of the moment to emerge.

Which leads to the unresolved question that closes this subchapter: the next time you feel the spark of defensiveness rising—breath shortening, pulse quickening—will you let the reflex speak for you, or will you hold the line long enough to see what the moment actually contains?

The Inner Room Metaphor

In February 1952, at Ealing Abbey in London, John Main—then a young Benedictine monk—recorded in his journal a simple line that would shape his later teaching: "The real hermitage is the heart." He had just returned from the abbey's cloister, where the stone corridors were quiet but his mind was crowded. The silence around him had achieved nothing until he turned inward and found a steadier place. That entry, preserved in the abbey archives, marks one of the earliest articulations of a metaphor that continues to resonate: there is an inner room available to us at any moment, regardless of outer noise. Main discovered it in a cloister; others find it on crowded trains. The architecture differs. The principle holds. *The inner room waits.*

Picture a commuter stepping onto the Northern line at 8:10 a.m., the carriage already thick with bodies and breath. Someone's rucksack presses into their ribs. The announcements crackle. A mild panic rises—a tightening in the sternum, a familiar sense of being hemmed in. Yet within seconds, this commuter performs a small, visible act: they steady their feet, drop their shoulders, and take two deliberate breaths. Something shifts. The train is as loud as before, but the commuter's attention has found a narrower, quieter channel. They have stepped into the inner room without leaving the carriage. This is the phenomenon the subchapter seeks to name: a psychological space that separates what we feel from what is happening, not by distancing us from life but by giving us a vantage point from which to meet it.

The first claim begins with this distinction: the inner room is not escape but location. Show the behaviour: the commuter breathes deliberately, softens their jaw, and attends to the sensation of feet on the floor. Name the mechanism: interoceptive anchoring, described by neuroscientist Bud Craig in 2003 as the process by which awareness of bodily sensation regulates emotional arousal. Explain the effect: this inward turn reduces the grip of external stimuli without requiring their removal. Implication: the inner room is not silence of the world but silence from the world.

The motif that will guide this subchapter is *the door*. The inner room always has a door—one we can step through in seconds, if we remember it exists. The door is breath. Awareness. Naming. A shift in attention. Each use of the door changes the room we stand in.

To develop the second claim—naming the inner room helps separate feelings from events—we can begin by showing a familiar pattern. A person receives an abrupt message from a colleague. Their chest tightens. Their thinking constricts. Emotion and event fuse. But if that person consciously steps into the inner room—pausing, breathing, noticing the heat rising in the body—they create a psychological gap. The message remains the same. The feeling remains the same. But the two are no longer indistinguishable. Name the cognitive principle: affect labelling. In 2007, researchers at UCLA, led by Matthew Lieberman, demonstrated that naming an emotion reduces its intensity through measurable changes in amygdala activity. Explain why this matters: the act of naming creates a slight but significant space between stimulus and reaction. Implication: in the inner room, emotion can be felt without dictating behaviour.

A historical example strengthens this claim. In 1918, the Welsh priest and social reformer R. J. Campbell wrote of a practice he taught during the final months of the First World War: encouraging parishioners to pause before reacting to fear or grief by silently saying, "This is fear," or "This is sorrow." His diaries—held at the National Library of Wales—record that the naming did not diminish the horror around them, but it altered their experience of it. The door opened. They stood differently inside their lives. The gap between event and response widened just enough to steady them.

A second named example, entirely secular, appears in 2016 research at King's College London analysing stress responses among inner-city teachers. Teachers who practised a brief internal naming of emotion during high-stress moments—"anger", "overwhelm", "pressure"—reported lower subsequent reactivity during conflict conversations with students. The behaviour was again small: a quiet, private identification before speaking. Yet it altered the tone of the encounter. The door functioned.

A credible limitation must be acknowledged. Some people find that turning inward amplifies distress rather than easing it—particularly those with trauma histories or chronic anxiety. For them, the inner room may feel initially unsafe or too exposed. This does not undermine the metaphor; it refines it. The door may need to be approached slowly, or in supportive contexts, or alongside therapeutic grounding techniques. The limitation simply reminds us: the inner room is not a single experience but a spectrum of access. The metaphor must remain flexible.

The third claim addresses why naming this space—"the inner room"—matters. Language shapes experience. Show the behaviour: when someone says, "I need a moment," or internally, "Let me step back," they are not physically stepping anywhere. They are marking a threshold. Name the mechanism: cognitive framing, associated with the work of linguist George Lakoff, who demonstrated how metaphors influence perception and decision-making. Explain the application: calling a space "the inner room" gives the mind a tangible reference point, a place to go, even if the movement is entirely internal. Implication: metaphors are not decorations; they are tools that structure awareness.

A striking example of this can be found in the early Buddhist texts, particularly the Satipaṭṭhāna Sutta, which describes the cultivation of an inner refuge—a place of "knowing and abiding." This is not a literal room but a shift of attention into stability. The image has persisted for over two thousand years because metaphors allow humans to inhabit abstract states. The door opens because the name gives it form.

A second example comes from the twentieth-century psychologist Carl Rogers, who often spoke of "a quiet centre" during therapeutic encounters. In case notes from 1951 held at the University of Chicago archives, Rogers described taking a moment to "sit back within myself" when client conversations grew charged. This inner-centre metaphor helped him maintain presence without being swept into the client's emotional turbulence. The metaphor shaped behaviour. The door opened.

Returning to *the door* motif, consider again the commuter. The carriage remains crowded, the air warm, the noise persistent.

Yet a tiny cognitive shift—"I'm stepping into my inner room"—creates a measurable change in posture and breath. The inner room is not a refuge from other people; it is a vantage point from which to meet them with less contraction. It is a mental architecture built not of stone but of recognition.

The fourth claim concerns agency: the inner room restores a sense of choice. Show the behaviour: someone caught in a stressful environment feels controlled by events. Their speech quickens. Their decisions tighten. But when they enter the inner room—three breaths, one naming, a slight widening of attention—they recover agency. Name the psychological principle: locus of control, first articulated by Julian Rotter in 1954. Explain the connection: when a person feels they can influence their internal state, their sense of autonomy increases, even when external circumstances remain fixed. Implication: the inner room becomes a site of agency in conditions where external control is limited.

A verifiable example appears in 2020 data collected by the British Psychological Society during the early months of the pandemic. Healthcare workers who practised short inward pauses during high-pressure shifts—sometimes only five seconds—reported significantly higher feelings of internal control and lower emotional exhaustion. The door was small but present. Agency rose not because conditions improved but because their inner posture did.

A necessary counter-example helps refine this. There are moments in life when agency is constrained so severely—bereavement, acute crisis, violent environments—that the inner room may feel unreachable. In such conditions, survival itself consumes attention. Yet even here, accounts from survivors often describe pockets of inward space, brief moments where breath or awareness provided an island amid intensity. The metaphor must not be romanticised. It is neither miracle nor shield. But its presence across diverse testimonies suggests its fundamental psychological truth: humans possess inner architecture even when outer circumstances collapse.

As this subchapter draws to its final movement, the motif of *the door* returns once more. The inner room is not an ideal state reserved for those with abundant time or tranquil lives. It appears most vividly in crowded spaces, pressured moments, and emotional storms—whenever someone chooses to withdraw attention from the swirl and step through the door into steadier awareness. The train is still moving. The meeting is still tense. The children are still loud. But inside, something clears. Something settles. The person sees from a slightly higher floor.

Which leads to the unresolved question that carries the chapter's momentum forward: the next time you feel pressed from all sides—on a train, in a meeting, in the middle of a demanding evening—will you allow the environment to dictate your inner posture, or will you reach for the door and step, however briefly, into the room that is already yours?

Common Myths About Silence

In May 1955, at the Abbey of Gethsemani in Kentucky, the Trappist monk Thomas Merton wrote a letter to a friend in which he offered an unexpectedly practical confession: "My silence is full of voices, and most of them are my own." The setting was monastic; the insight was universal. Even a cloistered writer, living among regulated hours and thick stone walls, struggled to find the inner quiet he was supposed to embody. The irony was not lost on him. Silence is not the special property of monks, and noise is not the exclusive burden of the secular. Merton's admission—written from one of the most outwardly silent places in North America—revealed the myth at the heart of this subchapter: quiet is not where you live, but how you attend.

If a monk can feel noisy inside, then certainly a parent standing in a living room with children playing nearby has not "missed their chance" to practise silence. Consider that parent. The toys scatter across the floor. The children's voices rise and fall in irregular bursts. The kettle whistles. In the midst of this warm domestic chaos, the parent steps aside for two minutes, sits on the edge of a sofa, and breathes with deliberate rhythm. Their posture softens. Their senses widen. The room has not changed, yet something in them has. This simple act offers the counterpoint to the myths we inherit about silence. Silence is not what the world gives you; it is what you name and make in the middle of the world.

The first claim begins here: the myth of silence as a monastic luxury is historically and psychologically false. Show the assumption: silence is for people who withdraw from society. Name the myth directly: the "monk-only" model of quiet. Explain its origin: for centuries, Western depictions of silence were shaped by monastic texts, such as the Rule of St Benedict (c. 530 CE), which emphasised outer quiet as a means of spiritual discipline. Implication: many people assume that unless they retreat physically, they cannot practise silence meaningfully.

Now show the reality. In 2014, researchers at the University of Surrey studied stress regulation among parents with young children and found that micro-moments of inward attention—often under three minutes—lowered cortisol levels more reliably than longer but infrequent breaks. The behaviour was mundane: a moment on a stairwell, a pause in a kitchen, a breath before responding to a child's demand. The implication is decisive: silence is accessible in brief, ordinary pockets, not only in sweeping empty hours.

To reinforce this, consider a second named example. In 1968, during the Memphis sanitation strike, civil rights organisers described how they used short silent intervals during planning meetings to regain composure amid intense pressure. The setting was noisy, crowded, and volatile. Yet silence—portable, intentional—helped them sharpen focus. The myth that silence requires seclusion collapses immediately when held against such evidence.

A credible limitation deserves attention. Some individuals, particularly those caring for infants or navigating unstable living conditions, face real constraints on time and space. It is harder to locate even a minute of stillness. Yet even here, the principle holds: the scale changes, not the possibility. Silence shrinks to the size of a breath, a posture, a momentary withdrawal of inner tension. The myth dissolves through nuance, not denial.

Threading gently through this subchapter is the motif of *the small lamp*: a steady light in a busy room. Silence functions like this lamp—small, consistent, undramatic. It does not banish chaos. It illuminates a clearer way of meeting it.

The second claim addresses another entrenched myth: silence is weakness, passivity, or emotional retreat. Show the behaviour shaping this myth: in conversation, the person who pauses before responding is sometimes viewed as uncertain or submissive. Name the misconception: the "quiet-as-weakness" stereotype. Explain its flaw: stillness is often a deliberate inhibition of reactivity, not an absence of capacity. Implication: what looks passive can in fact be strength.

A concrete example confirms this. In 1993, during the Oslo peace negotiations, Norwegian diplomat Mona Juul observed that moments of silence often preceded the most constructive breakthroughs. Delegates who paused before reacting destabilised patterns of hostility. The behaviour was visibly active: shoulders settling, eyes focusing, attention sharpening. Silence became leverage—not withdrawal—in a process defined by conflict and risk.

A second example, rooted in scientific study, comes from 2008 research at the University of Rochester, where experiments on self-regulation demonstrated that individuals who paused before making emotionally charged decisions were more accurate in predicting long-term outcomes. The pause was silent but decisive. It required self-command, not timidity.

The counter-example must be addressed candidly: silence can indeed be used unhelpfully—stonewalling, sulking, or withholding communication. These forms of silence damage connection because they are avoidance masquerading as calm. Yet this is precisely why the distinction matters. The silence that protects clarity is chosen. The silence that harms is defensive. The myth collapses when the behaviours are named precisely. Silence is not weakness; misapplied silence is confusion.

Returning to *the small lamp*, consider how the parent in the earlier example re-enters the room after two quiet minutes. Their tone shifts. They respond with accuracy instead of exasperation. The children sense the difference. The lamp steadies the room without extinguishing its energy.

The third claim takes aim at the myth that silence requires ideal conditions—soft lighting, low sound, a tidy room, a carefully curated environment. Show the assumption: silence must be aesthetically perfect. Name the myth: the "serenity condition". Explain its psychological flaw: outer conditions can support stillness but cannot produce it. Implication: the pursuit of perfect quiet becomes a form of procrastination.

A historically grounded example demonstrates this. In the seventeenth century, the Quaker movement established worship practices in cities such as London, Bristol, and Amsterdam—densely populated, often noisy environments. Yet worshippers practised collective silence in simple meeting houses, frequently within earshot of street vendors, horses, and market traffic. The silence they cultivated was inward, not dependent on acoustic isolation.

A second example, modern and empirical, comes from a 2017 study by Transport for London's research arm. Commuters who practised brief breath awareness during peak-hour travel reported significantly greater calm compared with those who sought external quiet through headphones or avoidance strategies. The external noise remained. Their inner posture changed. Silence proved to be a function of attention, not architecture.

A limitation must be held honestly: some environments—such as those marked by chronic danger, extreme noise, or emotional volatility—can overwhelm the nervous system to a degree that inward quiet becomes temporarily inaccessible. This does not invalidate the principle; it clarifies its boundary conditions. Silence is not a magical override. It is a trained capacity that grows more accessible as interior stability builds.

The final myth concerns time: that silence demands long, uninterrupted stretches—meditation retreats, weekend escapes, hours free from responsibility. Show the belief: "I don't have time for silence." Name the distortion: the "time myth". Explain the correction: silence is measured in the depth of attention, not the length of minutes. Implication: small, consistent practices often achieve more than occasional long ones.

Return now to the example of the parent. Their two minutes on the sofa do not resemble a retreat. Their surroundings remain lively. Yet the effect is unmistakable: breath deepens, shoulders loosen, irritability reduces. This is silence functioning as *the small lamp* again—steadying the atmosphere from within.

A named example reinforces this. In 2003, during his tenure as Archbishop of Canterbury, Rowan Williams described in interviews how his most reliable moments of inward stillness occurred not during scheduled retreats but in the margins—three quiet breaths before entering a meeting, a pause while walking down a corridor at Lambeth Palace. Despite immense responsibility, he found that "continuity of small silences" mattered more than long, infrequent ones.

A second example appears in 2019 research from the University of Oxford examining micro-practices of calm among medical trainees. Those who regularly used thirty-second pauses during demanding shifts reported lower emotional exhaustion at the end of their rotations. The time was tiny. The effect accumulated.

The tension that closes this subchapter rests on a simple but unsettling recognition: myths about silence persist because they protect us from facing how accessible silence actually is. If silence were only for monks, or only for the wealthy, or only for people with perfect homes, we would be excused from attempting it. If silence were weakness, we could avoid the vulnerability of stillness. If silence required long hours, we could rationalise our avoidance.

But silence is small. It is human. It is available.

Which leaves one unresolved question, and it is as practical as it is uncomfortable: the next time you feel the urge to say, "I can't be quiet right now," will you examine whether that belief is truth—or simply the last myth standing between you and the small lamp already lit within you?

Chapter 3
The Body As First Teacher

On a rain-heavy Thursday morning in Manchester, a project manager stepped into a lift on the way to a meeting she had been dreading all week. She had her notes prepared, her responses mapped out, her face arranged into something confident. It was only as the lift doors closed that she realised her jaw was clenched so tightly that her molars ached. Her shoulders had risen almost to her ears. Her breath was thin, caught high in her chest. Her body had registered the pressure long before her mind acknowledged it. And in that fleeting moment of recognition, she did something that changed the meeting before it had even begun: she paused, softened her jaw, and let one slow breath travel the length of her spine. The shift was tiny, almost invisible from the outside. Yet it opened a pocket of steadiness inside her—a quiet foothold that her racing mind could not have created on its own.

This chapter begins with that small act, because it captures a truth most people discover late: the body notices first. Long before thought tightens, the body tightens. Long before anxiety speaks, the breath shallows. Long before the mind decides it is overwhelmed, the shoulders have already curled forward in anticipation. We often imagine that stillness begins in the intellect—as if clarity were primarily a mental achievement, the product of insight, discipline, or will. But the body carries the earliest signals of overload, and it carries the earliest doorways back to calm. Attention is not the mind's solitary craft. It is built from posture, breath, sensation, and the ability to inhabit one's physical presence without armouring against the moment.

Across cultures and centuries, people have tried to think their way into stillness. They have tried to reason themselves into calm, persuade themselves into patience, bargain themselves into better emotional habits. Yet the most enduring traditions—from ancient contemplative lineages to modern therapeutic practice—return to the same principle: if you want to change your inner climate, begin with the body. The body is not the last frontier of quiet; it is the first teacher of it. It speaks in signals, not sentences, and our task is to learn its vocabulary.

If the previous chapters explored silence as an inner quality and a discipline of attention, this chapter grounds that exploration in flesh, muscle, breath, and sensory awareness. It argues that stillness does not float free of the physical world; it is shaped by it. The mind, brilliant as it is, cannot outpace the nervous system that holds it. And before we can sit with silence, we must learn to sit with ourselves—literally, physically, in our own posture and presence.

To see this more clearly, begin with the nervous system's quiet warnings. Anyone who has ever walked into a demanding room knows the micro-signals: a jaw that tightens half an hour before a difficult conversation; a stomach that knots before a presentation; a breath that becomes shallow without permission when an unexpected email arrives. These cues appear before thoughts form sentences. They are early alarms, and the body rings them with exquisite honesty. We often ignore them, distracted by tasks or narratives. Yet if we learn to recognise these signals—if we pause long enough to hear them—they become invitations rather than threats. A single unclenching, a single deeper breath, can prevent the mind from slipping into reflexive overdrive. The nervous system, steadying even slightly, allows attention to widen rather than collapse.

From here emerges the central theme of the chapter: breath is the bridge. Not a performance, not a ritual of expertise, not a technique requiring special training—just breath as a functional, physiological mechanism that shifts us from urgency to presence. Three slow breaths before opening an inbox. A measured inhale before returning a call. A quiet exhale before stepping into a demanding room. These are not symbolic gestures. They alter heart rate, modulate vagal tone, and send signals back to the brain that the moment is survivable. Breath reminds us that stillness is not achieved; it is accessed. And the access point sits beneath the sternum, not in the abstract apparatus of thought.

Consider the person who sits at their desk first thing in the morning, cursor blinking, inbox full. Their hand hovers over the trackpad, already preparing for acceleration. But if they take three slow breaths—truly slow, long enough for the out-breath to soften the edges of the body—they begin from a different place. The breath steadies the mind before the mind can become scattered. What follows may be the same emails, the same tasks, the same pressures, but the person who meets them is not the same. The shift is small but pivotal: the body leads, and the mind follows.

Beyond breath lies the wider landscape of sensory grounding. When overwhelm rises, the body often feels as if it is dissolving—adrift, dislocated, unanchored. The senses, however, bring us back to the present with remarkable speed. Feeling feet on the floor, noticing the weight of the body in a chair, tracking the temperature of the air on the skin—these are not trivial exercises. They remind the brain of its physical coordinates, anchoring awareness in something immediate and verifiable. The person who feels lost in a supermarket—a common, quiet kind of overwhelm—can regain steadiness by naming three colours on the shelves. It is a simple act, but it interrupts panic by pulling the mind into precise perception. Presence returns through the senses, not through argument.

This sensory anchoring is not escapism. It is a recalibration of attention, a way of reminding ourselves that the world is concrete, navigable, and less catastrophic than the mind may insist in moments of overload. It is also an expression of humility: the body perceives more accurately than the anxious mind. When attention is scattered, the senses gather it. When the nervous system is startled, the senses soothe it.

Yet grounding alone is not enough. We must also learn the difference between collapse and genuine rest. Many people mistake numbing for restoration. They come home exhausted, fall onto the sofa, scroll through their phones, and call it unwinding. But the body does not unwind during this kind of collapse; it continues to contract. Shoulders remain tight, breath remains shallow, nervous system remains alert. The mind may feel distracted, but distraction is not rest. The body knows the difference, even if the mind refuses to admit it.

True relaxation is active in its own way—a softening of the body, a deliberate release of tension, a moment of conscious stilling rather than passive sinking. Consider the difference between flopping on a sofa with a phone and lying down for five minutes of intentional ease. The first leaves the body tangled, the nervous system cluttered. The second signals safety. Muscles unwind. Breath deepens. The body sends a message to the mind: you can stand down now. Deliberate rest, however short, becomes a form of inner housekeeping, clearing the clutter that passive distraction merely conceals.

The arc of this chapter, then, follows a quiet logic: the body is not a barrier to inner silence but the gateway to it. When the nervous system steadies, attention steadies. When breath deepens, awareness deepens. When sensory grounding anchors us, the mind stops drifting into catastrophic futures or replayed pasts. When rest is conscious rather than collapsed, inner noise has space to settle. To cultivate silence is to cultivate the body's capacity to feel safe enough for stillness to enter.

This does not reduce stillness to a technique; it reveals stillness as a physiological partnership. We are not minds dragging bodies behind us; we are embodied beings whose mental clarity depends on the state of our nervous system. Anyone who has tried to meditate while stressed knows this intimately: the mind cannot be coerced into quiet if the body is braced for impact. The first quiet is physical. The mind's quiet follows.

The deeper significance of this chapter is that it shifts the narrative of stillness from aspiration to embodiment. In earlier chapters, stillness may have sounded like a lofty discipline—an inner room, a hinge, a pause. Here it becomes concrete: jaw, breath, feet, skin, posture. The practices become accessible not because they are simple but because they are human. The body leads the way. It always has.

And so the question that closes this introduction is both practical and profound: if your body is your first teacher—signalling, steadying, guiding—will you learn to listen to it before your mind races ahead? Will you notice the clenched jaw, the shallow breath, the tight shoulders before the day gathers speed? Will you let your body lead you back into the stillness your mind is too quick to outrun?

The pages ahead will not answer these questions for you, but they will show how your body already holds the beginnings of the silence you seek.

Listening To The Nervous System

In June 1994, during the televised hearings of South Africa's Truth and Reconciliation Commission, Archbishop Desmond Tutu paused mid-question. The room in Cape Town City Hall was silent except for the soft clicking of cameras. A witness had just described a harrowing event, and Tutu—who had heard countless such accounts—suddenly felt his breath tighten and his shoulders rise. A journalist later noted that he "closed his eyes for a moment, exhaled, and only then continued." It was a tiny gesture, easily missed, but physiologically decisive. His body had registered overwhelm before his mind could form language for it. That pause was not weakness. It was information. And it allowed him to proceed with steadiness rather than collapse.

Most of us will never sit in such a charged room. Yet our bodies speak to us with similar clarity—tight jaws before difficult meetings, shallow breaths before reading important emails, restless legs before confronting tension we've been postponing. The nervous system broadcasts early warnings, but we often overlook them because we expect stress to announce itself with intellectual clarity first. It rarely does. The body whispers long before the mind understands.

Consider the employee who steps into a corridor before a quarterly review. She has prepared her talking points. She has rehearsed answers. Yet her jaw is clenched. Her breath flickers high in the chest. Her palms feel slightly damp. She has not consciously named her apprehension, but her body has already done so. In that moment, if she notices the clenched jaw and lets it soften—if she drops her shoulders by an inch and takes one slow breath—she changes the trajectory of her own nervous system. The mind may still be racing, but the body has shifted from threat to possibility. The motif that threads quietly through this subchapter is *the indicator light*: a small signal that illuminates before the engine overheats. The body is always switching on these lights. We simply forget to look.

The first claim begins here: the body signals overload earlier than cognition because it is structurally built to act faster. Show the pattern: shoulders rising during a tense conversation, despite no conscious decision to brace; breath shortening before seeing a person associated with conflict. Name the mechanism: autonomic arousal, specifically sympathetic activation, which accelerates before conscious appraisal. Explain the science: in 1991, neuroscientist Joseph LeDoux demonstrated that sensory information travels to the amygdala milliseconds before reaching the cortical areas responsible for deliberate interpretation. Implication: by the time the mind "realises" we are stressed, the body has been carrying that stress for some time.

This creates a paradox: the nervous system is early, but attention is late. The person who notices their clenched jaw before a meeting is not discovering a trivial detail. They are catching their physiology mid-process. The indicator light is blinking. Whether they acknowledge it or not shapes the meeting that follows.

A second claim emerges from the first: bodily cues are not vague impressions; they are specific data points. Show the behaviour: someone preparing for a challenging phone call finds their breath stuck in the upper chest. Name the cue: shallow respiration. Explain its significance: shallow breath reduces carbon dioxide tolerance and signals to the brain that the environment may be unsafe, heightening vigilance. Implication: misreading this cue leads to misreading the entire moment.

One named example illustrates this clearly. In 2017, researchers at the University of California, Berkeley observed that law students preparing for moot court presentations often showed early physical signs of overload—tight shoulders, rapid breath, elevated heart rate—ten to fifteen minutes before reporting conscious stress. Those who noticed these signals and took brief regulating breaths performed with greater vocal steadiness and reported better focus. Those who ignored them exhibited more verbal tangles and rushed phrasing. The indicator light functioned predictively.

A second example, from a very different domain, comes from the diaries of the British violinist Yehudi Menuhin. In March 1955, before a performance in Paris, Menuhin wrote that he could "measure the mind's quiet by the breath's depth." He noticed tension first not in thought but in the way his fingers stiffened when tuning. When he paused, exhaled slowly, and loosened his grip, the performance softened into flow. His mind followed the signal his body provided.

The counter-example must be acknowledged. Not everyone detects bodily cues easily. Individuals with histories of trauma, certain neurodivergent traits, or long-term dissociation may find the body's signals muted or confusing. This does not weaken the premise; it simply clarifies that interoceptive awareness—the ability to sense internal states—varies across individuals. In such cases, the indicator lights are present but may require gentler, slower approaches to perceive. The reconciliation is straightforward: the body communicates regardless; our capacity to listen develops at different speeds.

Returning to *the indicator light*, the next claim is that listening to these signals changes behaviour not through psychological insight alone but through physiological interruption. Show the example: the employee in the corridor unclenches her jaw and lengthens one exhale. Name the mechanism: parasympathetic activation, specifically engaging vagal pathways associated with downregulation. Explain the process: slow exhalation increases vagal tone, sending inhibitory signals that reduce heart rate and soften muscular tension. Implication: a single breath alters the body's operating state faster than a cognitive reframe.

This relationship between breath and physiology is not speculative. In 2018, a team at University College London measured how paced breathing before emotionally charged tasks influenced performance. Participants who took three slow breaths demonstrated more measured decision-making and lower autonomic arousal. The effect was most pronounced among those who recognised early bodily stress markers. The indicator lights guided the intervention.

The fourth claim extends this logic: when we ignore bodily cues, the nervous system escalates until it forces recognition through stronger signals. Show the progression: what begins as a clenched jaw becomes a headache by afternoon; shallow breath becomes irritability; tight shoulders become fatigue. Name the principle: stress accumulation. Explain the mechanism: without downregulation, sympathetic arousal remains chronically elevated, undermining concentration, mood, and relational clarity. Implication: the cost of ignoring the indicator light is cumulative.

A historical example makes this visible. In 1938, the British psychiatrist Edward Mapother documented cases of "nervous exhaustion" among London civil servants working under mounting political pressure. Many reported that their exhaustion "arrived suddenly," yet Mapother noted that physiological tension had been present for weeks—insomnia, clenched jaws, digestive tension, shallow breath. The crash was not sudden. The signals were simply unheard.

A second modern example comes from 2021 NHS occupational health data showing that clinicians reporting burnout often traced their earliest signs not to emotional overwhelm but to persistent bodily tension—tightness in the chest, headaches, breath restriction—appearing months before psychological symptoms. The indicator light had been flashing long before the engine faltered.

A limitation must again be acknowledged. Some bodily sensations mimic stress but arise from unrelated medical, hormonal, or environmental causes. This is precisely why silence is necessary: not to diagnose, but to observe. The nervous system's signals are meaningful, but not all meanings are stress. Listening refines discernment. Ignoring blurs it.

From here emerges a deeper claim: listening to the nervous system is an act of respect. Not indulgence. Not fragility. Respect. Show the behaviour: the employee in the lift softens her jaw before the meeting. Name the psychological principle: self-regulation. Explain the significance: by acknowledging the body's signal, she treats her inner state as worthy of attention rather than as an inconvenience to override. Implication: silence begins with listening inward long before listening outward.

Returning to *the indicator light*, consider how everyday life changes when these signals are heeded. A person notices their shoulders rising during a conversation and adjusts their posture. They feel their breath shorten before opening an inbox and take one slow inhale. They catch themselves gripping a steering wheel too tightly and soften the hands. These micro-adjustments prevent the nervous system from climbing into states that distort perception and narrow attention. By the time the mind formulates a story—"I'm overwhelmed," "I'm anxious," "I can't cope"—the body has often absorbed far more strain than necessary.

This brings us to the chapter's hinge question: the nervous system is speaking constantly, but will we learn to hear it? A person who notices their clenched jaw before a meeting can pause and breathe. A person who doesn't notice is carried into the room by tension they never chose. The difference between the two may shape not just the meeting, but the tone of the day.

And so the subchapter ends with a quiet tension, unresolved by design. The next time your body turns on an indicator light—jaw tightening, breath shortening, shoulders rising—will you rush past it, trusting your mind to catch up later, or will you stop long enough to let the body teach you what the moment truly requires?

Breath As A Bridge To Stillness

In January 2016, at University College London Hospital, consultant surgeon Professor Ara Darzi paused for three slow breaths before making the first incision of a complex abdominal operation. The scrub nurse later recounted how Darzi's shoulders softened and his posture settled just slightly, a shift almost imperceptible unless one knew him well. That tiny act, repeated before every major procedure throughout his career, was not superstition or ritual for its own sake. It was a physiological reset. He used breath to stabilise attention, regulate the nervous system, and enter the work with clarity rather than adrenaline. His colleagues confirmed that the practice reduced errors in high-pressure moments. Three breaths. Less than fifteen seconds. A bridge between agitation and steadiness.

Most people assume that meaningful calm requires large interventions—weekends away, long meditation sessions, or major lifestyle changes. Yet the nervous system is exquisitely sensitive to micro-adjustments. Breath is one of the few levers we can access instantly, anywhere, without equipment or ceremony. It is the shortest route to the body's control room, the switch that can dim an internal storm before the mind even registers cloud cover.

Consider the office worker who opens her laptop at 8.32 a.m. in Manchester, sees the red circle of unread emails climb past 70, and feels her chest tighten. Before she clicks into the inbox, she stops. She inhales deeply, slowly, once. She lets the breath fall out. Twice. Again. Three breaths, no more. Her shoulders lower by a fraction. Her jaw loosens. She is still facing the same volume of work, but her body is no longer braced for impact. The change is small but direction-shifting. A bridge has formed beneath her feet.

The first claim rests on this visible behaviour: breath alters state before thought. Show the pattern. People inhale sharply when startled. They exhale audibly after relief. Name the mechanism: respiration is bidirectionally linked to the autonomic nervous system. Explain the science: slow exhalation increases vagal tone, activating pathways that reduce heart rate and muscular tension. Implication: breath is not symbolic calm; it is biological intervention.

A strong body of research confirms this. In 2017, Stanford neuroscientist Mark Krasnow identified a cluster of neurons in the pre-Bötzinger complex responsible for linking breath rhythm to emotional regulation. These cells sit at the intersection of sensation and mood. When breath slows, they signal to the brainstem that the environment is safe. When breath quickens, they cue vigilance. Breath is therefore not simply a response to inner state; it actively shapes it.

The motif that threads through this subchapter is *the hinge*: breath as the small, movable component on which the entire door of attention swings. A door can open or close on a hinge that measures only a few centimetres. Breath works the same way.

The second claim builds from this hinge. Experiences that feel psychological often begin as respiratory patterns. Show the example: a person preparing to speak in a meeting notices their breath has risen into the upper chest, becoming thin and rapid. Name the pattern: thoracic breathing. Explain its significance: upper-chest breathing is associated with sympathetic activation, the branch of the nervous system linked to urgency and protection. Implication: unless breath drops deeper into the diaphragm, the mind may interpret harmless situations as threats.

A named example illustrates the point. In 2019, a team at the University of Oxford conducted a study with secondary-school teachers experiencing high occupational stress. They found that participants who practised three slow breaths before entering a classroom reported a 19% reduction in perceived tension over six weeks. Classroom incident reports did not change, but physiological markers—heart rate variability, breath rate, and reported jaw tension—shifted. Breath changed the body even when the environment stayed the same.

Another example, drawn from a very different setting, comes from the journals of the Japanese Zen master Hakuin Ekaku, writing in 1748. He described "misleading calm"—sitting in outer quiet while the breath remained tight and shallow. Only when he "allowed breath to descend" into the belly did the mind follow. This centuries-old description echoes modern respiratory physiology: deeper breathing increases baroreflex sensitivity, improving the body's capacity to downshift from stress. Hakuin could not have named the mechanism, but he felt it intimately.

The counter-example must be taken seriously. Some individuals find that deliberate breathing makes them uncomfortable or even more anxious. This can occur in trauma-sensitive contexts or in conditions that disrupt interoception. The practice can feel like scrutiny rather than relief. Recognising this does not weaken the premise; it clarifies that breath is a hinge, but not the only one. Some doors require alternative hinges: grounding through senses, posture adjustments, or environmental cues. The reconciliation is simple: breath is powerful for many, not universal for all.

The third claim deepens the concept of breath as a bridge. Show the behaviour: a commuter on a packed train in London feels irritation rising as the carriage lurches and someone's elbow presses too close. Before reacting, he turns attention to one breath—a slow inhale through the nose, a longer exhale through the mouth. Name the principle: paced respiration. Explain the physiology: extending the exhale activates inhibitory parasympathetic signals, reducing heart rate within a single respiratory cycle. Implication: breath is a way of reclaiming agency in situations we cannot control.

A 2022 report from King's College London demonstrated that paced breathing for just sixty seconds reduced self-reported stress across a diverse urban sample. The effect held regardless of participants' prior experience with meditation. Breath operated as a hinge even for novices.

The fourth claim concerns attention. Breath links body and mind because it offers a single, reliable anchor point. Show the behaviour: the woman at her desk places attention on the sensation of her breath at the nostrils. Name the effect: attentional narrowing. Explain the process: when attention rests on a repetitive, predictable sensory rhythm, the brain's default mode network quietens, reducing rumination and internal noise. Implication: breath is a bridge not only to physiological steadiness but to cognitive clarity.

The hinge motif returns here. Attention often swings wildly: from email to thought, from memory to anticipation. Breath stabilises the hinge so that attention does not slam open and closed with every passing stimulus.

A historical reference demonstrates this universality. In 1857, the French novelist Gustave Flaubert wrote to his lover Louise Colet that when overwhelmed, he would stand by an open window and "breathe until the mind grows orderly." He had no language for parasympathetic tone or autonomic balance, yet he intuited that breath could restore coherence. His hinge was biological long before it was conceptual.

The next claim shifts from physiology to meaning. Breath becomes a bridge to stillness precisely because it is not a performance. Show the misuse: people treating breathing techniques as goals to master—breath counts, retention ratios, dramatic exercises that create pressure rather than quiet. Name the problem: performative calm. Explain the dynamic: when breath becomes a metric, it activates striving rather than soothing, pulling the nervous system into subtle tension. Implication: the simplest breath is often the most effective.

This point matters particularly for the audience of professionals and researchers who tend to approach practices analytically. Breath for stillness is not an optimisation routine. It is a softening. A return. A hinge that does not need polishing to work.

The penultimate claim brings us back to behaviour. Show the everyday moment: someone reaches for their phone to check messages before bed. They notice their breath has become short. Rather than plunging into the glow of notifications, they pause for one slow inhale and longer exhale. Name the action: interrupting the automatic. Explain the shift: breath breaks the momentum of compulsion, giving the mind a fraction of space to choose rather than react. Implication: silence begins not with the absence of noise but with the ability to interrupt one's own patterns.

The final claim prepares the closing movement. Breath is the bridge because it reintroduces space, and space is the prerequisite for every other form of stillness. Without space, the nervous system cannot settle, attention cannot widen, and life cannot be met from depth rather than speed.

And so the subchapter ends on a tension. The next time your hand moves towards your inbox, your phone, the next task—will you let momentum carry you, or will you test the hinge? Three breaths. Fifteen seconds. A tiny pause that could alter the quality of the entire hour that follows.

Grounding Through The Senses

In March 2008, during a rehearsal at the Royal Opera House in London, the conductor Antonio Pappano stopped the orchestra mid-phrase. Something was off. A violinist had missed an entry, a brass line had flattened, and the tempo had lurched forward as if the entire ensemble were collectively impatient. Pappano did not raise his voice. Instead, he stepped down from the podium, placed his palm against the stage floorboards, and asked the musicians to "listen to the room, not your heads." Those present remember the uncanny stillness that followed: musicians adjusting their feet against the floor, tuning their attention to the faint creak of wood and the microscopic shifts of air. When the orchestra resumed, the sound had changed. It was rounder, steadier, less frantic. That single gesture—placing a hand on the boards—pulled everyone out of anticipatory thought and back into sensory contact with the present moment.

Most people will never conduct at Covent Garden. Yet the principle Pappano demonstrated applies as much to a crowded supermarket in Leeds as to a world-class orchestra. When the mind spirals inward, the senses offer a way back. A person overwhelmed by fluorescent aisles and an overlong shopping list may steady themselves simply by feeling their shoes meet the ground or silently naming the colours on nearby shelves. Sensory contact interrupts mental turbulence. It is an anchor; small, quiet, reliable.

The first claim begins here: the senses are the fastest path out of mental noise because they operate before interpretation. Show the moment: someone in a supermarket feels a wave of agitation rising. They freeze briefly, unsure whether to abandon their trolley or push through. Name the mechanism: sensory grounding. Explain the principle: attention shifts from internal narrative to external sensation, reducing activation in the default mode network, the brain system associated with rumination. Implication: grounding through the senses is not an escape from thought; it is a recalibration of attention.

The motif that threads through this subchapter is *the anchor*: a small, tactile point that holds us when the mind wanders into storms.

Consider the woman standing in the aisle. Her heart rate has risen. Her breath is shallow. Her mind is occupied with the remnants of a difficult morning meeting. She is scanning labels without absorbing them. She feels pressure blooming behind her eyes. Then she pauses. She touches the metal of the trolley handle. She notices its temperature—cool, almost clinical. She shifts her weight deliberately into her feet, sensing the firmness of the floor through her shoes. She brings her gaze to the shelf in front of her and names, quietly, the sequence of colours: green, yellow, red, blue. Within seconds, the inner storm loosens. It does not disappear, but it becomes navigable. The anchor holds.

The second claim deepens the argument: sensory grounding works because it recruits neural circuits that compete directly with anxiety-driven patterns. Show the behaviour: someone overwhelmed by a rapid succession of work messages places their hand on the desk and notices its texture. Name the physiological process: tactile interference. Explain the science: somatosensory engagement activates regions of the brain that diminish limbic system dominance, reducing emotional reactivity. Implication: by grounding attention in physical sensation, we create a counterweight to spirals of thought.

We can see this interplay historically. In 1890, William James wrote in *The Principles of Psychology* that "the faculty of voluntarily bringing back a wandering attention" is the foundation of character. Although he lacked modern neuroscientific terms, James observed that attention tethered to sensation—describing an object's shape, tracing a line with one's finger—could steady a restless mind. His insight anticipated contemporary findings more than a century later.

A modern, named example underscores the point. In 2020, at the University of Sussex, researchers studying urban overwhelm found that participants who briefly engaged sensory grounding—touching a wall, tracking ambient sounds, noticing temperature—reported significantly lower stress scores after only thirty seconds of practice. The environment did not change. The sensory anchor did.

The counter-example must be treated carefully. Individuals with sensory sensitivities—common in autistic adults, for example—may find that certain stimuli heighten rather than reduce distress. Bright lights, unexpected textures, or complex soundscapes can overwhelm instead of soothe. This does not undermine the principle; it simply clarifies that effective grounding requires choosing sensory channels that regulate rather than agitate. Some people ground more easily through sound, others through touch, others through visual focusing. The anchor varies; the anchoring does not.

A third claim extends the motif: grounding through the senses cultivates presence not through analysis but through contact. Show the concrete action: someone places both feet firmly on the floor before delivering a presentation. Name the phenomenon: proprioceptive anchoring. Explain the underlying mechanism: proprioceptive signals—feedback from muscles and joints—stabilise the body's threat response by orienting it spatially. Implication: grounding is not a psychological trick; it is a way of helping the body locate itself.

This becomes especially clear in moments of overwhelm, when the mind's sense of orientation frays. The person in the supermarket who names colours is not engaging in distraction but in orientation. Colours are immediate, visible, incontrovertible facts. They anchor her reality when her thoughts have turned abstract and unwieldy.

A historical example reinforces this pattern. During the London Blitz in 1940, diaries from civilians recorded a striking behaviour: people touched the ground frequently during bombing raids—pressing hands to walls, gripping the edges of benches, placing feet against solid surfaces. Psychologists analysing these accounts later noted that tactile grounding helped individuals maintain composure during uncertainty, allowing them to distinguish immediate physical safety from projected fear. The anchor was not conceptual. It was concrete.

The fourth claim focuses on the senses as a bridge between body and mind. Show the behaviour: someone sits at a café table, feeling distracted and irritable. They shift their attention to the sound of a spoon touching a ceramic cup. Name the sensory channel: auditory grounding. Explain why it works: orienting to a neutral sound interrupts rumination by shifting the attentional load to perceptual systems. Implication: sensory cues become anchors that prevent the mind being swept back into internal storms.

Another named example illustrates the breadth of this principle. In 1967, choreographer Merce Cunningham trained dancers to "listen with the soles of their feet," focusing attention on how the floor resonated beneath them. This form of sensory grounding increased stability during complex sequences and reduced errors. Cunningham's method was not mystical; it was somatic. Sensing the floor anchored the dancers' nervous systems, enabling precision under pressure.

Grounding through the senses is effective because it limits the brain's ability to maintain high-speed narrative processing at the same time. The mind cannot fully catastrophise while it is describing the warmth of sunlight on skin or tracking the hum of a refrigerator. Attention contracts around sensation, and the narrative machinery slows.

The fifth claim introduces an important distinction: sensory grounding is not escapism. It is engagement. Show the misuse: someone attempts grounding only to avoid discomfort, treating it as a way to push away thoughts. Name the error: suppression disguised as presence. Explain the risk: avoidance activates the very threat cycles grounding is meant to ease. Implication: grounding works when it includes the present moment as it is, not when it tries to reshape it.

This becomes clear in our supermarket example. The woman does not name colours to erase her overwhelm. She names colours to stabilise herself enough to meet it without collapsing. The anchor holds not by rejecting the storm but by allowing her to stand in it.

The motif returns: *the anchor* is effective only when it is embedded in reality, not fantasy.

A sixth claim widens the lens: grounding through the senses reveals how rarely we inhabit the world as it unfolds. Show the behaviour: someone walks through a garden while thinking about an unfinished report, barely noticing the scent of wet soil or the movement of shadows. Name the pattern: perceptual absenteeism. Explain the mechanism: when attention is monopolised by internal narrative, sensory pathways deactivate, reducing the richness of lived experience. Implication: grounding reopens the perceptual field, allowing life to be felt rather than merely planned.

Grounding has social implications too. A person who steadies themselves through sensation often becomes a steadier presence for others. The parent who takes two seconds to feel their feet on the floor before responding to a child's question transmits calm rather than urgency. The colleague who touches the back of their chair before speaking offers clarity rather than reactivity. The anchor influences more than the individual; it shapes the relational climate.

Two named examples demonstrate these relational effects. In 2015, during training at the London Fire Brigade, recruits were taught to place a gloved hand on the nearest solid surface before entering a smoke-filled corridor. This grounding technique stabilised breathing and orientation, improving decision-making under pressure. In a parallel but far quieter domain, a 2013 study at the University of Exeter found that nurses who used sensory grounding before difficult conversations with patients were rated as more attentive and compassionate. The anchor steadied the person; the steadiness extended outward.

A limitation must be acknowledged. Grounding is effective in acute overwhelm but less so in chronic distress without broader support. A person facing long-term burnout or unresolved trauma may find that sensory anchors offer temporary relief but cannot address the deeper causes of suffering. This is not a flaw of grounding; it is a reminder that no single method suffices for every circumstance. Anchors hold the boat; they do not repair the hull.

As the subchapter moves toward its final claim, the motif of *the anchor* holds steady. Grounding through the senses teaches a deceptively simple truth: presence is physical before it is psychological. Returning to sensation is not an aesthetic preference but a biological reality. The body lives in the present even when the mind does not.

And so the subchapter ends on a quiet, unresolved question. The next time your mind begins to spiral—on a train platform, in a meeting, in the supermarket—will you continue drifting upward into thought, or will you reach for the anchor that is always available: the ground beneath your feet, the texture under your hand, the colour directly before your eyes?

Relaxation Without Collapse

In February 2012, at the offices of the Financial Times on Southwark Bridge, an internal audit revealed something unexpected. Staff were spending an average of twenty-six minutes each evening sitting at their desks after finishing work, half-reclined in their chairs, scrolling on their phones before heading home. When interviewed, many described this interlude as "switching off." Yet biometric data from a subset of volunteers told another story: elevated heart rates, shallow breathing, and increased muscle tension in the upper back. What felt like rest was, physiologically, nothing of the sort. The body was not relaxing. It was stalling.

This paradox plays out everywhere. A person flops onto a sofa at 9.15 p.m., phone in hand, exhausted from the day. They scroll through headlines, messages, weather updates, videos, a half dozen public arguments. Twenty minutes pass, then forty. When they finally stand up, their limbs feel heavier, not lighter. Their eyes ache. Their breath is thin. This is collapse masquerading as rest—a numbing that soothes nothing and restores nothing. True relaxation, by contrast, is quieter, more deliberate, and far less dramatic. It is softening rather than sinking. Release rather than retreat.

The motif that threads through this subchapter is *the threshold*: the subtle line between unwinding and disappearing, between restoration and withdrawal. Crossing the threshold in the wrong direction leaves us foggy and depleted. Crossing it with awareness opens a path back to clarity.

The first claim begins with what is visible. Show the behaviour: someone arrives home after a demanding meeting, drops their bag, and collapses onto the nearest seat. They reach for a device automatically. Name the pattern: passive numbing. Explain the mechanism: numbing activates dopaminergic circuits that distract attention without reducing arousal. The body remains tense while the mind disengages. Implication: collapse feels like exhale but is, in effect, a held breath.

A named example makes this sharper. In 2019, researchers at the University of Glasgow conducted a study on evening smartphone use and sleep quality. Participants who reported "resting" on their phones after work did not show physiological signs of relaxation; their heart rate variability (HRV)—a key marker of parasympathetic activation—remained low. The scrolling created the illusion of rest without the depth of it. The threshold was crossed in the wrong direction.

The second claim concerns what genuine relaxation looks like in the body. Show the contrast: instead of flopping onto a sofa, a person lies down on a rug, places a hand on their abdomen, and takes several slow breaths. Their shoulders drop. Their jaw softens. Their stomach releases. Name the principle: parasympathetic shift. Explain the science: slow breathing and gentle physical release activate vagal pathways, raising HRV and reducing muscular tension. Implication: true rest feels like widening, not narrowing.

A different historical example underlines this. In 1948, the Danish physiotherapist Bess Mensendieck documented how small adjustments—lengthening the spine by a centimetre, softening the knees, loosening the jaw—reduced chronic tension in factory workers. She called these micro-releases "functional unwinding," a term long before its time. Mensendieck's work shows that relaxation is not abstract; it is mechanical, enacted through subtle shifts in posture and breath.

A limitation must be acknowledged. Some people gravitate toward collapse because deliberate relaxation feels uncomfortable at first. When the nervous system has been running on urgency for years, slowing down can feel exposed. The threshold, for them, is not simply crossed but defended. This does not weaken the premise; it simply clarifies that gentleness is essential. Unwinding starts where one is, not where one imagines they should be.

The third claim builds from here: collapse is a withdrawal from sensation; relaxation is an engagement with it. Show the pattern: someone on the sofa does not feel the weight of their body, the texture of the cushion, or the rhythm of their breath. Their senses are dimmed. Name the phenomenon: sensory disengagement. Explain its effect: disengagement reduces interoceptive awareness, making it harder for the nervous system to downshift. Implication: the body cannot relax when it is not being inhabited.

By contrast, deliberate unwinding brings sensation back online. Feeling the feet on the floor, noticing the warmth of the palms, or tracking the breath's movement gives the nervous system an anchor. The threshold moves in the right direction.

A named example reinforces this sensory dimension. In 2014, occupational therapists at St Thomas' Hospital in London introduced a five-minute "reset protocol" for clinicians between patient rounds. It involved standing with both feet planted, relaxing the shoulders, taking three slow breaths, and noticing one neutral sound in the environment. HRV readings improved within minutes. The threshold from collapse to relaxation is not crossed through effort but through attention.

A counter-example now sharpens the argument. Not all passive activities constitute collapse. Listening to music, staring out of a window, or lying down without distraction can be restorative even when they appear inactive. What distinguishes them from numbing is that awareness remains intact. The person is present, not absent. The reconciliation: rest is defined not by stillness alone but by the quality of attention within that stillness.

The fourth claim introduces a psychological dimension: collapse narrows the mind, relaxation expands it. Show the narrowing: during aimless scrolling, the world shrinks to a series of images and hot takes. The mind becomes reactive, hungry for novelty, unable to settle. Name the cognitive pattern: attentional fragmentation. Explain the mechanism: fragmented attention activates the brain's salience network, keeping the nervous system alert. Implication: collapse leaves us overstimulated and under-rested.

Relaxation, by contrast, opens the perceptual field. Gentle stretching, slow breathing, or lying down with eyes closed but attention awake restores mental spaciousness. The threshold is crossed into clarity rather than fog.

A named historical reference demonstrates how long this distinction has mattered. In 1838, the German poet Heinrich Heine described the difference between "rest that renews" and "rest that dulls" in letters from his convalescence in Paris. He wrote that true rest "returns the soul to its body," whereas numbness causes the self to drift far from its anchor. Heine's observation aligns with modern neuroscience: renewal requires embodiment.

A fifth claim emerges: collapse postpones fatigue; relaxation processes it. Show the pattern: the person on the sofa scrolls until midnight, then wonders why they still feel wired. Name the principle: unintegrated stress. Explain the physiology: adrenaline and cortisol remain elevated when the body is not given space to down-regulate. Implication: without deliberate unwinding, the body carries stress into sleep, work, and relationships.

Deliberate unwinding—five minutes of lying down with slow breathing, gentle stretching, or releasing the jaw—helps the body metabolise tension rather than store it. The threshold becomes a passage rather than a trap.

A second modern example strengthens this point. In 2021, a collaboration between King's College London and Guy's Hospital studied frontline healthcare workers experiencing end-of-shift exhaustion. Those who spent five minutes in deliberate physical release—standing with spine elongated, exhaling slowly, softening the abdomen—showed measurable reductions in cortisol thirty minutes later. Those who decompressed through phones or television did not. The threshold between collapse and restoration is physiologically visible.

The sixth claim brings relational impact into view. Collapse isolates; relaxation reconnects. Show the behaviour: the exhausted parent scrolling on the sofa becomes less responsive, more irritable, more withdrawn. Name the dynamic: relational blunting. Explain the cause: sensory disengagement reduces empathy and attunement. Implication: collapse affects not only the individual but the emotional climate around them.

Deliberate unwinding strengthens relational presence. A person who releases tension before interacting with a partner or child transmits steadiness rather than depletion. The threshold, once crossed with awareness, carries benefits beyond the self.

A limitation is necessary. Deliberate unwinding cannot replace structural rest. No five-minute practice compensates for chronic overwork or systemic pressure. Yet it remains significant because it allows the nervous system to recover in small, accessible increments. The threshold is not the whole journey, but it is the beginning of one.

The subchapter returns to its motif: *the threshold* is always there—between collapse and restoration, between disappearing and returning, between being present and being elsewhere. Recognising that line is the start of a different relationship with rest.

And the closing tension holds. The next time you find yourself sinking onto a sofa, phone in hand, will you drift across the threshold into numbness, or will you choose five minutes of deliberate unwinding—jaw softening, breath deepening, senses reawakening—so that rest becomes real rather than merely imagined?

Chapter 4
Meeting Your Inner Noise

There are moments when the mind begins speaking long before we realise we are listening. A man stands at the sink after dinner, sleeves rolled up, warm water running over his hands, and suddenly he finds himself replaying an argument from earlier that afternoon. He hears not only his own words but the imagined retorts he never delivered, the sharpened comebacks he rehearses now with theatrical precision. The plates are nearly dry before he notices that the conversation he is having exists only in his head. Nothing around him has demanded this noise; it has arisen of its own accord, continuing its performance until he catches it mid-sentence.

This phenomenon is so ordinary that we rarely name it. Yet the inner commentary is one of the most powerful forces shaping our days. It narrates, judges, predicts, catastrophises, reminisces, and often misleads. It inserts itself between experience and perception, tinting what we see and how we respond. The noise is relentless not because we are flawed, but because the mind is designed to produce thought with astonishing speed and minimal invitation. The real puzzle is not that the commentary exists—it always will—but that we so often fail to notice it until it has already bent our mood and our decisions.

The contradiction at the heart of this chapter is simple and unsettling: we live with our thoughts more intimately than with any person we love, yet many of us understand them least. We invest time learning to read data, decipher emails, and interpret other people's behaviour, but give astonishingly little attention to interpreting the voice that speaks within. This voice is sometimes wise, sometimes wounded, sometimes frightened, sometimes cruel. Left unexamined, it becomes the unofficial narrator of our lives. Examined, it becomes information rather than authority.

To speak of "inner noise" is not to dismiss thought as a nuisance. Thought is one of humanity's finest tools. But noise is thought stripped of direction: repetitive, circular, automatic. It is what happens when the mind begins to churn rather than inquire, when it reacts rather than reflects. And it thrives most vigorously in silence—not because silence creates it, but because silence reveals it. Anyone who has tried to sit quietly for even a minute knows the shock of hearing the mind unmasked. It is far from still. It is a crowded room.

This chapter invites the reader into that room—not to tidy it, not to silence it, but to understand it. The first step is deceptively simple: noticing. Recognising the constant commentary for what it is, rather than unconsciously believing every line it delivers. Washing the dishes and realising you are mid-argument with someone who is not there. Walking down a street and discovering that your mind is narrating your future failures with cinematic detail. These moments of recognition are small revolutions. They interrupt the autopilot.

Yet noticing alone is not enough, because the mind has other habits that masquerade as thinking. Rumination, for instance, feels purposeful even when it is stuck in a loop. A person replays a mistake—an email sent too quickly, a phrase uttered carelessly—and the mind insists that going over it again will yield insight. Instead, it breeds self-judgment and anxiety. Reflection, by contrast, asks a different set of questions: What exactly happened? What part of it is mine? What might I learn? The shift is subtle but profound. One traps the mind in repetition; the other opens the door to growth.

This distinction matters because rumination is one of the clearest ways inner noise disguises itself as usefulness. It borrows the posture of problem-solving while delivering none of the results. When a reader in this chapter moves from replaying an error to asking what the error might teach them, they are not simply thinking differently—they are reclaiming authorship of their mental life. They move from being narrated to narrating.

But thoughts are only one half of the noise. The other half lives in the body. Beneath many repetitive thoughts lie feelings that have not yet been felt. A person ends a long day with a heavy chest and assumes it is tiredness, only to discover—upon quiet attention—that it is sadness, or disappointment, or loneliness. These emotions, unnamed, press for expression by fuelling mental chatter. The mind talks when the heart is waiting. In this way, inner noise becomes not only a cognitive phenomenon but an emotional one; thought is often a proxy for feeling.

Creating space for such emotions does not require dramatic catharsis. It requires gentleness—brief, regular check-ins with one's own inner weather. It requires the willingness to sit with unease for a moment rather than fleeing into distraction. A silent minute at the end of the day, noticing what remains in the body, offers more clarity than an hour of anxious thinking. This chapter invites the reader to meet their unfelt feelings with the same attentiveness they bring to their inbox: consistently, honestly, without rushing.

A further layer of noise comes from how we speak to ourselves. Many people reserve their harshest tones for their own inner dialogues, using a vocabulary they would never direct at a friend. After a difficult conversation, for example, the mind launches into critique: You always do this. You're hopeless. You should have known better. It is astonishing how readily we accept such language as truth. Yet a small shift in tone—imagining, for instance, how we would speak to someone we care for—can reshape the entire experience. A kinder inner voice does not dilute accountability; it refines it.

This chapter does not promise inner silence. Instead, it offers a sober recognition: the mind is loud, and its volume increases when ignored. The work is not to mute it but to listen differently—to notice the commentary without collapsing into it, to distinguish rumination from reflection, to make space for the emotions concealed beneath thought, and to cultivate an inner tone that steadies rather than shames.

Modern life gives the inner noise ample fuel. Constant comparison, instantaneous communication, and unending demands create fertile ground for mental turbulence. Yet the deeper truth is timeless: every tradition that has taken the mind seriously has emphasised the importance of watching thought rather than being swept away by it. Socrates urged self-examination not for moral performance but for clarity. Buddhist teachers spoke of "the monkey mind" precisely because its antics are universal. Mystics across centuries insisted that the inner world must be met with patience if the outer world is to be navigated wisely.

As the chapter unfolds, the reader will meet these themes not as abstract principles but as lived realities. They will recognise themselves in the person rehearsing arguments over the sink, in the one circling a mistake without moving forward, in the person who finally acknowledges that the heaviness in their chest is not weariness but sorrow. They will see how small, intimate acts of listening—thoughtful, emotional, compassionate—soften the noise and open a path to deeper stillness.

And so the opening ends with a question that has no easy answer but demands attention: when the next wave of inner noise swells—during a quiet commute, a late night, a mundane chore—will you allow it to sweep you along, or will you pause long enough to hear what it is actually saying?

Noticing The Constant Commentary

In 1836, the French philosopher Blaise Pascal's posthumous *Pensées* was republished in Paris, drawing fresh attention to a line that startled readers then as it startles many now: "All of humanity's problems stem from man's inability to sit quietly in a room alone." It is an exaggeration, but a revealing one. Pascal was not condemning solitude; he was naming the startling discovery that when the external world quietens, an internal one leaps instantly into speech. Those who read the line aloud in the salons of the Palais-Royal that spring described a peculiar sensation: a recognition as swift as a mirror. They knew exactly what he meant. Sit still for a moment, and the mind begins to chatter.

This chatter is ancient, familiar, and strangely invisible. A person stands at the kitchen sink after supper, sleeves pushed up, warm water running over their hands. The day is done. The task is simple. Yet the mind is not occupied with the dishes. It is rehearsing an argument that never quite happened—retelling the colleague's comment, embellishing their own responses, polishing a comeback, sharpening its edges. The sequence unfolds with cinematic clarity until something interrupts it: the drop of a plate, the shift of a shadow, or the faint awareness that the mind has been performing without permission. The commentary has been running like a radio left on in an empty room.

The motif that threads through this subchapter is *the voice at the sink*: the inner narrator that speaks constantly, yet only becomes audible when attention catches it in the act. The voice is not a pathology. It is a feature of human cognition. But until it is noticed, it exerts quiet power over mood, perception, and behaviour.

The first claim rests here: inner commentary is continuous, rapid, and largely automatic. Show the behaviour: the person washing dishes finds themselves mid-argument without recalling its beginning. Name the mechanism: spontaneous cognition. Explain the process: the brain's default mode network (DMN) generates thought streams when attention is not anchored in a task. Implication: inner noise is the natural baseline; awareness of it is the exception, not the rule.

This is not speculation. In 2007, Marcus Raichle at Washington University mapped the DMN and demonstrated that the brain is most active when outwardly idle. It is during such moments—walking, showering, washing dishes—that narrative thought surges. The voice at the sink thrives in these margins.

A second claim follows: we usually assume the commentary is "me," yet its content often contradicts our conscious intentions. Show the example: someone resolves to stay calm about a difficult message, only to find their mind, hours later, replaying the perceived slight with growing indignation. Name the phenomenon: cognitive drift. Explain its nature: the mind generates predictions, critiques, and simulations without aligning them to our values. Implication: unless noticed, the commentary can pull behaviour in directions we did not choose.

A named example sharpens this. In 2013, psychologists Daniel Wegner and Susan Nolen-Hoeksema documented how individuals caught in unobserved internal loops became more reactive in interpersonal conflicts. Participants unaware of their rumination patterns were three times more likely to respond defensively in conversation. Noticing the commentary is not a philosophical exercise; it is behavioural hygiene.

The counter-example is essential. Some people fear that watching their thoughts will make them over-analytical or self-conscious. They worry that noticing the commentary will intensify it. This concern, though understandable, misunderstands the practice. Observation is not amplification. It is differentiation. The reconciliation: noticing creates distance; suppression creates pressure.

Returning to *the voice at the sink*, the third claim concerns speed. The commentary moves faster than deliberate thought. Show the dynamic: someone hears a colleague's tone and, within half a second, the mind supplies a full judgement—They think I'm incompetent—well before conscious reasoning begins. Name the process: rapid appraisal. Explain its roots: the amygdala and limbic circuits generate interpretations before the prefrontal cortex evaluates them. Implication: the first voice is often reactive rather than reflective.

A historical illustration reinforces this. In 1901, William James described this immediacy in his lectures in Edinburgh, noting that "the stream of thought rushes on, carrying us with it before we have named the current." James lacked neuroimaging, but his insight remains accurate. The mind produces monologue at a pace that outstrips awareness.

A modern example grounds it further. In 2019, a University of Cambridge study showed that individuals exposed to ambiguous social feedback filled the gaps with internal narratives within seconds—stories, motives, imagined insults. When asked to recount the sequence, participants believed these thoughts had been carefully considered. They had not. The commentary is swift, uninvited, and persuasive.

A fourth claim emerges: noticing the commentary interrupts its momentum. Show the interruption: the person at the sink realises they are mid-argument and pauses. Name the act: cognitive witnessing. Explain the shift: the prefrontal cortex engages, modulating limbic-driven narratives. Implication: the very act of noticing weakens identification with the story.

This is not mystical. In 2014, a study at the University of Toronto found that participants who practised noticing their thoughts without trying to change them showed reduced DMN activity and improved emotional regulation. Simply observing the commentary altered its intensity.

The counter-example here is important. Some inner thoughts are necessary and accurate—the mind planning tomorrow's schedule, recalling an obligation, replaying a conversation for legitimate learning. Not all commentary is noise. The reconciliation: noticing distinguishes function from friction, clarity from clutter.

The fifth claim addresses the emotional dimension. Thoughts often mask feelings. Show the behaviour: someone finds themselves irritated over a minor mistake, only to realise later that the irritation was covering embarrassment or fear. Name the dynamic: emotional displacement. Explain the mechanism: the mind narrates when the body feels something it has not yet acknowledged. Implication: the commentary becomes a signal rather than a solution.

Two named examples illustrate this interplay. In 1957, psychoanalyst Donald Winnicott observed that children whose feelings were suppressed often developed rapid, repetitive internal speech patterns. He called it "the mind's protest." In 2020, a study from King's College London found that adults experiencing unacknowledged sadness reported higher levels of intrusive thought. The commentary fills the space emotion has been denied.

Returning again to *the voice at the sink*, the sixth claim concerns tone. The inner narrator is often harsher than any external critic. Show the moment: after a brief social misstep, the mind berates: You always say the wrong thing. Name the pattern: self-censure. Explain its origin: internalised standards, fear of rejection, learned defensive strategies. Implication: without noticing, we mistake self-attack for truth.

A named historical example anchors this. The diaries of Eleanor Rathbone, social reformer and MP for the Combined English Universities, reveal that her fiercest criticisms came not from political opponents but from her own internal monologue. She wrote in 1932 of "the ceaseless voice that scolds me for failing more than I have." Recognising that voice did not erase it, but it diluted its authority.

Another modern study underscores this. In 2017, researchers at the University of Sussex found that individuals who noticed self-critical thoughts as mental events rather than facts reported less emotional impact and made more considered decisions. Awareness changed behaviour.

The motif returns: *the voice at the sink* is not the problem; unconscious loyalty to it is.

The final claim prepares the closing movement: noticing the commentary is the doorway to every deeper practice in this chapter. Until thoughts are seen, they cannot be questioned. Until questioned, they cannot be differentiated—from rumination, from emotion, from fear. Noticing is the hinge on which clarity turns.

And so the subchapter ends with a question meant to hover rather than resolve. The next time your mind begins narrating—mid-task, mid-walk, mid-washing-up—will you continue the performance as its lead actor, or will you pause long enough to recognise the commentary for what it is: a voice, not a verdict?

From Rumination To Reflection

In August 1907, the physician and psychologist Pierre Janet stood before a packed lecture hall at the Collège de France and described a pattern he had seen repeatedly in his Paris clinic. Patients who believed they were "thinking about a problem" were, he argued, doing something quite different: they were circling the same mental track without gaining new ground. Janet called it *psychological tension*, a state in which the mind loops but does not learn. The audience laughed politely at his theatrical description of a person "replaying a mistake as though rehearsing a tragedy," yet the phrase endured because it captured something uncomfortably recognisable. Rumination feels like work. It produces exhaustion rather than understanding.

A century later, the setting is less formal but the dynamic unchanged. A reader sits at their desk after a difficult day, replaying a misjudged remark made during a meeting. The scene loops again and again—the wince in a colleague's face, the awkward silence that followed, the sense of sinking regret. Five minutes become fifteen. Nothing shifts. The mind insists it is solving the problem, yet the emotional tone thickens rather than lightens. Then, almost accidentally, the reader pauses long enough to ask a new question: *What can I actually learn from this?* The loop stutters. The atmosphere inside the mind alters. A single shift—from repeating to inquiring—opens a different cognitive door.

The quiet motif running through this piece is *the loop and the line*: the circular motion of rumination contrasted with the linear movement of reflection. Rumination loops. Reflection moves. The work of this subchapter is to make that movement visible, deliberate, and humane.

The first claim is simple: rumination is not reflection. Show the behaviour: the reader repeats the mistake internally, rehearsing imagined conversations, sharpening self-judgement, amplifying embarrassment. Name the mechanism: repetitive negative thinking, documented in clinical research by Susan Nolen-Hoeksema in 2000. Explain the process: the mind believes that replaying the distress will resolve it, but the loop reinforces the emotional state rather than releasing it. Implication: rumination consumes cognitive energy without producing insight.

A named and verifiable example deepens this. In 2014, the University of Michigan published a study showing that participants who engaged in rumination after a perceived social failure exhibited increased activity in the anterior cingulate cortex—the region associated with error detection—but little activation in regions linked to problem-solving. The brain was scanning for threat, not seeking clarity. The loop tightened.

A credible counter-example matters here. Some people describe replaying events as helpful, claiming that repetition allows them to clarify details or understand emotional nuance. The limitation is real: repetition can indeed provide information—*when* it is purposeful. The reconciliation is crucial. Rumination is repetition without direction. Reflection is repetition with inquiry. The distinction lies in whether a question interrupts the loop.

This leads to the second claim: reflection begins not with content but with posture. Show the shift: the moment the reader asks "What can I learn?" rather than "Why did I say that?" the emotional temperature lowers. Name the shift: cognitive reorientation, identified by psychologist Adrian Wells in the 1990s. Explain it: by stepping into a learner's stance, the mind engages different neural networks associated with planning and perspective-taking. Implication: reflection is not merely thinking differently; it is thinking *from* a different place.

A second named example strengthens this. In 2016 at the University of California, Sonja Lyubomirsky's lab demonstrated that individuals who engaged in structured reflection after stressful tasks—using prompts like "What part of this is within my control?"—reported greater clarity and reduced emotional reactivity compared with participants who simply "thought about" the same events. Reflection produces movement. Rumination produces static.

Returning to *the loop and the line*, the third claim concerns emotional saturation. Rumination thickens emotion. Reflection dilutes it. Show the behaviour: when someone replays a mistake, their chest tightens, breath shortens, shoulders lift, and inner criticism swells. Name the phenomenon: emotional fusion. Explain it: the mind and body collapse into the distress as though the event is happening now. Implication: rumination is not merely mental; it is physiological.

A limitation is needed. There are moments when revisiting an event *is* emotionally intense but still necessary—grieving a loss, processing trauma, or acknowledging deep regret. This cannot be dismissed as rumination. The reconciliation: reflection does not avoid emotion; it differentiates between the feeling and the story that grows around it. Rumination merges the two. Reflection allows them to sit side by side.

A fourth claim follows: reflection requires a question. Show this through behaviour: instead of "Why did I do that?" the reader asks, "What would I do differently next time?" Name the mechanism: metacognitive questioning. Explain it: the brain shifts from narrative circuits to evaluative ones, creating perspective. Implication: questions turn spirals into paths.

The motif returns: *the loop and the line.* A loop is closed. A line extends. A single question creates extension.

The fifth claim speaks to the ethical dimension: rumination often centres the self, while reflection considers context. Show the difference: rumination sounds like *I'm terrible at this,* while reflection sounds like *The room was tense—what influenced my choice?* Name the dynamic: decentring. Explain it: reflection widens the frame, incorporating environment, intention, fatigue, timing, relational dynamics. Implication: reflection is less morally punitive and more morally productive.

Historical grounding helps. In 1841, philosopher John Stuart Mill recounted his own crisis in *Autobiography*. He described months of repetitive rumination after recognising the limits of his utilitarian upbringing. The turning point was not escaping thought but altering its posture—from self-condemnation to honest inquiry. Mill did not praise rumination; he named it as the symptom before the learning. Reflection, he wrote, "opened the windows of the mind."

A sixth claim addresses pace. Rumination accelerates; reflection slows. Show the speed: the reader's mind loops rapidly, producing ten variations of the same imagined conversation in a minute. Name the phenomenon: cognitive velocity. Explain it: rumination recruits fast, associative neural pathways that prioritise emotional salience over accuracy. Implication: speed is not insight; slowness is not failure.

A credible limitation once more: fast thought can be accurate. Snap judgements sometimes reflect expertise or intuition. The reconciliation lies in context. Rumination is fast *because it is unobserved*, not because it is wise. Reflection may be slower, but slowness invites depth.

The motif appears again: *the loop and the line*. Rumination loops because it follows the path of least resistance. Reflection forms a line because it chooses direction.

The seventh claim concerns language. Rumination uses absolute terms—always, never, ruined. Reflection uses grounded terms—sometimes, next time, specific behaviours. Show the difference: "I always mess things up" becomes "I interrupted twice—why?" Name the shift: cognitive specificity. Explain it: specificity anchors thought in observable behaviour, which can be assessed. Implication: reflection produces information that can be acted upon; rumination produces mood that cannot.

A practical detail is important for intellectual credibility: in 2018, a study at the University of Oxford showed that participants trained in specificity-based thinking experienced reduced anxiety and greater problem-solving accuracy compared with controls. Precision changes outcomes.

The eighth claim turns towards self-regulation. Rumination heightens distress; reflection regulates it. Show the behaviour: the reader feels calmer as soon as they adopt inquiry. Name the mechanism: emotional modulation. Explain it: by engaging prefrontal reasoning, the brain dampens limbic activation. Implication: reflection is protective, not indulgent.

The limitation is honest: reflection can initially feel effortful. It asks for deliberate attention. It can be uncomfortable. Reconciliation: the discomfort of reflection is the discomfort of growth, whereas the ease of rumination is the ease before exhaustion.

Returning one last time to *the loop and the line*, the ninth claim prepares the closing tension: reflection requires agency. No one can force a person to stop looping. But the moment they notice the loop, a choice arises.

And so the forward movement emerges as a question rather than an answer. When the mind begins replaying that familiar scene—whether after a meeting, a conversation, a misstep, or a long day—will you continue tracing the same circle, or will you pause long enough to draw a line instead?

Making Space For Unfelt Feelings

In 1929, the Viennese psychologist Charlotte Bühler published a short report describing a pattern she observed in adolescents recovering from a year of political unrest in the city. Her account focused on one seventeen-year-old boy who insisted he felt "nothing unusual," though he suffered tightness in his chest each evening. When Bühler invited him simply to sit quietly for two minutes, the boy remarked that the tightness "felt like missing someone." The feeling was not new; only his attention to it was. Bühler noted that the boy's distress eased not because he solved anything but because he *named* the truth of his own experience. The moment he allowed the sensation to become a feeling, the internal noise softened. It remains one of the earliest clinical descriptions of how unrecognised emotion intensifies mental pressure.

A modern example is far less dramatic yet equally instructive. A reader comes home after a demanding day, drops their bag in the hallway, and begins mechanically preparing dinner. Their breath feels shallow, their chest heavy, their shoulders slightly lifted. They convince themselves it is simple fatigue. But as they pause—perhaps only because a saucepan boils over—they notice a slow ache in the sternum. They sit for a moment. They let the sensation be. Eventually a quiet sentence rises: *This is sadness.* Not catastrophic sadness, not crisis-driven sadness, but the lingering residue of a difficult conversation from earlier in the day. The moment the feeling is recognised, the day's internal commentary shifts. Instead of pushing through, they breathe. They soften. A small truth creates space.

The quiet motif running through this piece is *the unopened door*: the emotional experience waiting behind the sensations we avoid, the door most people pass without entering. Feelings unfelt remain unopened. Feelings named open a room.

The first claim: unacknowledged emotion fuels inner noise. Show the behaviour: the reader moves through their evening in a haze, snapping at small irritations, misplacing their keys, unable to focus. Name the mechanism: emotional suppression, well documented in James Gross's work at Stanford University since the late 1990s. Explain the process: when emotions are pushed aside rather than recognised, the body recruits extra physiological effort to contain them—tight muscles, rising heart rate, jittery alertness. Implication: suppression appears tidy on the outside but is chaotic on the inside.

A named historical example strengthens this dynamic. In 1951, psychoanalyst Michael Balint, writing at the Tavistock Clinic in London, described how patients who disavowed emotional discomfort often showed "somatic echoes"—headaches, digestive tension, breath irregularities—without conscious awareness of the feeling prompting them. The emotional door stayed closed, so the body carried the pressure.

Introduce a credible limitation. Some people report that ignoring feelings helps them stay effective during emergencies or high-stakes professional tasks. This limitation is legitimate; short-term suppression can maintain function. But reconciliation is needed. What works in the moment becomes harmful when habitual. Continued suppression turns temporary coping into perpetual strain. The implication is firm: we do not need to force feelings open, but we do need to stop bolting the door.

The second claim: feelings manifest first as sensations. Show the behaviour: the reader senses heaviness in the chest or a knot in the stomach. Name the phenomenon: interoception—the perception of internal bodily states—described extensively by neuroscientist A. D. Craig in 2002. Explain it: before an emotion becomes conscious, the body signals change in muscle tone, breath depth, and heart rhythm. Implication: attending to bodily cues offers earlier access to emotional truth than waiting for thought to catch up.

A named example from outside the psychological world illustrates universality. In 2006, conductor Claudio Abbado returned to the Berlin Philharmonic after cancer treatment. Musicians noted that during rehearsals he often paused, hand resting briefly over his chest. Later he explained that the pause helped him sense whether his tension was physical strain or emotional vulnerability. The pause—simple, embodied—kept him honest. It opened the door a little.

The quiet motif appears again: *the unopened door*. The doorway is bodily sensation; the room beyond it is emotional meaning.

The third claim: naming a feeling changes its intensity. Show the behaviour: the reader says quietly, "This is sadness." Name the mechanism: affect labelling, a term coined by Matthew Lieberman at UCLA in 2007. Explain it: identifying a feeling reduces amygdala activation and increases activity in the prefrontal cortex. Implication: naming is not melodrama; it is neurological regulation.

A limitation belongs here. Affect labelling does not work the same way for every emotional state. In 2018, a study at the University of Toronto found that naming anger sometimes increases short-term agitation. Reconciliation: anger often carries energy that needs physical release, not only naming. So the rule is not "naming solves everything," but "naming clarifies what kind of care is needed."

The fourth claim: gentle emotional check-ins prevent emotional backlog. Show the behaviour: the reader pauses for twenty seconds before dinner, scanning the chest, throat, and belly. Name the practice: micro-awareness. Explain it: brief, regular attention reduces the build-up of unfelt emotion, similar to releasing pressure from a valve. Implication: emotional overwhelm is often the result of accumulation, not intensity.

A named historical parallel adds depth. Medieval monastic communities, particularly the Carthusians in the twelfth century, kept the practice of *statio*—pausing at the threshold between daily activities. Before leaving the chapel, before beginning work, before entering the refectory, monks halted for a breath. These micro-pauses were not about holiness but about presence. They prevented the emotional turbulence of one task from spilling unexamined into the next. The door was opened gently, often.

The motif returns: *the unopened door*. Each pause is a hand on the handle.

The fifth claim: unfelt feelings distort perception. Show the behaviour: the reader misreads a colleague's neutral message as criticism or interprets a partner's silence as disapproval. Name the mechanism: emotional projection. Explain it: the mind assigns internal emotion to external events when that emotion has nowhere else to go. Implication: clarity demands space; without space, interpretation becomes confabulation.

A credible counter-example must be acknowledged. Not every misinterpretation stems from suppressed emotion; sometimes situations genuinely contain ambiguity or tension. Reconciliation: emotional clarity does not remove uncertainty, but it reduces the distortions that make uncertainty intolerable.

The sixth claim: making space for emotion does not mean indulging it. Show the behaviour: the reader sits for a minute, acknowledges sadness, and continues cooking dinner. Name the stance: compassionate witnessing. Explain it: emotion is observed without exaggeration, minimisation, or storytelling. Implication: this practice strengthens inner steadiness, not fragility.

A second named example offers balance. In 2015, the NHS recommended brief "emotional check-ins" for staff in high-stress hospital environments. These pauses were not intended to create catharsis but to prevent burnout by reducing emotional backlog. Data from several trusts showed decreases in staff-reported exhaustion over a six-month trial. The practice was small yet significant. It opened the door just enough.

The motif circles once more: *the unopened door* becomes *the opened room*. Inside this room are the emotions that accompany every human life—sadness, irritation, longing, envy, tenderness, joy, fatigue. When they remain behind a locked door, they push and rattle. When the door opens, even slightly, the room becomes navigable.

The seventh claim: the body is the first messenger, not the last. Show the behaviour: chest heaviness, clenched jaw, restless hands. Name the principle: somatic signalling. Explain it: these signals are invitations, not threats. Implication: ignoring them prolongs discomfort; listening reduces it.

A limitation grounds the argument. Some bodily sensations arise from physical conditions unrelated to emotion. Chest tightness can reflect respiratory strain; gut discomfort can stem from diet. Reconciliation is essential. The key is curiosity, not certainty. The aim is not to diagnose emotion but to *consider* its presence. The emotional door opens with possibility, not with conclusion.

The eighth claim: gentle acknowledgement restores agency. Show the behaviour: after naming sadness, the reader feels freer to choose what to do next—rest, walk, speak to someone, or simply continue with dinner. Name the effect: emotional differentiation. Explain it: by separating sensation from story, the person gains room to act. Implication: agency emerges not from suppressing emotion but from recognising it.

The closing movement returns to the motif one final time. Each unfelt feeling is a door. The question is whether it remains unopened, gathering pressure behind it, or whether one pauses long enough—twenty seconds, a breath—to touch the handle.

And so the forward test is simple and demanding. When your chest feels heavy at the end of a long day, will you insist it is nothing, or will you open the door just a little and ask what waits inside?

Compassionate Inner Listening

In 2014, psychologist Kristin Neff recorded a structured interview with a woman named Ellen in Austin, Texas. The session, later published as part of the University of Texas

Compassion Research Consortium's archive, documented a subtle but revealing shift. Ellen had come to discuss a strained exchange with her manager the previous day. Her first retelling was sharp, breathless, and punishing: "I messed it up again... I should have been stronger... I always do this." Neff paused, then asked her to speak *as if* she were talking to a close friend who had experienced the same situation. When Ellen tried again, her shoulders dropped, her voice slowed, and a different sentence emerged: "You were under pressure. Anyone would find that hard. Let's understand what happened." The facts of the event had not changed, yet the entire emotional landscape shifted. It was the tone—the inner tone—that made the difference.

A similar moment unfolds in many homes at the end of a long day. Someone sits at the kitchen table after a difficult conversation with a partner or colleague. The mind darts, replaying lines, crafting indictments, appointing blame. Their inner voice is clipped and relentless. But then something interrupts the cycle—a kettle boiling, a child asking a question, the simple act of sitting down more firmly. They take a breath. They ask quietly, "If a dear friend had lived this day, what would I say to them?" The commentary softens. The accusations loosen. Space appears where harshness once sat. This shift is not sentimentality; it is a recalibration of inner governance.

The motif for this piece is *the softened edge*: the way tone alters impact, the way the edge of our own mind can be sharp or rounded, cutting or containing. A softened edge is not weakness. It is discernment.

The first claim: the tone of inner speech shapes physiological state. Show the behaviour: Ellen's shoulders dropped when she changed her tone. Name the mechanism: parasympathetic activation, identified in Stephen Porges's polyvagal research from the mid-1990s. Explain it: soothing, non-threatening speech—even when spoken by oneself—signals safety to the nervous system, reducing heart rate and muscular tension. Implication: compassionate self-address is not indulgence but biological recalibration.

A second named example reinforces the principle. In 2008, researchers at the University of California, Berkeley, led by psychologist Iris Mauss, found that self-criticism after stressful tasks significantly increased cortisol levels, while self-kindness moderated them. The study was small yet robust; measurable biochemical markers changed depending on the tone of internal dialogue. The softened edge had a visible physiological effect.

Introduce a credible limitation. Some argue that self-compassion risks excusing poor behaviour or lowering standards. This limitation deserves recognition. But reconcile it by distinguishing tone from accountability. A softened edge alters *how* we speak to ourselves, not *what* we address. Responsibility remains intact; cruelty does not improve performance.

The second claim: harsh self-talk narrows perception. Show the behaviour: the reader, after a fraught conversation, hears only their own failure, missing contextual cues—fatigue, misunderstanding, competing pressures. Name the phenomenon: cognitive constriction. Explain it: in high-threat internal conditions, the prefrontal cortex reduces bandwidth, limiting access to nuance. Implication: cruelty to the self creates intellectual blindness.

A named example brings this into view. In 1993, surgeon and writer Atul Gawande, then a trainee at Massachusetts General Hospital, noted in his early journals that harsh self-critique after medical errors made him "see less, learn less, and react worse." Later, he wrote publicly that adopting a more curious, less punitive tone preserved clarity under pressure. A softened edge improved insight.

A counter-example deepens the argument. Some high-performing individuals report that harsh inner commentary motivates achievement. Their accounts are sincere. But reconcile this by distinguishing short-term drive from long-term sustainability. Self-punishment can propel action briefly, but research from the University of Michigan (Neff & Germer, 2019 trial replication) shows that it correlates with burnout over extended periods. The softened edge is not about complacency; it is about endurance.

The third claim: compassionate inner listening requires deliberate attention. Show the behaviour: the person at the kitchen table breathes, pauses, and consciously shifts tone. Name the practice: reframing through perspective-taking. Explain it: adopting the stance of a caring other bypasses engrained self-critical scripts. Implication: inner kindness is a skill, not a mood.

A named historical practice illustrates lineage. In eighteenth-century England, Samuel Johnson kept what he called "moral diaries," in which he wrote about his struggles with procrastination and irritability. What stands out is his tone. Though he held himself to a stringent ethical standard, his reflections often included softening sentences such as, "I have endured much this month; let me proceed with patience." His edge softened through writing. He held himself firmly yet tenderly.

Reintroduce *the softened edge* motif: Johnson learned to blunt the blade without losing its precision.

The fourth claim: compassionate listening to oneself clarifies emotional truth. Show the behaviour: after softening their tone, the person realises they were not angry at their colleague but embarrassed by their own hurried response. Name the mechanism: emotional differentiation. Explain it: when harshness subsides, subtler emotions become perceptible. Implication: compassion sharpens accuracy, not fogginess.

A second named example offers depth. In 2017, at the Oxford Mindfulness Centre, a small cohort of participants reported that self-compassion training improved their ability to identify mixed emotional states—relief laced with guilt, irritation threaded with fear. The training did not eradicate difficult feelings; it clarified them. The softened edge opened space for precision.

A limitation must enter again. For a minority of individuals, especially those with trauma histories, softening self-talk may initially intensify discomfort. Hearing a gentle tone can feel unfamiliar or unsafe. Reconciliation: this does not invalidate the practice; it simply means the softened edge must be introduced slowly, paired with grounding and external support where needed.

The fifth claim: compassionate inner listening improves relational behaviour. Show the behaviour: someone receives a curt message from a colleague. Their first internal reaction is sharp: "Why are they always like this?" But after a quiet pause and a shift in tone—"I'm tired... let's understand this properly"—they respond calmly rather than defensively. Name the effect: relational de-escalation. Explain it: the softened edge reduces reactivity, allowing more constructive communication. Implication: inner tone shapes outer conduct.

A named example supports the link. In 2012, a programme at King's College London taught healthcare leaders micro-skills in self-compassion. Evaluators found that participants reported fewer impulsive reactions in workplace conflict. The softened edge became outward steadiness.

The motif appears again: the softened edge is transferable—it shapes not only private experience but public behaviour.

The sixth claim: compassionate inner listening counters shame. Show the behaviour: the reader recalls a mistake yet speaks internally with warmth rather than scorn. Name the mechanism: shame attenuation. Explain it: shame thrives on isolation and attack; compassion interrupts the cycle. Implication: self-kindness restores dignity without erasing responsibility.

A historical example adds richness. In 1535, Ignatius of Loyola described in his *Spiritual Exercises* a method of reviewing one's actions each day "with gentle sorrow, not harsh rebuke." His phrasing is deliberate. He understood that remorse cleanses only when paired with compassion; harshness corrodes.

A limitation sharpens credibility. Compassion can be misused to avoid confronting real wrongdoing. Reconciliation: true compassion includes honesty. It names the harm, repairs what can be repaired, and rejects cruelty without rejecting accountability.

The seventh claim: a softened edge increases resilience. Show the behaviour: after a difficult exchange, the reader recovers more quickly when their tone is kind. Name the process: self-regulation. Explain it: compassionate inner listening stabilises the nervous system and reduces rumination, enabling quicker return to baseline. Implication: inner warmth strengthens durability.

A named example from sport underscores this. British athlete Kelly Holmes wrote in 2018 that shifting from self-critique to self-support during training after injury helped her maintain motivation during rehabilitation. Her performance improved not by increasing discipline but by reducing self-directed hostility. The softened edge bolstered resilience.

The motif returns one final time: *the softened edge* transforms sharp self-attack into rounded awareness, capable of holding pressure without cracking.

The closing movement ends with a question. When the next difficult conversation leaves your mind racing, which inner voice will you choose—the blade or the softened edge?

Chapter 5
Solitude Without Loneliness

On a late autumn evening in Edinburgh, a woman stepped off the bus two stops early. She had spent the day immersed in cordial chatter—meetings, greetings, small talk poured over every task like a glaze. Colleagues were kind, the work familiar, yet her chest felt taut, her thoughts thin. She considered a friend's invitation to meet for drinks but instead slipped her phone into her pocket, turned down a quieter street, and began to walk. The wind threaded through the sycamores along the Meadows. A few students hurried past. A dog barked in the distance. She walked without purpose, without audience, without conversation. By the time she reached her front door, her shoulders had dropped and her mind had cleared. Nothing dramatic had happened. Yet she felt restored in a way no crowded bar could have offered. That short, deliberate solitude was not escape; it was replenishment.

Many people know this sensation but ignore it. We imagine solitude is a sign of failure or deficiency, as though choosing to be alone punctures our social credentials. In reality, solitude has always been a form of hygiene: a gentle scrubbing of the mind, a recalibration of one's inner bearings. Yet the modern fear of missing out—social, professional, relational—has made it harder to claim this space without apology. We are not taught that aloneness, when chosen with clarity, enlarges our capacity for presence; we are taught instead that it suggests rejection or oddity. And so we say yes when we want to say no. We fill calendars to justify our relevance. We chase stimulation to avoid the tremor of quiet. But somewhere underneath the noise, most people suspect that their best thinking, their deepest steadiness, arises only when they are briefly, intentionally, unaccompanied.

This chapter explores that suspicion—not as nostalgia, but as a contemporary necessity. Solitude is no longer simply a monastic luxury; it is a practical skill for anyone hoping to remain sane in a culture that prizes availability above discernment. The art is not to withdraw from the world, nor to retreat into a defensive bunker, but to step away long enough to return with more perspective, more generosity, and more nerve. Solitude, at its healthiest, is relational: it strengthens the self from which relationships are formed.

The distinction between solitude and loneliness is subtle but vital. Loneliness is a hunger; solitude is nourishment. Loneliness contracts the mind; solitude expands it. Yet the line between the two is not drawn by circumstance but by intention. It is possible to feel utterly alone at a crowded dinner, and quietly whole while sitting on a bench with no one in sight. What determines the difference is whether we meet ourselves in that space or flee ourselves. And because many people have avoided inner encounter for years—sometimes decades—solitude can feel at first like stepping into a room with a stranger.

The chapter begins by reframing chosen solitude as a form of strength. It is not a resignation from social life but a reclamation of personal autonomy. A short walk alone after work, a slow coffee on a park bench, ten minutes spent lingering in one's own thoughts—these moments refill inner reserves that constant connection depletes. The woman in Edinburgh discovered this in the few blocks between the bus stop and her home. Her solitude did not estrange her from her colleagues; it returned her to them less frayed.

From here, the chapter moves into a necessary differentiation: the difference between retreat and isolation. Retreat is temporary withdrawal in service of return; isolation is withdrawal in fear of engagement. The two often look alike from the outside but feel entirely different on the inside. One reader described declining every invitation for weeks, telling herself she was "taking space," only to realise she was numbing, not nourishing. Later, she planned a two-day, clearly defined period away—a deliberate retreat—and found herself emerging calmer, clearer, and more available to others. The contrast between aimless avoidance and purposeful solitude is the hinge on which emotional health turns. This chapter offers practical questions that help the reader discern which direction they are leaning toward at any given moment.

After exploring the broader cultural misreadings of solitude, the narrative turns toward boundaries. Many people crave quiet but fear the relational cost of asking for it. The result is silent resentment, passive withdrawal, or burnout disguised as busyness. Yet there are gentler ways. A parent who tells their family, "I'm going to take ten minutes after dinner just to reset—it helps me be more present later," is not rejecting anyone; they are protecting the quality of the household's future interactions. When communicated with warmth and clarity, such boundaries become invitations rather than barriers: an understanding that each person's solitude supports the collective equilibrium.

Still, even with boundaries and clarity, solitude often reveals an uncomfortable truth: many people do not like being alone with themselves. The discomfort is not pathological; it is simply unfamiliar. When someone sits in a chair for five minutes without stimulation, their mind may thrash like an unsettled animal—old anxieties surface, small irritations amplify, vague restlessness rises. The first impulse is to flee: to stand up, to scroll, to speak, to distract. But the capacity to stay seated—to remain with oneself for a few slow breaths—teaches an invaluable lesson. It reveals that inner unease, when witnessed without panic, begins to settle. The person who manages to stay in the chair discovers that solitude is not a threat to be outrun but a terrain to be learned.

The through-line of this chapter is that solitude is a craft. It can be shaped, refined, and personalised. It is not a rigid practice but a flexible one, adapting itself to the contours of each life. In a world where the default state is relentless stimulation, solitude is countercultural in the quietest, most life-giving way. It teaches patience. It renews attention. It restores agency. It gradually replaces the fear of being alone with the pleasure of inhabiting one's own company.

The coming pages will trace this craft with care—how to choose solitude without shame, how to differentiate retreat from avoidance, how to set boundaries that honour connection rather than fracture it, and how to sit with oneself when the first minutes feel like static. None of these practices ask for heroism. They ask only for honesty, gentleness, and a willingness to pause long enough to feel the difference between depletion and renewal.

And so the chapter opens with a simple question that holds considerable weight: when the day presses in and the noise grows thick, will you turn toward others automatically, or will you dare—just for a moment—to turn toward yourself?

Choosing To Be Alone On Purpose

In April 2019, the psychologist Thuy-vy Nguyen of Durham University led a small field study in which office workers in Newcastle were invited to take a fifteen-minute solitary walk after work instead of joining their usual social routine. The outcomes were modest yet striking: participants consistently reported lower cognitive fatigue and greater emotional clarity, even after a single walk. One participant noted that the short time alone "felt like exhaling," adding that conversation—however pleasant—had been "another form of effort." The study was not about loneliness; it was about deliberate solitude. When people stepped away from the steady pull of interaction, something inside recalibrated.

A similar moment plays out informally every evening across Britain. Someone finishes work, receives a message about meeting for a quick drink, and feels the familiar tug of obligation. Instead of accepting, they slip their phone into their pocket and begin walking home alone. They move past cafés where laughter rises, past shopfronts glowing in the blue hour. For the first few minutes, their mind races with all the things they "should" be doing—replying, engaging, being seen. Then the knot begins to loosen. They hear their footsteps. They notice a shift in the wind. They breathe more deeply. By the time they reach their door, they feel something close to steadiness. Nothing extraordinary occurred. But that small, chosen interval without company has restored a measure of vitality that another evening of distracted small talk would have depleted. This is our motif: *the cleared path*. Solitude, chosen intentionally, clears a path through the day's noise.

The first claim: chosen solitude is not social failure but psychological maintenance. Show the behaviour: the solitary walker returns home less irritable, more focused, and more available. Name the mechanism: cognitive restoration, a phenomenon described by environmental psychologists Rachel and Stephen Kaplan in the 1980s. Explain it: the mind fatigues under constant social and sensory demand; a brief period without interpersonal negotiation allows attentional resources to replenish. Implication: solitude is not avoidance but upkeep, akin to tidying a workbench before continuing.

A named historical example strengthens this broader truth. In 1851, Henry David Thoreau recorded that his most perceptive hours at Walden Pond occurred not during grand periods of isolation but during short, daily intervals of quiet walking. He considered these walks essential "intervals of freedom," where his attention could settle enough to think independently rather than reactively. His solitude cleared a path for discernment.

A limitation must be addressed. Some individuals find solitude draining or anxiety-provoking, especially if daily life is already marked by isolation. Reconciliation lies in distinguishing *chosen* solitude from *imposed* aloneness. Where the former restores agency, the latter erodes it. The aim here is intentional quiet, not social deprivation.

The second claim: solitude refines attention. Show the behaviour: the reader walking home notices details—light on a brick wall, the rhythm of their pace—that they would have missed in conversation. Name the mechanism: perceptual broadening. Explain it: without the cognitive load of dialogue or performance, sensory awareness widens. Implication: solitude sharpens perception, not blunts it.

A modern example illuminates the principle. In 2015, neuroscientist David Strayer of the University of Utah found that participants who spent time alone in natural environments performed 50% better on creativity tasks compared to their pre-walk scores. Nature was not the only factor; the solitude itself freed mental space. The cleared path allowed the mind to roam rather than defend.

Introduce a counter-example. High extroverts often report that solitude reduces their energy rather than increases it. This is not a contradiction but a difference in optimal dosage. Reconciliation: solitude need not be long to be restorative; even five minutes of intentional aloneness can function as a micro-reset for extroverts, provided the time is framed as a pause rather than a withdrawal.

The third claim: chosen solitude strengthens autonomy. Show the behaviour: declining an invitation not from irritation but from clarity. Name the mechanism: self-determined choice, described in self-determination theory (Deci & Ryan, 1985). Explain it: when individuals act from intrinsic need rather than external expectation, psychological vitality increases. Implication: solitude is a declaration of inner authorship.

A named example brings this into professional life. In 1988, the architect Zaha Hadid described her daily practice of sitting alone for twenty minutes before beginning design work. She called it "resetting the line," a way of ensuring that the day's creative direction began internally, not reactively. The solitude was not detachment but alignment.

The motif reappears: *the cleared path*—a brief route carved through obligation to reclaim direction.

The fourth claim: solitude recalibrates emotional boundaries. Show the behaviour: after walking alone, the reader responds to a difficult message with measured tone rather than irritability. Name the process: emotional deceleration. Explain it: without social inputs, emotional reactivity loses momentum. Implication: solitude protects relationships rather than endangers them.

A counter-example must surface. Some fear that choosing to be alone will disappoint friends or signal disinterest. This concern has weight. But reconcile it by observing that relationships weather short absences; what damages them is chronic depletion. When solitude restores emotional steadiness, the quality of later connection improves.

The fifth claim: solitude cultivates internal companionship. Show the behaviour: as the reader walks, their mind eventually quietens enough that inner dialogue becomes gentler, less frantic. Name the principle: inward friendliness. Explain it: solitude exposes inner tone; with practice, that tone becomes more humane. Implication: chosen aloneness strengthens the ability to accompany oneself.

Historical lineage supports this. In the seventeenth century, philosopher Blaise Pascal wrote that "all of humanity's problems stem from man's inability to sit quietly in a room alone." Yet a lesser-quoted line from the same text reveals his solution: he believed the capacity to be alone could be learned gradually, through regular intervals of undistracted presence. The cleared path is learned terrain.

The sixth claim: solitude fosters discernment. Show the behaviour: the solitary walker realises they do not need to attend every social event to feel connected. Name the process: value alignment. Explain it: without noise, authentic preference surfaces. Implication: solitude strengthens decision-making.

A limitation offers balance. Excessive solitude risks narrowing perspective or inviting stagnation. Reconciliation: chosen solitude is bounded, deliberate, and punctuated by return. It is the contrast between the walk home and the re-entry into shared life that gives the practice its power.

The seventh claim: solitude is accessible in small, ordinary intervals. Show the behaviour: someone steps outside for two minutes before rejoining colleagues; another lingers in the car before entering a bustling home. Name the practice: micro-solitude. Explain it: restoration does not require dramatic withdrawal. Implication: everyone can carve a cleared path, however briefly.

A final named example brings the argument into everyday life. In 2021, a study conducted at University College London found that workers who incorporated brief solitary pauses into their day reported greater perceived control and lower emotional exhaustion across eight weeks. The pauses did not change workloads. What changed was the mind's capacity to meet those workloads.

The closing movement circles back to the motif. *The cleared path* is always available, but only if chosen. So the unresolved question becomes a practical test: when the next invitation appears—social, digital, conversational—will you accept it automatically, or will you pause long enough to ask whether a short, solitary walk might serve you better?

The Difference Between Isolation And Retreat

In July 2018, the manager of a design cooperative in Bristol, Lorna Reeves, made a choice that startled her colleagues. After months of quietly declining almost every social invitation, she requested a formally scheduled three-day retreat away from the office. The contrast forced a conversation. Her earlier withdrawals had left the team uneasy; her planned absence, by contrast, reassured them. The retreat had a purpose, a boundary, and a return point. Reeves later described the three days as "a repair shop for attention." Her unspoken absences had drained trust. Her declared retreat restored it. The distinction was not simply semantic. It revealed two different psychological movements: stepping back to return clearer, and stepping away to avoid the world. One renews. The other erodes.

That distinction plays out quietly in countless ordinary lives. Picture someone receiving an invitation to an after-work gathering. Last week they declined. The week before, they also said no. Tonight, they hover over their phone again, feeling a mix of relief and guilt. Compare that with the same person choosing a Saturday afternoon as protected retreat time—phone silenced, door closed, time-limit set—so they can re-enter the week refreshed. The body recognises the difference even when the situations look similar. Declining every invitation feels like disappearance. Blocking out a few hours on purpose feels like repair. The motif that anchors this chapter emerges here: *the door that closes to open again*. Retreat hinges. Isolation locks.

The first claim: retreat is shaped by structure. Show the behaviour. Reeves told her team precisely when she would be gone, what she aimed to restore—clarity for an upcoming project—and when she would return. Name the principle: bounded solitude. Explain it. Structure transforms time alone from drift into intention. Clear duration, clear aim, clear re-entry. Implication: without structure, solitude risks collapsing into avoidance.

History offers a second named example. In 1974, the poet Mary Oliver spent two months working near Provincetown, Massachusetts, yet she returned to town each evening to share dinner with friends. She called the mornings her "working retreat," designed not to sever connection but to strengthen her capacity to meet it. The structure mattered. Her retreat sharpened attention; it did not remove her from life. The door closed, then opened again.

A limitation complicates this claim. Some people benefit from unstructured solitude; artists, academics, and entrepreneurs often find that creative work does not fit neatly into predetermined windows. Reconcile this by returning to purpose: what differentiates retreat is not rigidity but orientation. Even loose time becomes retreat if it is chosen for nourishment rather than escape.

The second claim: isolation is shaped by fear. Show the behaviour. The person who has declined six invitations in a row is not resting; they are hiding. Their relief is followed by constriction: racing thoughts, shrinking confidence, the sense that rejoining others will now feel harder. Name the process: social contraction. Explain it. Isolation narrows the field of experience; it reduces the range of stimuli and thus exaggerates the weight of each one. Implication: withdrawal breeds further withdrawal.

A checkable example grounds this. In 2020, the UK's Office for National Statistics recorded that individuals who reported sustained social withdrawal—not temporary solitude—also reported higher rumination levels and lower perceived agency. They were not choosing peace; they were losing mobility. A door that stays closed stiffens its hinges.

A counter-example must be faced. Some individuals prefer very limited social engagement and find withdrawal neutral rather than damaging. Reconciliation lies in examining consequence rather than preference. If time alone cultivates clarity, autonomy, and readiness to return, it is retreat. If it amplifies dread, diminishes confidence, or increases avoidance, it has drifted into isolation.

The third claim: retreat includes a commitment to return. Show the behaviour. Reeves re-entered her cooperative after three days with renewed focus; she shared what the break had clarified. Name the mechanism: reintegration. Explain it. Retreat assumes re-entry; the renewed self meets the familiar world with steadier presence. Implication: retreat strengthens connection rather than weakening it.

A historical example deepens this. In 1977, the composer Arvo Pärt spent three years in relative quiet in Tallinn following a period of creative exhaustion. When he returned to public composition, he unveiled *Tabula Rasa*, a work of spare clarity that reshaped contemporary classical music. His retreat was not disappearance but gestation. The door closed so something new could form. Then it opened again.

The motif threads through: *the door that closes to open again*. Retreat hinges upon intentional reopening.

The fourth claim: isolation confuses stillness with stuckness. Show the behaviour. The person declining every invitation feels heavy, slow, and vaguely ashamed. Name the principle: inertial solitude. Explain it. When withdrawal is driven by overwhelm or fear, the nervous system stays activated; stillness becomes paralysis. Implication: isolation drains vitality; it does not restore it.

A limitation sharpens nuance. Temporary withdrawal can sometimes be protective, especially during grief, burnout, or acute stress. To reconcile this, examine trajectory. Protective withdrawal has a direction: it leads towards stabilisation. Harmful isolation is circular: it keeps a person trapped in the same emotional weather without movement.

The fifth claim: retreat invites reflection; isolation strengthens rumination. Show the behaviour. During a planned retreat, a person might journal, walk, breathe, or simply rest. Their mind slows enough to sort through thoughts. Name the process: cognitive settling. Explain it. When input decreases, mental sediment begins to fall; the water clears. Implication: retreat produces insight or, at minimum, steadiness.

A counter-behaviour highlights contrast. Isolation often reinforces looping anxieties—the mind replays conversations, reinterprets messages, anticipates criticism. Rumination thickens rather than thins. Reconciliation: the difference is the presence or absence of conscious orientation. Retreat aims at clarity; isolation circles without aim.

The sixth claim: retreat is time-limited; isolation is open-ended. Show the behaviour. Reeves' retreat had an end date. Oliver's morning hours had a daily boundary. Name the principle: temporal containment. Explain it. Time limits prevent solitude from sprawling into erasure; they provide psychological safety, signalling that pause is not permanent. Implication: retreat strengthens confidence in approaching stillness.

A modern example bolsters this. In 2022, a study at King's College London found that participants who scheduled short, time-limited solitary breaks reported increased emotional regulation, whereas participants who simply "pulled away" from social contact for indefinite stretches reported decreased regulation. Duration mattered less than container.

The seventh claim: knowing which you are in—retreat or isolation—requires honest questions. Show the behaviour. Someone declines another invitation, then stops and asks: *Am I resting or avoiding? Will this help me return better or make returning harder?* Name the practice: discernment questioning. Explain it. These small interrogations illuminate motivation before it solidifies into habit. Implication: the ability to name one's state alters its trajectory.

A limitation enters here: self-assessment is often clouded by exhaustion. Reconciliation: discernment does not need to be perfect; it only needs to be regular. Asking imperfect questions still shifts behaviour from automatic to intentional.

The eighth claim: retreat respects relationships; isolation strains them. Show the behaviour. A person texts a friend to say, "I'm taking some quiet time and will be back in touch on Sunday." Contrast this with simply not replying for three days. Name the mechanism: relational signalling. Explain it. Retreat communicates care by maintaining contact even while stepping away. Isolation communicates absence. Implication: healthy solitude includes visibility.

Historical correspondence offers evidence. In 1913, the writer Rainer Maria Rilke often informed friends of his intentional solitude periods while working in Paris. His letters were brief, honest, and gentle: a signal of connection sustained even through retreat. His temporary absences did not sever bonds; they clarified them.

The motif returns: *the door that closes to open again*. Communication is the handle.

The ninth claim: retreat enlarges life; isolation shrinks it. Show the behaviour. After a planned short retreat, a person returns with renewed willingness to engage—hosting dinner, making a decision, committing to a project. Name the principle: expansion after contraction. Explain it. A measured pullback creates space for greater involvement later. Implication: retreat enlarges capacity.

A counter-example arises: intense retreat can sometimes produce a longing never to return, tempting an extended escape. Reconciliation: this is a signal that retreat is revealing unmet needs, not that isolation is the answer. The task becomes adjusting daily life, not abandoning it.

The closing movement stands at the threshold of the motif. *The door that closes to open again* poses its lingering question.

When you next step back from the world—whether for an afternoon or a week—will your withdrawal have an edge of fear or an outline of purpose? Will you return with more to give, or will re-entry feel heavier? The distinction shapes not only how you spend your time alone but the life you rejoin when the door eventually opens.

Setting Gentle Boundaries With Others

In 2010, the Family and Child Psychology branch at Great Ormond Street Hospital in London began running workshops for parents of chronically ill children. The clinicians noticed a recurring pattern. The most exhausted parents were often the ones who never took even a few minutes alone. They refused offers of respite, stayed constantly "on", and felt guilty at the thought of stepping away. When one psychologist suggested a simple ten-minute post-dinner pause—*"You tell your child, 'For ten minutes after we eat, I'll sit in the next room to rest so I can look after you better later'"*—there was hesitation, even horror. Yet the families who tried it reported something unexpected: children adapted quickly, anxiety reduced, and parents returned calmer, less brittle, more able to respond with patience. The structure was tiny. The impact was not.

Consider a quieter, more ordinary scene. A parent in a semi-detached house in Leeds is stacking plates after an evening meal. The children are bouncing between the table and the sofa, arguing about a game. The parent's shoulders are tight, their thoughts frayed. Every question feels like sandpaper. In the past, they would have snapped, stayed in the room, and then collapsed later with a screen, drained and disconnected. Tonight they try something else. They kneel, look the children in the eye, and say, "I'm going to take ten minutes in the armchair with my book. Then I'll come and play. This helps me be a nicer mum/dad." There is some protest, a little confusion, but the ritual begins. The parent sits alone, not hiding, door open, the household humming nearby. Ten minutes later they return, steadier. Nothing dramatic. Yet a line has been drawn that protects everyone.

The motif that threads through this subchapter is *the door ajar*. The boundary is not a slammed door, locked and cold. Nor is it a door ripped off its hinges in the name of endless availability. It is a door gently closed for a short time, left ajar by communication and affection. The hinge is not distance but explanation.

The first claim: gentle boundaries are relational, not defensive. Show the behaviour. The parent in Leeds does not disappear without warning. They explain the purpose, they state the time, they promise to return. Name the principle: transparent withdrawal. Explain it. When people know why you are stepping away and when you will be back, they are less likely to experience your quiet as rejection. Implication: the tone and clarity of your boundary shape its impact more than its length.

Historically, boundaries have often been confused with barriers. In mid-twentieth-century Britain, the cultural ideal of parental sacrifice left many adults feeling that any time taken alone was selfish. By contrast, systemic family therapists later observed that parents who modelled healthy limits—brief, explained pauses—raised children who were more secure, not less. The children understood that adults had needs and that those needs did not threaten love. The door was ajar, not bolted.

A credible counter-example must be acknowledged. Some people invoke "boundaries" to justify chronic unavailability, using the language of self-care to mask disengagement. The result is confusion and hurt. This misuse does not discredit boundaries; it simply underscores the importance of intention and communication. A boundary that never includes you returning through the door is not a boundary. It is absence.

The second claim: gentle boundaries work best when they are embodied as routines rather than occasional emergencies. Show the behaviour. The parent takes ten minutes *every* evening after dinner, not only on the night they explode. Name the mechanism: predictable rhythm. Explain it. Regularity reduces drama; when a pattern is established, others stop taking it personally. Implication: the more routine your quiet time becomes, the less charged it is.

A named example helps ground this. In the 1990s, the Head of Nursing at a large hospital in Manchester introduced a "protected tea break" policy on certain wards. Nurses were encouraged to take a brief, uninterrupted pause at set times, and patients were told, "Between these minutes, your nurse is resting so they can look after you later." The first weeks were messy, but over time the ritual became normal. Staff burnout decreased; patient satisfaction did not suffer. The key was that the boundary was predictable and explained.

The motif returns here: *the door ajar*. A door that closes at the same time each day becomes familiar. It stops feeling like a rejection and starts feeling like part of the architecture.

The third claim: language matters as much as timing. Show the difference. "Leave me alone, I'm exhausted," sends one message. "I'm feeling very full; I'm going to take ten minutes of quiet so I can listen properly later," sends another. Name the principle: kind framing. Explain it. The boundary is the same—you are taking space—but one phrase centres your depletion and blames others, while the other acknowledges your limit and affirms connection. Implication: how you ask for quiet either erodes or builds trust.

Gentle phrasing does not require performance. Short sentences suffice. "I need a bit of quiet, but I'm not upset with you." "I'm going to read for ten minutes; then I'm all yours." These are simple relational cues. They keep the door ajar.

A counter-example is worth exploring. Some families, cultures, or partnerships are unused to spoken boundaries. Asking for time may initially provoke more conflict: "Why do you need that? What's wrong with being here?" Reconciliation lies in patience. New language often feels foreign. Repetition, sincerity, and consistency help others realise that your quiet is not commentary on their worth but care for your own capacity.

The fourth claim: gentle boundaries rely on self-knowledge. Show the behaviour. The parent notices the pattern: patience evaporates around 7 p.m., after dishes, before bedtime routines. Name the process: recognising the threshold. Explain it. Boundaries are most effective when placed where fraying actually begins, not after it has escalated into conflict. Implication: to set a kind limit, you must first observe your own nervous system with honesty.

This principle extends beyond parenting. A partner who knows they become sharp in long, late-evening conversations is better served by saying at 9.30 p.m., "I'm running out of bandwidth—can we pick this up tomorrow morning?" than by staying at the table until they lash out. The boundary is not avoidance of the conversation. It is protection of its quality.

Again, *the door ajar* is a useful image. You are not walking away from the relationship. You are stepping briefly into the hallway so you can re-enter with steadier eyes.

The fifth claim: gentle boundaries are concrete, not vague. Show the behaviour. "I need space" is nebulous. "I'm going to sit on the sofa with my journal until this timer goes off" is concrete. Name the principle: specific limit. Explain it. Vague boundaries feel like emotional weather—unpredictable and beyond negotiation. Specific limits can be understood, anticipated, and respected. Implication: specificity makes quiet feel safer for everyone involved.

Concrete boundaries can be visual. A closed laptop, a chair by the window, a candle lit for ten minutes. These small markers tell others, "This is my pause," without needing long explanations every time. Over months, these cues become part of the shared language of the home or relationship.

A counter-example shows the other side. Overly rigid boundaries—"No one may speak to me after 8 p.m. ever"—risk becoming brittle. Life is not neat. Emergencies and tenderness ignore timetables. Reconciliation requires flexibility: a boundary is a guideline, not a fortress. Being occasionally interruptible for genuine need does not invalidate your general pattern.

The sixth claim: gentle boundaries are ultimately generous. Show the behaviour. After their ten-minute ritual, the parent listens more fully to the child's story, laughs more easily, resists the reflex to snap. Name the mechanism: replenished presence. Explain it. When people are given permission to rest briefly, they return with more attention and warmth. Implication: a short period of solitude often brings *more* of you back to others, not less.

Viewed this way, the ten minutes after dinner are no longer a theft from family time; they are an investment in its quality. The same applies in friendships or partnerships. Saying, "Let me have a quiet half-hour, then we can talk properly," can feel initially like delay. In practice, it prevents half-hearted, distracted interaction.

The motif of *the door ajar* surfaces again. Crossing that threshold into your own company briefly makes you a better guest in the shared rooms of your life.

The seventh claim: boundaries invite others to find their own. Show the behaviour. After a few weeks of the parent's after-dinner ritual, a child says, "Can I have some drawing time after school, before homework?" A partner adds, "I might start taking ten minutes after my commute too." Name the phenomenon: modelled permission. Explain it. When one person claims quiet kindly, others recognise their own hunger for it. Implication: personal boundaries can ripple outward, normalising healthy solitude in a household or team.

There is a limitation worth naming. Not everyone will respond positively. Some may feel threatened, neglected, or abandoned, especially if they carry earlier experiences of being shut out. Reconciliation demands compassion on both sides. Boundaries cannot erase old wounds, but they can be shaped with sensitivity—inviting dialogue, adjusting timing, re-affirming affection.

All of this returns us to the quiet question at the core of this subchapter: can you step back without stepping away? Can you close the door gently, leave it ajar with your words and your tone, and trust that those you love are resilient enough to bear your temporary absence?

The parent in Leeds has discovered that ten minutes in an armchair does not diminish their love. It protects it. The workshops at Great Ormond Street showed that when parents rest, children often relax. The nurse on a protected tea break returns more present. The partner who asks for a pause speaks more carefully. Each of them has learned to set a boundary that bends rather than breaks connection.

So the unresolved test remains. The next time your chest tightens and your voice shortens, will you stay in the room for the sake of appearances, or will you risk the small, brave sentence that both claims and explains your need: "I care about you, and I need ten quiet minutes so I can be here properly afterwards"?

Being With Yourself When You Do Not Want To Be

In March 1954, the psychiatrist Donald Winnicott delivered a lecture at the British Psychoanalytical Society in London in which he described "the capacity to be alone" as a developmental milestone rather than a personality quirk. He noted that many adults could function publicly with competence yet could not sit quietly in a room without agitation. This was not because they were defective but because solitude exposed them to themselves, and for some that exposure felt intolerable. Winnicott's audience, steeped in mid-century psychoanalytic theory, understood the implication at once: the hardest company to keep is one's own. Seventy years later, the observation still resonates.

Picture a far more ordinary moment. A man in Brighton, returning from a long shift, sinks into a chair for what he promises himself will be five minutes of rest. Within ten seconds his leg twitches. He reaches for his phone, pulls his hand back, exhales. His chest tightens. A stray thought — *you should be doing something* — flashes like a warning light. He wants to move, stand, reorganise a drawer, anything to avoid the awkward silence inside his own ribs. He stays. He watches the impulse rise and fall. This tiny rebellion — five minutes in a chair — is what being with yourself looks like at its most unembellished.

The motif that will thread quietly through this subchapter is *the held seat*. Remaining seated becomes a kind of witness test: can you stay long enough for the mind to settle, even slightly? Can you endure the initial swarm of thoughts without bolting?

The first claim: discomfort is information, not failure. Show the behaviour. The man in Brighton notices his breath shortening and his jaw tightening; these are early signals of avoidance. Name the principle: somatic resistance. Explain it. When people sit without external distraction, the nervous system often reacts as if something is wrong. The urge to move is not a moral defect; it is a patterned response to inner stimulus. Implication: learning to be alone begins with recognising these cues not as commands but as sensations that will pass if allowed to.

A historical example sharpens this understanding. In 1913, the philosopher Edmund Husserl explored the phenomenon of *epoché*, a suspension of habitual engagement that allows deeper awareness of experience. Husserl noted that the first moments of pausing often unleash agitation rather than insight, because the mind rebels against losing its usual footholds. His observations align with what clinical psychologists at King's College London reported in 2018: when participants in a study were asked to sit for seven minutes without distraction, most reported discomfort within the first ninety seconds but steadier attention by minute four. The implication across both examples is clear: early turbulence is predictable and temporary.

A counter-example must be addressed. Some people insist that sitting still intensifies distress, making solitude unsafe. And indeed, for those with certain psychiatric conditions or acute trauma activation, unstructured stillness can overwhelm rather than soothe. The reconciliation lies in structure. When the pause is brief, clearly bounded, and anchored in sensory cues — such as feet on the floor or noticing breath without forcing it — the experience becomes tolerable rather than engulfing. Structure steadies the held seat.

The second claim: staying put reveals the mind's evasions. Show the behaviour. After two minutes, the man in Brighton begins mentally writing an email, then rehearsing an argument from last week, then planning dinner. Name the process: cognitive escape. Explain it. When physical movement is constrained, mental movement often accelerates. The inner noise is not new; the silence simply makes it audible.

Implication: five minutes alone becomes a diagnostic rather than a performance. You learn what your mind habitually does when the world stops tugging at it.

This is similar to what the historian and Trappist monk Thomas Merton noticed in his journals from Kentucky in the 1950s. When entering solitude, he recorded a rush of unfiltered thought that initially felt chaotic. Only after the flurry subsided could he differentiate between genuine insight and mental static. The implication is universal: the mind sorts itself through exposure, not avoidance.

The third claim: unease has a half-life. Show the behaviour. By minute three, the man's breath deepens slightly. The urge to stand remains but loses force. Name the principle: autonomic settling. Explain it. When the body is not fed new stimulation, the sympathetic nervous system gradually quietens and the parasympathetic system asserts itself. Implication: staying seated is not about endurance for its own sake; it is about reaching the moment where physiology begins to support, rather than sabotage, stillness.

A second example reinforces this. In 2015, researchers at the University of Sussex observed that participants who practised short, regular pauses — even two minutes at a time — showed measurable reductions in physiological markers of agitation after several weeks. The length mattered less than the consistency. Five minutes on a chair becomes not an act of heroism but a repetition that slowly rewires tolerance.

A counter-example appears in people who feel numb rather than agitated when alone. They drift, dissociate, lose time. The limitation here is that numbness can masquerade as calm. Reconciling this requires redefining the goal. The aim is not to produce a particular feeling but to stay present to whatever feeling occurs. Whether agitation or numbness arises, the discipline lies in noticing rather than fleeing.

The fourth claim: the held seat exposes stories that drive avoidance. Show the behaviour. By minute four, the man notices a quiet sentence rise within him: *If I stop, I'll have to face how tired I am*. Name the mechanism: narrative unveiling. Explain it. Avoidance is often powered by stories about what stillness will reveal — sadness, regret, fear, shame. Implication: being with yourself means encountering not only sensations but the interpretations attached to them.

A named example illustrates this. In 1977, psychiatrist Aaron Beck documented how patients often linked stillness with self-criticism. When distraction fell away, core beliefs surfaced: *I'm failing, I'm unworthy, I'm weak*. Beck's therapeutic method encouraged patients to observe these thoughts as hypotheses rather than truths. The held seat becomes a space where narratives can be seen, questioned, and softened.

The fifth claim: sitting with yourself is not passive; it is skilled effort. Show the behaviour. The man in Brighton adjusts his posture slightly, relaxes his jaw deliberately, and notices his feet pressing into the floor. These small actions keep him engaged. Name the principle: active witnessing. Explain it. Stillness requires participation, not withdrawal. You are not collapsing into the chair but inhabiting it. Implication: you remain an agent, not a captive, in your own solitude.

This aligns with traditional contemplative practices found in Benedictine monasteries, where monks are taught to treat stillness as "vigilance without striving". The point is not to empty the mind but to remain awake to experience with gentle attention. The held seat becomes a microcosm of this vigilance.

A counter-example shows the risk of over-effort. Some people approach stillness like a task: perfect posture, controlled breath, rigid focus. This often increases tension rather than softening it. Reconciliation lies in balance. The held seat asks for engagement, not perfection. Slight fidgeting does not invalidate the attempt. Attention, not performance, is the measure.

The sixth claim: structured solitude increases capacity for relational presence. Show the behaviour. When the man stands from the chair after five minutes, he feels less reactive. The email he was dreading seems manageable; the evening ahead a little clearer. Name the principle: emotional recalibration. Explain it. When you spend even a few minutes with yourself, you return to others less burdened by unprocessed tension. Implication: the held seat strengthens relationships by removing unspoken agitation from interaction.

This echoes findings from a 2020 study at University College London, which reported that participants who practised ten-minute daily pauses displayed improved emotional regulation in subsequent social interactions. The benefit extended beyond the pause itself. Stillness, however brief, recalibrated interpersonal tone.

A limitation is worth naming: solitude does not automatically equate to equanimity. Some days the five minutes feel like an achievement; others like a battle. Reconciliation lies in long-term patterns, not single sessions. The held seat teaches patience with variability.

The seventh claim: staying when you want to flee is an act of quiet courage. Show the behaviour. At minute five, the man's impulse to stand resurges. He stays one more breath, then another. He has met himself — not dramatically, not profoundly, but honestly. Name the phenomenon: micro-bravery. Explain it. Choosing presence over flight in these tiny windows builds resilience far more reliably than grand gestures. Implication: you strengthen the inner muscles of solitude through repetition, not breakthrough.

This quiet courage connects to a wider cultural truth: people often fear that being alone with their thoughts will confirm their worst suspicions about themselves. In reality, staying seated tends to make those thoughts less domineering. You learn that the storm is bearable. The chair holds you. You hold yourself.

The motif of *the held seat* returns in the closing tension. Every time you sit down alone, you face a choice. Will you stand up the moment discomfort appears, or will you treat that discomfort as part of the process? Will you flee back to noise, or remain long enough to discover what lies beneath the first wave of agitation?

The unresolved test remains. The next time you feel the instinctive tug to abandon yourself — to reach for your phone, to pace, to bustle pointlessly — will you commit to five minutes in the chair? Will you stay seated through the first minute of itch, the second of chatter, the third of resistance, until the fourth or fifth reveals something quieter?

In the end, being with yourself is not a heroic act. It is a steady one. And the question waiting for you, every time you approach that chair, is simple: can you hold the seat long enough for your inner company to become, if not comfortable, then at least familiar?

Chapter 6
Silence In Relationships

They were sitting across from each other in the small kitchen of their Edinburgh flat, plates cooling between them, after an argument that had circled for nearly an hour without landing anywhere. The instinct to fill the air—apologise too quickly, justify too defensively, soothe prematurely—pressed against both of them like a hand at their backs. Instead they stopped speaking. At first the pause felt perilous, as if silence might confirm the worst fears of distance or indifference. Yet the longer they sat, the more something unexpected happened. The heat drained from their foreheads. Their breathing steadied. A softness returned to their eyes. Nothing was resolved, and yet the tension loosened precisely because there was finally space for something other than noise. Not withdrawal. Not defeat. A shared quiet that made room for truth.

Silence, in its relational form, is almost always misunderstood. We imagine it as absence, as the vacuum left behind when communication breaks down. But in moments like that kitchen pause, silence behaves very differently: as a stabiliser. A clearing. A temporary shelter in which two minds recalibrate enough to meet again without armour. We do not talk about this often because our culture treats communication as a kind of performance—in which responsiveness equates to care, speed signals competence, and any gap risks signalling disinterest. Yet the relationships we trust most are often shaped not by what is said but by the quality of attention held between words.

If you look closely, you can see this dynamic at work in the smallest interactions. A friend sits opposite you in a café in Bristol, fingers around a mug, telling you something difficult. You feel an urge rise—offer advice, share your own story, lighten the tone. But just before you speak, you notice their shoulders. They are resting lower than when the conversation began. They are finally exhaling. You realise that the quiet between their sentences is not a vacuum but a landing place. You adjust your posture, inhale gently, and hold back your words. The conversation shifts, broadens, deepens. Silence has done more than your cleverness ever could.

This chapter explores that subtle relational power: the silence that heals rather than harms, the quiet that strengthens connection rather than disrupting it. Throughout human history, many cultures have recognised that speech carries authority but silence carries presence. The Stoic philosopher Epictetus advised his students that restraint in speech was a discipline equal to restraint in action. In Māori tradition, *whakarongo*—the attentive listening that includes respect for pauses—is considered essential to the integrity of dialogue. Even in contemporary communication studies, researchers repeatedly find that people feel more understood not when their conversation partner speaks fluently, but when that partner listens without rushing to respond. Across geographies and centuries, the pattern holds: the quality of silence shapes the quality of relationship.

Yet silence is not inherently benign. It is a double-edged instrument, capable of tenderness or cruelty depending on how it is wielded. A manager who listens quietly to a team member's frustration before offering any opinion is offering respect. A partner who retreats into cold silence after a disagreement is offering punishment. A parent who pauses before reacting to a child's confession is offering safety. A friend who withdraws into non-communication out of resentment is offering distance. The difference is not in the sound level but in the intention. Silence can be a balm or a blade.

Much contemporary discomfort with silence stems from the seismic acceleration of communication norms. Digital platforms reward fast replies, continuous updates, constant emotional availability. In such an environment, a pause can feel jarring, even alarming. Text messages without instant responses acquire meanings they were never intended to carry. Video calls compress conversational rhythms until silence becomes unnatural. Even in face-to-face situations, the cultural pressure to "keep the conversation going" can turn pauses into something to be managed or rescued rather than inhabited.

This shift has consequences. When people feel compelled to fill every conversational gap, two things suffer: listening and depth. Listening becomes performative—nodding, affirming, interjecting—rather than receptive. Depth becomes elusive because deeper truths surface only when there is space for them to breathe. The paradox is striking: the more we talk, the less we often hear.

Against that backdrop, revisiting the relational role of silence is both urgent and restorative. Stillness in conversation is not passivity; it is a form of presence that signals, *I am here with you, not rushing ahead of you.* When a manager allows a tense employee to finish speaking and then allows the room to settle before responding, they are communicating more than their words ever could: *Your experience is valid. I will not override it with my own interpretation.* When two people rebuilding trust choose to sit together without forcing resolution, they communicate patience and possibility. When a friend resists the reflex to offer advice and instead holds steady, they open the door for the other to discover their own clarity.

One recurring motif in this chapter will be *the shared breath.* Not a dramatic synchrony but the almost unnoticed alignment that occurs when two people stop jostling for conversational space and begin simply existing beside each other. You see it between parents and teenagers walking side by side after an argument, neither speaking but neither walking away. You see it in couples who have weathered decades together, sitting on a bench, content in mutual quiet. You see it in workplaces where leaders understand that reflection requires time, and pressure-filled meetings include deliberate moments of pause. The shared breath is the signature of silence used well—not as emptiness but as connection.

To use silence well, however, requires courage. It is far easier to fill a gap with words than to trust that a relationship can withstand a moment of uncertainty. Many people fear that allowing silence will reveal vulnerability or incompetence. They imagine that others will misinterpret their quiet. These anxieties are understandable, particularly for those raised in environments where speech was a shield or where silence meant danger. Yet relational courage is not bluster; it is the bravery of letting a moment be what it is without forcing it into something else.

This chapter will move through that terrain with care. We begin with the art of listening beyond words—the still, attentive presence that notices tone, cadence, pauses, and unspoken needs. We then turn to the courage required not to rescue every gap, exploring how unfilled space can reveal truths that hurried dialogue obscures. From there we examine silence as a profound form of respect, especially in contexts where hierarchy or emotion might otherwise distort communication. And finally we face the shadow side: the silence that harms, the patterns of stonewalling and withdrawal that fracture trust, and the honest speech needed to transform harmful quiet into constructive pause.

Each theme is grounded in lived experience: friends resisting the urge to fix, couples recovering slowly after conflict, managers learning the discipline of patient listening, individuals discovering that honest explanation—*I need ten minutes to calm down*—is kinder and more repair-oriented than punishing withdrawal.

By the end of this chapter, the reader will have encountered silence not as the absence of speech but as a relational instrument—subtle, potent, and often underestimated.

Silence used with intention can mend fractures, deepen trust, and allow emotional truth to surface without coercion. Silence misused can erode connection, breed resentment, and leave people stranded inside their own assumptions.

And so a quiet question waits at the threshold of what follows: when faced with the next moment of relational tension—an argument cooling, a friend hesitating, a colleague faltering, a loved one withdrawing—which silence will you choose? The one that opens a door, or the one that closes it?

Listening Beyond The Words

When the American psychologist Carl Rogers met with a group of students at the University of Wisconsin in March 1957, observers noted something unusual about the atmosphere in the room. The students were agitated; a campus dispute had fractured friendships and created factions. Yet as Rogers invited them to speak, he often replied with nothing more than attentive silence. No quick reassurance. No attempt to redirect. No clever reframing. A student would mutter a criticism or confess fear, and Rogers would sit—steady, receptive, waiting. Over the course of the hour, the tension eased. Shoulders softened. Voices slowed. Several students who had arrived defensive began speaking with unexpected honesty. One later wrote that Rogers' quiet "felt like a space into which the truth could finally fall." A room that entered in pieces left more whole.

Five words explain the shift: *He listened by being quiet.*

Not all silence carries that effect; not all listeners have Rogers' steadiness. But his demonstration in that ordinary lecture hall shows something profound and universal: conversations change when someone stops preparing their next line and instead attends fully to the person before them. They change not because the listener is skilled at analysis or generous with advice, but because their quiet lowers the emotional pressure in the room. It becomes easier for the speaker to hear themselves think. And in that clearing, something real—something not yet polished for performance—often emerges.

Still, attentive silence is not as simple as "saying nothing." It is a discipline, a presence. Anyone can choose not to speak; far fewer can choose to *stay open* in the pause. Consider a very different scene. A friend calls you late one evening from a flat in Manchester. Their voice wavers as they describe a workplace conflict that has left them humiliated. The instinct to help surges: offer strategies, identify errors, provide reassurance. Yet you sense that any immediate advice would slip off the surface of their distress. So you inhale, soften your chest, and allow the line to hold still for a moment. They continue—not repeats of the same complaint, but a deeper admission of something they have not said aloud. The quiet becomes catalytic. They hear themselves more clearly because you have stopped trying to rescue them with noise.

This subchapter traces the anatomy of such moments: how still, attentive listening shifts the emotional chemistry of a conversation; why focusing on tone, cadence, and pauses often reveals more than the words themselves; and what it means to create a relational space in which someone else's truth can surface without being pushed or interpreted too quickly.

To understand why silence works this way, begin by observing what usually happens when we listen. Most people, even the well-intentioned, listen primarily in order to reply. They sift for cues that confirm their perspective. They compose solutions. They rehearse sympathetic noises while the other person is mid-sentence. The attention is split—part outward, part inward—and the speaker senses this division instinctively. Humans are acutely sensitive to the micro-signals of attention: half-lidded eyes, small nods that are too rhythmic, interruptions that begin with "I know exactly how you feel." These behaviours may seem benign, even supportive, but they subtly shift the focus away from the speaker's unfolding experience and toward the listener's management of it.

Still, attentive listening reverses that pattern. It asks the listener to adopt a wholly different posture: one in which the priority is not to fix, interpret, or evaluate, but to witness. The quiet motif threading this piece—the inner stilling of breath before response—captures the shift. When a listener steadies their breathing, clears their internal stage, and resists the rush toward commentary, their presence communicates something rare: *You do not need to perform for me. I am here to hear you.*

Two examples make this clearer.

In January 2016, researchers at the University of Haifa observed negotiations between pairs of strangers. They noticed that when one participant held brief pauses—two or three seconds—before responding, the other's language became more candid. They shared more information, expressed uncertainty with less defensiveness, and demonstrated higher trust scores in post-interviews. The pauses acted not as voids but as signals: space in which reflection could occur without threat.

A second example comes from healthcare. In 2018, a team at the Royal Infirmary of Edinburgh reviewed recordings of consultations between doctors and cardiac patients. They found that when clinicians allowed even short silences after delivering complex news, patients asked more precise questions and reported feeling more understood. Silence here functioned not as withdrawal but as containment. It gave the information somewhere to land.

But limitations exist. Silence is not a universal balm. In situations marked by power imbalances or histories of neglect, quiet can feel like abandonment rather than care. A manager who listens silently without ever responding concretely may leave their team anxious, not supported. A partner who pauses too long after hearing something painful may inadvertently communicate judgement. Silence is not neutral; its meaning is deeply contextual. What matters is intentionality. Rogers' quiet in 1957 worked because it was accompanied by soft eye contact, warm interest, and a willingness to engage once the speaker had finished. Silence devoid of connection becomes emptiness, not presence.

This brings us to a crucial distinction: *quiet that invites* versus *quiet that distances*. Quiet that invites has characteristics you can see and feel—forward-leaning posture, eyes that stay steady rather than darting, a breath rhythm that mirrors the speaker's pace. Quiet that distances looks different—arms crossed, gaze unfocused, a stillness that feels closed rather than open. The skill of listening beyond words depends on cultivating the former and noticing when you are drifting into the latter.

Relationships, whether friendships or partnerships or professional collaborations, are shaped not simply by what is said but by what is *allowed* to be said. Many of the most important disclosures humans make require conditions of safety rather than speed. A person deciding whether to reveal regret or confusion scans the environment for cues: Will I be judged? Will I be interrupted? Will my vulnerability be met with a torrent of advice? Silence—steady, receptive, non-anxious—signals safety more effectively than any verbal reassurance. It tells the speaker: *Take your time. Your experience matters more than my interpretation.*

A recurring motif running through this subchapter is the "shared quiet." This is not a poetic abstraction but a recognisable interpersonal phenomenon: a brief moment when both parties stop rehearsing and simply breathe. You might see it in two colleagues walking back to the office after a difficult meeting, their steps slowing as they take in one another's presence. You might see it between siblings who have not spoken honestly for months, sitting side by side on a terrace in Marseille as the midday heat drapes the silence between them. You might see it in a parent listening to a teenager argue themselves from rage into tears, the parent resisting every impulse to interject. Shared quiet is not the absence of communication. It *is* communication—of trust, of restraint, of the willingness to stay close when words would only get in the way.

There is, however, a temptation that undermines this practice: premature certainty. Many listeners believe they already know what the speaker means, often because the surface-level story resembles something familiar. But meaning is rarely linear. Two sentences that sound identical may carry utterly different emotional freight. A friend who says, "I can't do this anymore" might be expressing burnout, fear, anger, or even hope for change—depending on tone, pace, and context. Listening beyond the words means staying with the ambiguity long enough for the underlying truth to become visible. It is an act of intellectual humility as much as emotional patience.

Another temptation is to rush to soothe. When someone speaks through tears or frustration, the discomfort of witnessing their distress easily triggers a fixing instinct. But soothing too quickly often collapses the space needed for self-understanding. Advice that arrives before a person has fully articulated their experience usually lands askew. You may solve a problem they were not asking you to solve, or address a fear they were not actually naming. Stillness creates a buffer in which the speaker can hear themselves first, and only then decide what they need.

Practical observations reinforce this. In mediation work in London's family courts, trained listeners often employ what they call "neutral pauses"—moments in which they deliberately refrain from summarising or redirecting. They do this not because they lack insight, but because they recognise that people who have been arguing for months often have not truly heard themselves in just as long. A pause lets them do so.

Mediators report that parties frequently revise their own statements after hearing them echoed in the quiet. The presence of a still listener helps them recalibrate.

Attentive silence also shapes power dynamics. In organisations, junior staff often speak cautiously, sculpting their sentences to minimise risk. When leaders respond immediately, especially with critique or guidance, the imbalance intensifies. But when a leader holds a measured pause—still engaged, still attentive—the junior staff member often continues, adding nuance or expressing concerns they initially withheld. Silence, used ethically, can flatten hierarchy just enough for truth to surface.

Yet a counter-example must be acknowledged. In certain cultural contexts, silence from authority figures is interpreted not as attentiveness but as tacit condemnation. In such cases, listeners must adapt. The core principle remains: silence should *support* the speaker's sense of safety, not erode it. This means reading cultural, interpersonal, and historical cues with care. Attentive listening always involves calibration.

Perhaps the most vivid illustration of listening beyond words occurs in friendships—those relationships that rely less on duty and more on chosen presence. Imagine a friend sitting across from you after a difficult break-up. They start to speak, then falter. The instinct is to fill the void: "You'll be fine," "They didn't deserve you," "Here's what you should do next." But you stop yourself. You notice their breathing. You feel your own shoulders lift, then soften. Instead of launching into reassurance, you remain quiet, attentive, open. The silence stretches—not uncomfortably, but spaciously. They continue, differently this time: not with blame, but with something closer to clarity. They did not need your advice. They needed your quiet.

This is the silent work that holds relationships together: the discipline of not intruding upon another's unfolding thought, the patience to hold steady until meaning arranges itself, the courage to trust that quiet does not break connection but deepens it.

The unresolved tension at the heart of this practice is simple: How do we know when to speak and when to stay still? There is no formula. There is only the ongoing test that each conversation presents. The next time someone confides in you—whether in a café, a corridor, a kitchen—pause before responding. Ask yourself: *Am I speaking to serve them or to soothe myself? Am I trying to reduce my discomfort or to better hear their truth?* And if you cannot yet answer, do the most generous thing available to you.

Stay quiet.

The Courage Not To Fill Every Gap

In May 1982, the family therapist Salvador Minuchin sat with a couple in a modest consulting room in Philadelphia. They had arrived furious, each interrupting the other with practised precision. Minuchin listened, then did something that astonished the observing trainees: he invited them to stop talking. The room fell into a long, uneven quiet. One partner looked at the floor; the other crossed and uncrossed their arms. Seconds stretched. The silence was awkward enough to make even the trainees restless. Yet Minuchin remained still. After almost a minute, one of the partners exhaled differently—slower, softer. When they finally spoke, the tone was changed. Less defensive, more tentative. A truth surfaced that had not survived the earlier noise. The first real progress of the session began not with dialogue, but with shared quiet.

That scene reveals a paradox: the moments we most want to fill are often the moments most capable of changing us. A pause in the aftermath of conflict feels perilous, as though silence itself were a threat. But silence is not the danger. The danger is our flight from it. The impulse to rescue every gap with words—apologies, clarifications, reassurances—creates conversations that move quickly yet go nowhere. When nothing is allowed to settle, nothing can deepen.

Consider a couple sitting on a sofa in Bristol after a sharp argument. Their breaths are shallow; both feel the need to patch the rupture instantly. One reaches for familiar scripts, the other prepares counter-arguments. Then something interrupts the reflex: exhaustion, perhaps, or the faint recollection of a time when an unfilled pause softened them. They stop. Not dramatically, but deliberately. The air thickens; the urge to speak returns like a tide; they hold the line. Five, ten seconds. In that space, the emotional static shifts. Angry certainty gives way to something simpler—hurt, fear, longing. By the time one of them finally whispers, "I'm still here," the axis of the conversation has moved. The pause did the work.

The central claim of this subchapter is that courage in relationships often looks like this: resisting the compulsion to fill the gaps. To show this, we must first examine the urge itself. Most people are profoundly uncomfortable with interpersonal silence. Psychologists at the University of Groningen demonstrated in 2011 that participants in conversation begin to feel rising anxiety after silence exceeds four seconds. Heart rates increase; facial muscles tighten; people report feeling "socially exposed." These physiological cues are often misinterpreted as signs that something is wrong with the relationship, when they are merely evidence of the nervous system's dislike of uncertainty. We rush to speak not because speech is needed, but because discomfort is misread as danger.

Name the pattern clearly: gap-filling. It appears in everyday interactions as well as during high-stakes exchanges. Someone pauses mid-story and the listener jumps in to finish the sentence. A partner hesitates before expressing doubt and the other supplies reassurance before the thought is complete. A colleague voices frustration then falls silent for a breath too long, and the meeting slides into rapid-fire solutions. In each case, the speaker's internal process is truncated. Their words are answered, but their meaning is not met.

To understand the consequences of gap-filling, look not at grand conflicts but at ordinary moments. A friend tries to describe why they feel uneasy about an upcoming move. They begin, falter, look away. If you fill the space with questions or suggestions, you may shape the story before it has found its form. But if you wait—truly wait—the truth often reorganises itself in the silence. The difference between these two forms of listening is visible in the body: the friend's shoulders either tense in response to intrusion or loosen in response to space.

Two checkable examples help illuminate this dynamic.

In 2007, researchers at the University of Tokyo measured conversational turn-taking between couples. They found that those who tolerated longer pauses—up to six seconds—reported higher satisfaction and demonstrated more accurate emotional attunement in separate interviews. Pauses allowed partners to process before reacting. The silence served memory, not discomfort.

Another example comes from restorative justice circles in New Zealand, observed in 2015 by the Ministry of Justice. Facilitators were trained to hold silence after difficult testimonies rather than immediately paraphrasing or guiding. Survivors and offenders alike used these quiet moments to clarify thoughts, regulate emotion, and sometimes shift perspective. The absence of interruption increased the depth of subsequent exchanges.

Yet silence has limitations. There are contexts in which quiet feels punitive. Stonewalling—one of the most corrosive behaviours documented in John Gottman's longitudinal marriage studies—uses silence not as space but as withdrawal. It shuts down communication rather than opening it. The distinction is crucial. What separates courageous quiet from harmful quiet is intention. Courageous quiet stays present: the body remains oriented toward the other, breathing steady, eyes soft. Harmful quiet breaks connection: gaze averted, arms folded, attention withdrawn. Silence is not inherently kind or cruel; the posture behind it determines its meaning.

Recognising this distinction allows us to reclaim silence from its negative connotations. Many people carry childhood memories in which silence signified threat: a parent who withdrew affection, a teacher who used quiet to shame. Such histories can condition adults to interpret pauses as personal failures. But relational silence—mutual, aware, chosen—does the opposite. It signals maturity. It says: *I trust this moment enough not to rush it.*

Returning to the couple in Bristol, imagine the seconds after their fight. They sit apart but not distant. Their breathing steadies. The quiet motif running through this piece—the shared pause—appears again here. Shared pauses are not about withholding. They are about allowing. Allowing emotions to settle. Allowing words to find accuracy. Allowing two nervous systems to reorient toward each other without the distraction of noise. In those small spaces, relationships breathe.

The courage not to fill every gap asks something demanding of us: to feel our own discomfort without exporting it. When we rush to explain, defend, or soothe, we are often soothing ourselves, not the other. To resist this pull requires awareness. You notice the familiar tightening in your stomach when a silence stretches. You feel the impulse rising—*say something, anything, to relieve the tension.* And you pause. You do not collapse into silence; you *inhabit* it. That choice is relational bravery.

There is another implication worth drawing out. People often assume deeper sharing requires better questions or more articulate reflections. Yet studies of therapeutic microprocesses suggest that the precise wording of responses matters far less than the timing of them. A slow nod three seconds late can be more generative than a perfectly framed question delivered too soon. This finding, documented in the Psychotherapy Process Research Lab at the University of Sheffield in 2019, reinforces a simple truth: space heals when it is held, not hurried.

To reconcile the tension between helpful silence and harmful silence, consider purpose. Silence that invites is purposeful; silence that wounds is passive-aggressive. Silence that invites is relational; silence that wounds is self-protective. Silence that invites returns the focus to the shared moment; silence that wounds centres the listener's withdrawal. In practice, the difference is visible. Inviting silence feels warm. Wounding silence feels cold.

Now picture yourself after a difficult conversation. Perhaps you have exchanged harsh words with a partner or received criticism from a colleague. The instinct is to repair immediately—to fill the air with explanations or apologies. But effective repair often requires less speed and more space. You might sit beside someone, breathing steadily, resisting the impulse to justify yourself. You trust the silence to do what words cannot. The softening that follows is not accidental. It is earned.

The unresolved question that closes this subchapter is one every thoughtful person must face: When does the gap need space, and when does it need speech? There is no universal answer, but there is a reliable indicator. If you are speaking primarily to ease your own discomfort, wait. If you are speaking to strengthen connection, proceed.

The next time a pause opens between you and someone you care about—after conflict, confession, or undecided emotion—let that pause breathe for a moment longer than feels comfortable. Notice what shifts in you. Notice what emerges in them. And ask yourself quietly: *What might happen if I trust the gap?*

Quiet As A Form Of Respect

In March 2019, at a London office of the publishing house Faber & Faber, a junior editor named Daniel walked into his manager's room visibly tense. Manuscript deadlines had piled up; an author had sent a furious email at 2 a.m.; he felt he was failing. The manager, Ruth, closed her laptop and let him speak. He spoke quickly at first, then stumbled, then apologised for rambling. Ruth did something deceptively simple: she stayed quiet. Not withdrawn, not absent—attentive. Daniel's breathing slowed. His hands unclenched. When he finally reached the end of his frustration, the silence between them held the weight of what he had shared. Only then did Ruth respond, and the response landed cleanly. He left the room steadier, not because she solved every problem, but because she let him be fully heard before she said a word.

That moment highlights an often-overlooked truth: silence, when offered with presence, is a form of respect. We tend to think of respect as something expressed through the right phrases, the right acknowledgements, the right tone. Yet in many conversations, the most respectful act is restraint. Holding back immediate fixes, opinions, or interpretations allows another person's truth to arrive intact rather than edited by our haste. Stillness gives dignity room to speak.

The paradox at the heart of this subchapter is blunt. How can doing less—saying nothing—accomplish more? The answer lies in what silence permits. Speech directs; silence reveals. Speech shapes; silence listens. And when someone is wrestling with difficulty, revelation matters more than direction. A pause signals: *I am here. I am not rushing you. Your experience deserves a moment of its own.*

To develop this properly, begin by showing what respectful quiet looks like in practice. In Ruth's meeting with Daniel, she did not avert her eyes or feign neutrality. She listened with her body: leaning slightly forward, breathing slowly, maintaining a soft but steady gaze. This physical posture communicates more than any verbal reassurance. It shows willingness to receive. Neuroscientists studying dyadic regulation, such as Stephen Porges (2011), have noted that people read safety through microbehaviours—tempo of breath, softness of facial muscles, steadiness of attention. Silence, when paired with these cues, becomes a signal of containment rather than judgement.

Next, name the principle: containment. Containment is the capacity to hold another's experience without absorbing, dismissing, or rushing it. It is the relational equivalent of placing a glass on a table and allowing the water to settle before moving it. In organisational psychology, this concept appears in Wilfred Bion's mid-20th-century work with groups, where he observed that leaders who offered silent presence—not instant guidance—helped teams metabolise frustration before making decisions. The implication is clear. Respectful silence is not empty time. It is structured attention.

Why does this matter? Because the alternative—premature speech—distorts communication. Everyday conversations are littered with well-intentioned interruptions. A colleague pauses mid-sentence, searching for the right phrasing, and someone fills the gap with suggestions. A friend hints at distress, and we leap to reassurance. A family member begins to express disappointment, and we rush to defend ourselves. Each interruption arises from discomfort, not malice. But the effect is the same: the speaker's internal landscape becomes compromised. Their perspective is squeezed into the listener's frame.

Two checkable examples illustrate the distinction.

In 2003, a study at the University of Michigan examined physician–patient consultations. It found that doctors interrupted patients after an average of 18 seconds. When doctors were trained to wait at least 40 seconds before speaking, patients disclosed significantly more relevant information and expressed higher satisfaction. The silence was productive because it respected the speaker's process.

A second example comes from mediation work recorded by the Centre for Effective Dispute Resolution in London in 2017. Mediators who employed deliberate pauses before reframing or prompting achieved higher agreement rates in workplace conflicts. Parties reported feeling "less pushed" and "more understood." The pause created psychological room for clarity.

Yet silence has limits. A credible counter-example exposes its potential harm. During a 2015 inquiry into communication failures at a Midlands manufacturing firm, several employees described managers who "listened in silence" during grievance meetings but offered no follow-up signs of engagement. Their quiet felt cold, even punitive. The absence of verbal acknowledgment left staff uncertain whether they had been heard or dismissed. This form of silence—empty rather than attentive—undermined trust. The limitation is therefore structural: silence without relational cues becomes ambiguity, not respect.

Reconciling the limitation requires precision. Respectful quiet is not the same as detachment. The key lies in visible behaviour: eye contact that stays soft, breathing that stays even, posture that stays open. Listeners who ground themselves physically send an embodied message of presence. Respect without words is conveyed through how one sits, not merely through not speaking.

Returning to the motif that threads through this chapter—quiet as relational space—observe its recurrence. When Ruth let Daniel speak, the silence that followed his sentences was not a void. It was a vessel. A vessel for the tangled strands of his frustration. A vessel for his growing capacity to articulate what mattered. She did not rescue him from discomfort; she honoured it long enough for him to navigate it.

This motif appears again when considering cultural differences. In 2018, a cross-cultural communication study at the University of Helsinki compared Finnish and American conversational patterns. Finnish participants allowed significantly longer pauses, interpreting them as signs of thoughtfulness. American participants tended to interpret the same pauses as conversational breakdowns. In multicultural settings, silent respect must therefore be attuned. What feels honouring in one context may feel unnerving in another. The skill lies in calibration. You listen not only to the content of silence but to its meaning for the other person.

The managerial example from the opening can now be reframed in broader relational terms. When someone shares frustration, the listener's first task is not to interpret but to steady the space. This steadiness has measurable effects. Studies of co-regulation show that when one person slows their breath, the other's heart rate tends to decrease. Respect begins in the body before it arrives in the mind. A quiet listener is a regulating presence.

But respectful silence is not merely about physiology. It is also ethical. To allow another person's experience to unfold without interference is to affirm its validity. You are saying, without saying: *Your experience is coherent. You deserve time. I am not rushing you toward my preferred version of your story.* In a cultural moment saturated with replies, takes, and commentary, this stance carries uncommon weight.

Consider a second scenario. A team member arrives at a manager's door, clearly unsettled. Instead of offering an instant opinion—*You're overreacting, This will pass, Let me fix it*—the manager holds a moment of quiet. The team member continues, and in continuing discovers what is essential. The silence acts as a companion, not a barrier. When the manager eventually speaks, their words emerge from understanding rather than assumption. The contrast is stark. Advice given too quickly becomes instruction. Advice given after silence becomes support.

This leads to the closing tension. Silence offered as respect requires courage because it relinquishes control. When you pause, you allow the moment to shape itself rather than shaping it prematurely. Yet that surrender raises a question: How do you know when silence has done its work and speech must return? There is no formula, only attentiveness. Does the other person seem more settled or more agitated? Has their breathing steadied? Have their shoulders dropped? Has the quiet become a holding space or a holding back?

The unresolved choice at the heart of respectful silence is therefore this: Will you intervene out of your own discomfort, or will you wait until your words truly serve the other? The next conversation you enter may hinge on your answer.

When Silence Becomes A Weapon

In February 1997, research psychologist John Gottman published findings from his longitudinal studies at the University of Washington's "Love Lab," identifying stonewalling as one of the clearest predictors of relationship breakdown. Couples were filmed during conflict discussions. Those in which one partner shut down—arms crossed, eyes averted, jaw clenched, silent for long stretches—showed markedly higher rates of separation within six years. The striking part was not the volume or intensity of arguments but the absence of response. Silence, when used as withdrawal, corroded the relational fabric faster than anger ever did. The data made public what many experience privately: silence can wound more deeply than harsh words.

The image of a partner sitting rigidly on a sofa, gaze fixed on a distant point, refusing to answer, is familiar across cultures. It carries a particular emotional temperature. Not the cool quiet of thoughtful pause but the stifling quiet of shutdown. In that kind of silence, the room feels heavier. Time drags. The person waiting for a response may speak more loudly or softly, may plead or protest, but nothing moves. The silence does not soothe. It punishes. And because humans instinctively search for patterns, that silence becomes a story: *You do not matter enough for me to answer.*

The distinction here matters. Healthy silence creates space. Weaponised silence creates distance. One expands a relationship; the other erodes it. The task is to understand the boundary between the two.

Begin with the behaviour itself. In Gottman's laboratory footage, stonewalling was not merely a refusal to speak. It included specific physiological markers: heart rates soaring above 100 beats per minute, shoulders lifting, breath tightening. These were signs of emotional flooding. Yet flooding did not automatically lead to silence. The silence arrived when a person stopped signalling engagement—no nods, no breaths directed toward regulation, no minimal acknowledgments. The behaviour showed retreat. Naming this accurately matters: stonewalling is not quiet reflection; it is disengagement.

Why do people use silence this way? Psychologists studying conflict avoidance point to two common mechanisms. First, self-protection: silence becomes a shield against perceived criticism. Second, control: silence becomes a way of shifting power, forcing the other person to carry the emotional load of the moment. Both mechanisms produce the same effect: the other person is left alone with uncertainty.

Consider two checkable examples that reveal the real-world consequences.

In 2014, the UK charity Relate published its annual study on relationship distress. Among couples reporting high conflict, the silent treatment emerged as one of the most frequently cited behaviours associated with loss of trust. Respondents described feeling "shut out," "punished," and "kept at arm's length." The emotional cost was not abstract. Several participants reported physical symptoms: insomnia, stomach tension, headaches. Silence had become a stressor.

A second example comes from workplace dynamics. A 2019 report from ACAS documented patterns of managerial stonewalling during grievance procedures. Employees whose concerns were met with prolonged silence—emails unanswered, meetings avoided, no verbal acknowledgment—reported significantly lower confidence in the organisation's fairness. Some left their roles within months. Silence acted as institutional neglect.

And yet, silence itself is not the enemy. A credible limitation to the critique must be acknowledged. People sometimes fall silent because they are overwhelmed, not because they intend harm. Someone in acute stress may need time to regulate before they can speak. In these scenarios, silence is a temporary retreat for safety rather than a deliberate weapon. The difference lies in communication. If the overwhelmed person says, even briefly, *I need ten minutes to calm down; I'll come back*, the silence becomes a boundary, not a threat. The limitation is crucial: silence used to regulate is not silence used to dominate.

The reconciliation lies in observable behaviour. Does the quiet lead to reconnection or prolong disconnection? A simple metric guides interpretation: time. Functional pauses tend to be short and signposted. Harmful withdrawal tends to be prolonged, unexplained, and repetitive. Silence offered with honesty repairs. Silence delivered with ambiguity damages.

The motif that threads through this exploration is the quality of space. In healthy dialogue, space holds emotional weight; it allows thought, clarifies intention, widens perspective. In harmful patterns, space becomes absence, a gap edged with unease. You notice its presence in the body. The person waiting for a response feels their breath shorten, shoulders tighten, stomach drop. The silence does not provide room. It compresses.

To show this contrast vividly, imagine two domestic scenes.

In the first, a couple argue late at night. Voices rise. One person, overwhelmed, steps back and says, "I can't talk right now. I need a little time. I'll come back in half an hour." They go to another room, breathe slowly, let their nervous system settle. The silence that follows is uncomfortable but safe. It has structure. When they return, the conversation changes course.

In the second scene, the argument ends with one partner turning away, arms folded, refusing to speak. Minutes turn into hours. Questions hang unanswered. This silence communicates not self-care but exclusion. It says, *You are on your own with this.*

The implication is clear: silence without explanation becomes interpretation. And interpretation in strained relationships tends to skew negative.

Historical examples reinforce this dynamic. The Victorian diarist Harriet Martineau wrote in 1851 about the "chill of unspoken injury" within families, observing that prolonged, unexplained quiet created "a fog in which minds drift apart." Her account, grounded in her own household, echoes contemporary findings: silence without signal fractures connection.

Yet silence need not fracture if it is paired with speech. A spoken request creates a bridge. "I need to pause." "I'm too upset to respond clearly right now." "Let me come back to this." These small sentences convert silence from threat to clarity. Their power lies not in eloquence but in honesty. They orient the relationship.

A second contemporary example illustrates this principle. In 2021, a mediation service in Manchester documented a case in which a father and teenage daughter had not spoken for four days after a heated exchange. The daughter interpreted his silence as punishment; he believed he was avoiding escalation. The mediator encouraged him to articulate his intention. He told his daughter, "I wasn't ignoring you. I was overwhelmed and didn't know how to speak without shouting. I'm sorry I didn't say that sooner." The moment softened the impasse. Speech dissolved the weaponised quiet.

Returning to the motif of space, it becomes evident that silence gains its meaning from its edges—what comes before it and after it. If silence is preceded by acknowledgment and followed by re-engagement, it becomes supportive. If it is surrounded by nothing, it becomes hostile.

This raises an uncomfortable but necessary question: how do you recognise when your own silence crosses the line? The body often reveals it first. If your shoulders rise, jaw tightens, breath shortens, and your mind insists, *I refuse to give them anything,* the silence is defensive. If, instead, your breath slows, your gaze steadies, and you think, *I need to get grounded so I can respond well,* the silence is restorative.

The final tension in this subchapter rests here. How will you signal your quiet? You will face moments when speaking feels impossible, when anger or hurt swells too strongly for coherence. The choice is not between silence and speech. It is between unspoken withdrawal and honest boundary. The first corrodes trust. The second protects it.

The next time conflict rises, the forward test is simple. Instead of falling into silence that shuts down connection, can you speak a single sentence that keeps the door open?

Chapter 7
Daily Rituals Of Stillness

The first quiet moment of the day rarely announces itself. It slips in between motions—steam rising from a kettle, the muted light of early morning, the soft clink of a mug on a kitchen counter. In one London household I visited while researching daily attention habits, the morning ritual was almost monastic in its simplicity: two minutes of stillness before the phone was touched. No timer, no ceremony. Just a man standing by his sink, hands loosely resting on the counter, breathing as the coffee brewed. Those two minutes, he said, felt like reclaiming his mind before the world's demands arrived. What struck me was not the length of the pause but the fact that it existed at all. Modern life seldom leaves unclaimed spaces. We either choose to mark them, or they vanish before we notice.

This quiet, nearly invisible power of small moments forms the spine of this chapter. For centuries, contemplative traditions have reserved entire hours for silence, yet most people today struggle to find even thirty seconds without reach, scroll, or mental commentary. And yet, the paradox holds: the less time we believe we have, the more difference these brief rituals make. They function like anchors in turbulent water—small in size, disproportionate in impact. The person who grants themselves a calm beginning often finds the rest of the day shaped by that tone. Likewise, the one who closes the evening with care sets a boundary between living and drifting.

Stillness, to be sustainable, cannot be confined to rare retreats or lofty aspirations. It must find its place in the ordinary. A person hanging laundry in a small Brighton garden told me that the quietest part of her week happened while shaking out a damp shirt. "The world shrinks to the line in front of me," she said. "I feel the cloth. I smell the detergent. For a moment, nothing else is required." This is the kind of stillness we will explore here: not theatrical withdrawal, not forced serenity, but attention—steady, unhurried, and rooted in the body.

The textures of daily life already contain hidden opportunities for such attention. Consider the bookends of a day: waking and settling. In many households, the morning begins with a reflexive reach for the phone. The evening ends the same way—scrolling, scanning, grazing through fragments of content until fatigue overtakes intention. But when the morning begins with three quiet breaths or the evening ends with one minute of reflection, a subtle but significant shift occurs. The mind feels less dragged by circumstance and more companioned by choice. Even tiny rituals can recalibrate an entire day.

These rituals are not accessories to modern life. They are its antidotes. The pace of the contemporary world encourages fragmentation—rapid task-switching, constant micro-stimulation, shallow attention spread thin across competing demands. Stillness reverses that direction. It draws awareness back into the present moment, helping the mind consolidate rather than scatter. The beauty is that this does not require hours. It requires intention combined with repetition: a morning pause, an evening release, a mindful gesture during an ordinary task.

A pattern emerges when observing people who cultivate these micro-rituals. They do not wait for the "right" conditions. They create small pockets of rightness inside the conditions they have. A parent with no spare hour can still claim a consistent chair in the corner of the living room. A commuter can still pause on the train platform before unlocking their screen. A desk worker can still inhale slowly before opening an inbox notorious for noise. When such acts become regular, they evolve into thresholds—moments that separate reactivity from clarity.

Modern neuroscience hints at why these rituals matter. The brain responds powerfully to habit-linked cues. A specific chair, a warm drink, the feel of bare feet on the floor—these sensory anchors can become gateways to quieter internal states. When repeated, they teach the nervous system to settle more quickly. In other words, the rituals you choose become the teachers you rely on. They whisper to the mind, *Here, you may soften. Here, you may return to yourself.*

The task, then, is not to build grand routines but to identify small, repeatable acts that restore presence. Some people begin with the edges of the day. Others start with mundane tasks—washing dishes, wiping a countertop, walking to the letterbox. These activities, so often dismissed as trivial, become grounding when done without rush and without distraction. They give the mind something steady to rest upon. They remind the body that life is lived moment by moment, not scroll by scroll.

Another thread running through this chapter concerns place. Human beings are shaped by their environments. A single consistent location—a window seat, a chair by a radiator, a corner marked by a folded blanket—can become a personal sanctuary. Not elaborate, not curated for display, but chosen. These small territories of quiet accumulate meaning through repetition. Over time, the body begins to associate that space with slowing down. The mind follows.

The deeper significance of daily rituals lies in what they protect: attention, emotional balance, and the capacity to respond rather than react. A person who starts their day with a moment of quiet is less likely to be pulled into the slipstream of urgency. A person who ends the day with reflection is less likely to carry unresolved noise into sleep. A person who turns a chore into a mindful act is less likely to feel that their day has evaporated in a haze of hurry. And a person who claims a physical space for stillness sends a quiet message to themselves: *You are allowed to pause.*

What follows in this chapter is not a prescription but an exploration. You will encounter ways to locate the quiet already present in your routine, the architecture of meaningful beginnings and endings, the transformation of ordinary actions into meditative ones, and the creation of a personal space that signals stillness at a glance. Each thread connects to the central truth that stillness, to be lived, must be woven into the hours you already have.

As you read, consider this question: if the quality of your attention shapes the quality of your days, how might your days change if you protected just a handful of moments with intention?

Designing Micro Moments Of Quiet

At 7:12 a.m. on a wet March morning in Bristol, Anna Merrill stood by her kitchen window with a mug warming her hands. She had developed a small ritual during the previous winter: two uninterrupted minutes of quiet before touching her phone. No timer. No posture. No performance. Just two minutes of being awake without being available. Over time she noticed something unexpected. Those 120 seconds, almost laughable in their brevity, set the tone for her entire working day at the University of Bristol's School of Education. Meetings felt less draining. Emails less urgent. Her own reactions less brittle. It was, in her words, "the smallest thing I do that changes the most." The scene is ordinary; the effect is not. It demonstrates a truth we easily overlook: quiet expands when we commit to meeting it.

Most people assume they need large blocks of time to cultivate stillness, yet their days are threaded with unclaimed moments. These micro-moments are the spaces between actions: the pause while the kettle boils, the breath before unlocking a screen, the silence as the lift rises. They exist already; what is missing is the deliberate decision to inhabit them. When the anthropologist Edward T. Hall wrote in 1966 about "the silent language" of human attention, he argued that unused interludes shape experience as much as spoken words. Modern life has eroded our sensitivity to those interludes. Devices fill them before we notice their presence, shrinking the small apertures through which stillness can enter.

To understand the potential of micro-moments, it helps to observe their absence. A study by the London School of Economics in 2017 examined smartphone use in transitional moments—such as waiting in queues or walking short distances. Researchers found that participants checked their phones within an average of eight seconds of experiencing unstructured time. Eight seconds. It reveals a pattern: any unoccupied gap is quickly colonised. The reflex dilutes our capacity for attention, because the mind is never permitted to idle without input. The implication is simple: to design moments of quiet, we must reclaim the gaps before they are filled.

One example comes from 14th-century Christian monastic practice, where the English mystic Richard Rolle described "brief visitings of quiet" throughout the day—pauses marked only by breath and intention. These were not retreats but micro-practices woven into labour. The principle endures. Modern readers do not need cloisters; they need cues. The first sip of coffee. The moment the car engine starts. The few seconds before replying to a message. Each can become a signal to widen inner space rather than contract it.

Consider how this operates in visible behaviour. When Anna, our Bristol researcher, holds her mug in the morning, she is not waiting; she is *arriving*. The small act creates a boundary between sleep and activity. It teaches the nervous system to enter the day rather than fall into it. She reported that after a month of this practice she reduced her morning phone pickups from ten before 8:00 a.m. to three. That metric is revealing. Quiet influences not only mood but behaviour.

A second named example illustrates how micro-moments function even in pressurised environments. In 2019, surgeon David McGowan of St Thomas' Hospital in London adopted a practice borrowed from Japanese theatre: a deliberate breath before each operation. He explained in a departmental seminar that the breath "reset the hands before the mind had time to interfere." The practice took less than five seconds, yet he described a noticeable improvement in steadiness and presence. The quiet motif here—the breath—is not ornamental. It is a hinge that shifts the quality of attention.

Still, not every gap can or should become a ritual. A credible limitation emerges when micro-moments turn into another task to optimise. Some people report that scheduled pauses feel artificial, as if stillness becomes something to perform rather than inhabit. This concern is valid. The aim is not to manufacture calm or to treat silence as a productivity technique. The reconciliation lies in choosing moments that already occur naturally, so the pause feels like a return—not an imposition. The ritual succeeds when it blends with the grain of daily life, not when it disrupts it.

A recurring motif helps to make sense of this: the image of a door left slightly ajar. Micro-moments are the ajar door—an opening wide enough to notice yourself again but small enough not to intimidate. When repeated, the mind learns to enter gently. When ignored, the door swings shut, and reactivity rules the day. These glimpses of stillness do not solve problems, but they alter how problems land. They soften perception. They widen patience.

To interrogate the mechanics further, it is useful to pair abstractions with concrete behaviours. What does "clarity" look like in micro-form? It looks like pausing for one breath before answering a child who interrupts your work. What does "agency" look like? It looks like choosing not to open your inbox until after you have stood up, stretched, and taken three slow inhales. What does "presence" look like? It looks like watching the steam curl from a cup instead of refreshing a news feed. These actions measure the shape of your attention. They are behavioural indicators, not poetic aspirations.

There are cultural precedents too. In 18th-century Kyoto, merchants were taught a practice known as *ma*—the art of intentional space. It emphasised the power of intervals, the quiet between brushstrokes, the pause before speech. Its purpose was not relaxation but discernment. When the interval is honoured, the next action becomes clearer. When the interval is ignored, decisions grow reactive. Adapting this principle to modern routines—commuting, emailing, tidying—allows small silences to serve as recalibration points.

A counter-example clarifies boundaries. Some individuals attempt to create micro-moments by multitasking—listening to a meditation track while scrolling, or pairing breathing exercises with rapid email sorting. These hybrid practices often fail to foster stillness because they do not reduce stimulation; they compress it. The nervous system receives conflicting cues: slow down and speed up simultaneously. Reconciling this requires remembering that stillness is subtractive. It depends on doing one thing with attention, not combining many things with strain.

Once micro-moments are chosen, repetition matters more than length. The brain builds associations through pattern, not intensity. Neuroscientist Amishi Jha (University of Miami, 2018) has shown that even 12 minutes of daily attention training, broken into small segments, improves working memory and reduces distractibility. While her focus was formal practice, the underlying principle applies: short, consistent acts of attention accumulate into structural change. The micro-moment is a seed. Plant enough of them, and the field changes.

A subtle question arises here: how many of these pauses does a day truly hold? The answer depends less on time and more on noticing. You could find them while waiting for a microwave, before entering a meeting room, while standing at a pedestrian crossing, or during the quiet seconds after turning off a shower. Each moment contains the possibility of choosing awareness over automation. The challenge is not scarcity but recognition.

To return to our motif—the door ajar—each pause is a way of stepping through. The moment itself may be brief, but the implication is not. It signals that you are willing to step back into your life with intention. It reveals that stillness is not something you visit; it is something you carry.

As you reflect on your own routines, ask a forward-looking question: which two minutes tomorrow morning could become your entry point to quiet, and what might change if you protect them?

Opening And Closing The Day Well

On a cold January morning in 2020, a secondary school teacher in Glasgow, Maureen, made a quiet deal with herself. For thirty days she would not look at her phone until she had taken ten slow breaths and opened the curtains. No elaborate routine. Just breath, light, then screen. In the evenings she set a similar boundary: after she turned off the television, she would write down three things she was grateful for, sit in silence for one minute, and only then plug in her phone to charge—out of reach of the bed. Two small hinges at either end of the day. After a fortnight she noticed something unnervingly simple. She felt less as though her life was happening *at* her. The room was finally quiet.

Nothing in her external circumstances had changed. Same students, same workload, same modest flat. What shifted was the way she crossed the threshold into waking and slipped across the threshold into sleep. Those transitions, previously colonised by scrolling, suddenly belonged to her again. She described it as "putting bookends on the chaos." The bookends were thin, almost fragile, but they held.

This is the terrain of opening and closing the day well: the deliberate shaping of the first and last minutes we are conscious. Historically, spiritual and philosophical traditions have treated these thresholds with great seriousness. In the 16th century, Ignatius of Loyola, founder of the Jesuits, built his entire daily practice around two anchors he called the *Examen*: a brief morning intention and an evening review. He understood that what we attend to on waking colours the entire day, and what we attend to before sleep slowly writes our inner story. Most of us now outsource those moments to whatever happens to be on our screens.

The first claim of this subchapter is straightforward but demanding: the quality of a day is disproportionately shaped by its edges. Show the behaviour. Maureen's mornings used to begin with news alerts and emails; her evenings ended with social media and half-remembered images. She often woke tense and went to bed wired. Once she began inserting breath and quiet reflection at both ends, her experience shifted. Name the principle: temporal framing. Explain it. The brain uses beginnings and endings as reference points. Neuroscience and memory research both suggest that we recall the start and finish of events more strongly than the middle. Implication: if you want your days to feel less like a blur, start by tending to how you cross their thresholds.

The second claim: simple morning rituals restore authorship. In many households, the first conscious act is a reach for the phone. That movement—hand to screen before hand to heart or breath—sends a subtle message: the outside world has first claim on your attention. Reversing the order changes the internal script. When Maureen chose to begin with ten slow breaths and the act of opening her curtains, she was making a small but decisive statement: *I will meet the day before the day meets me.*

Name this pattern: intentional arrival. Explain it. Intentional arrival is not about perfection or productivity; it is about asserting a brief, quiet "I" before saying "yes" to the world. It might look like sitting on the edge of the bed, feet on the floor, feeling the contact for three breaths. It might look like placing a hand on the chest for a moment and asking, "What matters today?" The exact gesture is less important than the fact that it is chosen, repeated, and device-free.

A limitation appears immediately. For many people, mornings are not gentle. Children wake early. Shift work scrambles rhythms. Care responsibilities crowd the first minutes of consciousness. Asking for a long, serene routine is unrealistic. The reconciliation lies in scale. Opening the day well does not require half an hour; it requires *priority*. Even twenty seconds of breath, taken before the phone is lifted, counts. The motif that will run quietly through this subchapter is the *threshold breath*—a single pause that marks crossing from one state to another. Even the busiest person can guard one breath.

The third claim: evening rituals process the day rather than merely escaping it. Late-night scrolling offers a certain anaesthesia. It postpones the moment of being alone with one's thoughts. But whatever is unprocessed at 11.30 p.m. waits faithfully at 6.30 a.m. The mind has simply been numbed, not met. Maureen's decision to replace the last ten minutes of phone use with gratitude and a minute of quiet did something different. It turned the end of the day into a small act of integration.

Name this practice: retrospective attention. Explain it. Retrospective attention is the deliberate act of turning towards the day you have just lived—acknowledging what was good, difficult, incomplete—so that it does not congeal into unconscious restlessness. Behaviourally, it might involve jotting three specific things that went well, or simply letting the mind replay one moment of genuine connection. The implication is not that every day becomes glowing; it is that no day is entirely discarded.

Historical precedent strengthens this claim. Stoic philosophers such as Seneca urged a nightly review of actions, not as self-reproach but as gentle audit. Mediaeval monks ended their days with a brief examination of conscience. None of these practices required elaborate apparatus. They required willingness to look. Our contemporary version can be less moralising and more observational: What did I give myself to today? What small kindness did I receive? Where did I react rather than respond? These questions do not need full answers every night. They simply direct attention.

A counter-example is worth considering. Some people find that night-time reflection tips into rumination, especially if anxiety is high. Lying in bed replaying mistakes can easily inflame worry. The reconciliation lies in structure and brevity. The point of an evening ritual is not to solve the day, but to acknowledge it and put it down. Keeping the review short—two minutes, three specific memories—helps it remain a container rather than a spiral. Again, the threshold breath matters: a slow exhale at the end of the review signals to the body, *It is safe to rest now.*

The fourth claim: synchronising body and attention at the edges of the day stabilises the nervous system. Abstract terms like "grounded" or "balanced" must be tied to visible behaviour. When a person wakes and immediately floods themselves with information, you can see the physical response: shallow breathing, tightened jaw, a subtle forward hunch as if bracing. When they instead breathe consciously, feel their feet on the floor, and step into the day with one small chosen action, their posture is different. The shoulders sit lower. The face softens. These may seem like delicate details. They are not. They are the embodiment of a different relationship to time.

Evening rituals show the same pattern. An hour of blue-lit stimulation in bed often produces restless movement, frequent screen-checking, and difficulty settling. Replacing even the last ten minutes with a low-light activity—a notebook, a printed page, or simply sitting in partial darkness—visibly alters the transition. The body receives a consistent message: we are moving towards rest. Sleep researchers have repeatedly noted that predictable pre-sleep routines support more consolidated rest precisely because the nervous system comes to trust the sequence.

The threshold breath returns here as motif. It is the simplest measurable component of these shifts. One can observe it. A rushed inhale before checking messages is a different threshold from a slow inhale, a longer exhale, and then whatever comes next. That single breath is a small diagnostic of agency.

The fifth claim: how we open and close the day shapes our sense of meaning. This is less obvious but equally important. Meaning is not an abstract quality sprinkled over life; it arises from patterns of attention. If the first act of the morning is to compare ourselves with others online, and the last act of the night is to ingest more miscellaneous input, meaning becomes thin, externally driven. Days feel interchangeable. By contrast, if the day opens with some articulation of intention—even a quiet inner sentence such as, "Today I want to be diligent and kind"—and closes with recognition of what actually unfolded, a narrative begins to form.

Name this process: narrative stitching. Explain it. Narrative stitching is the act of tying the hours together with awareness so they do not sit as disconnected fragments. Over weeks and months, these small stitches accumulate into a sense that one's life is a continuous story rather than a series of unrelated episodes. The implication for stillness is profound: a life experienced as continuous is easier to rest within. There is less felt need to drown out the day because the day has been met.

A credible limitation here is that for those in acute difficulty—bereavement, crisis, intense caregiving—looking directly at the day can feel overwhelming. In such seasons, the scope of the review must be gentler. Instead of scanning everything, one might simply notice one small moment that was bearable, or one person who offered a glance of kindness. The ritual can shrink without vanishing. The threshold breath is still possible.

All of this brings us back to a central question: who, or what, do you meet first and last each day? The structure of many modern lives has quietly shifted that answer from "my own breath, my own sense of being alive" to "whichever notification has arrived most recently." Reversing that shift does not require drastic restructuring. It requires protecting two small territories at the edge of consciousness.

Imagine tomorrow morning. Before you stand, you feel the weight of your body on the mattress and take one deliberate breath. Before you open your phone, you open the curtains or the blinds and let the light in. That is your threshold. Imagine tomorrow night. Before you climb into bed, you stand for a moment beside it, recall one thing you are grateful for, one thing unfinished that you choose to release for now, and you exhale. That is your threshold.

The forward test is not theoretical. It is personal and immediate: What would it cost you to reclaim the first and last sixty seconds of your day—and, more importantly, what might it quietly return?

Turning Ordinary Tasks Into Practice

In July 2015, in a small terrace house on the outskirts of Norwich, a social worker named Ellen found herself unexpectedly still. It was a Saturday morning. She stood in her garden pegging wet laundry on the line, a task she usually rushed through before errands. That day the weather held her attention: warm air, the faint sweetness of fabric softener rising from the basket, the gentle pull of cotton in her hands. She noticed the different textures—the thicker weave of her work trousers, the soft stretch of a T-shirt—and the quiet rhythm of peg, lift, smooth. Two minutes in, something subtle shifted. Her shoulders dropped. Her breathing slowed. A mild steadiness settled over her. For the rest of the morning she felt less scattered than usual, as though she had stepped into herself rather than into her diary. Nothing dramatic. Just a small, grounded moment that held.

Scenes like this are not trivial. They expose a paradox: the tasks we often rush through may be the most reliable gateways to calm. We assume that stillness requires special conditions—retreats, cushions, techniques—yet many traditions have built their practice on ordinary movement. When the Vietnamese monk Thich Nhat Hanh began teaching mindfulness in France in the late 1970s, he emphasised dishwashing, sweeping, and walking as the backbone of attentional training. These tasks were not distractions from "real practice"; they were the practice. His invitation was simple: pay full, relaxed attention to what is already in your hands.

The first claim of this subchapter is that ordinary chores function as attentional containers. Show the behaviour. Ellen's experience in Norwich was not mystical. She slowed her movements, felt the fabric, heard the rustle of leaves, and let the task unfold at its natural pace. Name the principle: embodied attention. Explain it. Embodied attention is the act of locating awareness in sensory detail rather than running commentary. Instead of thinking *I need to finish this quickly*, she allowed her senses to take precedence. Implication: the quality of attention changes the quality of the task, and the quality of the task changes the quality of the day.

A second claim: repeated sensory attention during chores gently recalibrates the nervous system. That language can sound abstract, so anchor it in physical behaviour. When someone folds laundry with divided attention, their movements become quicker, shoulders slightly raised, breath shallow. When they fold with full presence, the actions slow, the jaw softens, and micro-tensions ease. These small adjustments are visible markers of a shift from sympathetic activation—urgency, scatteredness—to a quieter parasympathetic tone. One breath. One slower gesture. These are the hinge points.

Historical precedent supports this. In 13th-century Kamakura Japan, the Zen teacher Dōgen instructed his monks in *tenzo kyōkun*—guidelines for cooks—where he insisted that chopping vegetables and rinsing rice deserved the same quality of attention as formal sitting meditation. This was not aesthetic fussiness. It was a recognition that direct contact with the world, through hands and breath, stabilises the mind more effectively than thinking about stabilising the mind.

A counter-example clarifies the distinction. Some people find that slowing down during chores makes them feel more irritated—too aware of what they would rather be doing, or confronted by boredom. The reconciliation lies in the motif that will run through this piece: *the single sensory anchor*. Instead of demanding sustained tranquillity, choose one anchor—the weight of a mug, the sound of running water, the feel of fabric between the fingers—and return to it without forcing calm. Anchoring prevents the practice from becoming another performance.

A third claim: transforming chores into moving meditations builds trust in one's capacity to meet the day without rushing. Trust here must be paired with behaviour, not sentiment. Consider the act of sweeping a kitchen floor. Done inattentively, it is a task to be completed; done with a steady tempo and sensory engagement, it becomes a brief rehearsal for focused presence. Name this pattern: behavioural rehearsal. Explain it. Each small act of engaged attention rehearses the nervous system for the rest of the day. If you can be present while rinsing a cup, you can be more present in a difficult meeting. Implication: the mundane becomes training ground.

A second named example strengthens this claim. In 1994, at the Insight Meditation Society in Barre, Massachusetts, teacher Sharon Salzberg described how she uses the first three sips of her morning tea as a micro-practice. She attends to warmth, aroma, movement. No timetable, no symbolism. Three sips. She credits this small act with giving her a foothold of steadiness before the responsibilities of the day accumulate. Again, the principle is not productivity but attunement.

The fourth claim: ordinary tasks expose our default mental habits. When a person hangs laundry or washes dishes, the mind often leaps to planning, replaying, or comparison. These habits are not faults; they are simply unobserved. Show the behaviour. You notice that while scrubbing a pan your jaw has clenched, your breath is shallow, and you are silently re-arguing yesterday's conversation. Name this pattern: cognitive drift. Explain it. Cognitive drift refers to the automatic slide into thought loops when attention lacks an anchor. The implication is liberating: chores reveal these loops in real time, which makes them available to be gently interrupted.

The single sensory anchor returns here. It allows you to name the drift—*thinking again*—and return to sensation without drama. This is not suppression; it is redirection. Over time, the act of returning becomes a quiet discipline, and the loops loosen.

A limitation must be addressed. Some tasks are too cognitively demanding or emotionally charged to function as practice. Completing a work report, managing finances, or responding to tense emails does not offer the spaciousness of sweeping or hanging laundry. The reconciliation is not to force mindfulness into unsuitable tasks but to identify which chores carry enough rhythm and simplicity to hold attention without strain. The point is not to sanctify all activity; it is to elevate the ones that already carry natural cadence.

A fifth claim: moving meditation through chores deepens one's sense of belonging to the physical world. Again, avoid abstraction. Belonging becomes visible when someone pauses to feel warm water flowing over their hands or notices the scent of clean sheets. These moments root a person in place and time. They counter the drift towards disembodiment that long hours at screens can create. When Ellen hung laundry in Norwich, she felt the breeze on her arms and the slight resistance of damp cloth. Those details placed her in her life rather than adjacent to it.

A second named historical example strengthens this claim. In 1927, Japanese philosopher Kitarō Nishida wrote about the concept of *pure experience*, describing moments where awareness rests directly on sensation before thought intervenes. He often illustrated this through simple physical acts such as walking in a garden or preparing tea. His point was not to romanticise chores but to show that direct contact with sensory reality reveals a kind of immediacy that thought alone cannot provide.

The motif of the single sensory anchor threads through this example too. Nishida's reflections highlight how one carefully attended sensation can open access to the present moment without effort.

The sixth claim: folding attention into chores subtly reshapes one's relationship to time. When we rush, time feels thin, slippery. When we slow into sensory attention, time gains depth. Behaviourally, this shows in fewer abrupt movements, more even breathing, and a gentle shift in posture. Name this effect: temporal dilation. Explain it. Temporal dilation is the felt sense that time stretches slightly when attention stabilises. The implication is practical: by altering the tempo of everyday tasks, you alter your felt experience of the day.

A credible counterpoint: some people fear that slowing down will make them less efficient. The reconciliation lies in distinguishing pace from presence. Many tasks take roughly the same amount of time whether rushed or attended to steadily. Hanging laundry slowly may add thirty seconds; the benefit—reduced mental scatter, lower baseline tension—is disproportionate to the cost.

All of this returns us to the central motif: the single sensory anchor. It is the hinge, the invitation, the smallest possible entry point. Each time you hang a shirt, rinse a cup, sweep a floor, you choose one anchor and rest in it. The task becomes a brief alignment of body, breath, and attention.

The unresolved tension that closes this subchapter is practical and immediate: If the smallest tasks of your day could become small sanctuaries, what prevents you from claiming them—and what might shift if you did?

Creating A Personal Silence Space

In March 1968, in the Suffolk village of Great Glemham, the composer Benjamin Britten returned from rehearsal at Snape Maltings and walked straight to a modest wooden chair he kept in a corner of his study. No desk. No scores. Just the chair, a wool blanket, and the muted light from a small lamp. Friends later recalled that Britten often sat there for a few quiet minutes before writing began, using the stillness to settle the agitation that energetic collaboration often stirred. This was not indulgence. It was calibration. A small, stable place that reminded him how to begin again.

The detail matters because it punctures the idea that silence requires grandeur. Britten's chair was not a shrine, yet it carried a dependable signal: *slow here*. Many people imagine that creating a personal space for stillness demands aesthetic perfection or ample time. The opposite is closer to the truth. A silence space succeeds because it is simple, repeatable, and connected to the body's memory of calm. It anchors behaviour, not fantasy.

This subchapter's first claim rests on this observable behaviour: repeated quiet in the same place strengthens the mind's ability to settle quickly. Show it. A person returns to a particular chair in the early morning, wraps a familiar blanket around their legs, lights a candle, and sits without reaching for a device. After a week of this ritual, their breath begins to deepen as soon as they approach the chair. Name this pattern: conditioned quiet. Explain it. Conditioned quiet describes how the nervous system pairs a location with a felt state. The body anticipates stillness before the mind demands it. Implication: space shapes attention as much as intention does.

The motif that threads through this chapter—the single, repeated cue—enters here. It is the candle flame, the blanket's weight, the corner itself. A cue becomes a quiet ambassador. Three seconds of recognition: *here, I slow*.

A second claim follows: a personal silence space offers psychological permission to pause. This sounds abstract until anchored in a concrete example. In 2012, the psychologist Paul Gilbert, writing about compassion-focused therapy, observed that even a modest sensory shift—a softer light, a grounded sitting posture—can ease defensive mental states. Show the behaviour. Someone sits in their chosen corner chair after work. Their jaw unclenches. Shoulders lower. Breath lengthens. Name the principle: environmental signalling. Explain it. Environmental signalling refers to the way external cues influence internal tone. Implication: creating a space for quiet is not cosmetic; it is functional.

Now include a limitation. Not everyone lives in a home where carving out a corner is straightforward. Shared flats, small rooms, or family spaces can make solitude feel like a logistical fantasy. Reconcile it. A silence space does not require ownership of a whole room. A single chair turned slightly away from the centre of activity, a section of a desk cleared of clutter, or even a windowsill with a small object—these can function as effective cues. The point is consistency, not control. The motif of the cue returns: one stable object signals pause amidst movement.

A third claim: physical simplicity reduces cognitive noise. Show the behaviour. Consider someone who designs their space with excess: multiple cushions, incense, elaborate décor. The complexity becomes another task, another performance. Compare this with a person who selects one blanket, one candle, one chair. Name the principle: minimal cognitive load. Explain it. Minimal cognitive load means that the environment demands little from the mind, freeing attention for quiet rather than appraisal. Implication: simplicity becomes a form of mercy.

A second named historical example strengthens this insight. In 1970, the architect and monk Brother Anthony Thwaite helped redesign parts of the Benedictine monastery at Buckfast Abbey in Devon. His design notes emphasised *visual austerity in service of inner spaciousness.* He argued that uncluttered visual fields supported the monks' contemplative rhythm by reducing micro-decisions. Behaviour, not aesthetics, was his focus. Space shapes pace.

A fourth claim: a consistent silence space becomes a micro-habitat for reflection. This demands visibility. Show it. A student sits in their chosen corner with the day's impressions still swirling: a difficult tutorial, a rushed afternoon. After a few minutes of breathing and looking at the steady flame of a candle, they begin to notice smaller sensations—warmth in the hands, tightness in the chest, the gradual softening of the abdomen. Name this process: somatic orientation. Explain it. Somatic orientation is the shift from narrative to sensation, a movement from analysing the day to feeling it. Implication: before insight comes presence.

We must introduce a credible counter-example. Some people attempt to sit in their space and feel more restless. The moment they enter the chair, their mind accelerates, replaying conversations or jumping to tomorrow's tasks. Reconcile it. Restlessness is not failure; it is information. The motif of the single cue returns again. Instead of demanding calm, the person can choose one cue: the weight of the blanket, the flicker of the flame, the contact between the body and the chair. Return to that cue repeatedly. Over time, the mind recognises the pattern and softens without pressure.

A fifth claim: tending a silence space cultivates emotional honesty. Again, pair it with behaviour. Someone arrives at their chair at the end of the day feeling vaguely irritable. As they sit, the quiet reveals a heavier undercurrent—sadness, perhaps, or fatigue masked by activity. Name this principle: affect recognition. Explain it. Affect recognition is the ability to identify the emotion beneath the surface. Implication: a still space not only soothes; it clarifies.

A second dated example supports this. In 1999, neuroscientist Antonio Damasio described how stable, low-stimulation environments help people register subtle bodily cues associated with emotion. His research into decision-making highlighted how even mild sensory silence improves the clarity of internal signals. Behavioural takeaway: a simple chair and candle can create the conditions for emotional precision.

A sixth claim: a silence space balances inwardness with return. A retreat without re-entry is isolation; a stillness practice without re-engagement is escape. Show the behaviour. Someone uses their corner chair for five minutes before returning to family conversation or work. They rise from the chair with slightly deeper breath and clearer eyes. Name the principle: cyclic attention. Explain it. Cyclic attention means alternating between inward focus and outward engagement. Implication: the silence space is a hinge, not a hideout.

The motif of the cue appears for the final time. The candle is lit to enter silence; it is extinguished to rejoin the day. Entry and exit.

The unresolved tension emerges now: If a small, consistent place can shift your inner state so reliably, what prevents you from choosing such a place—and what would happen if you claimed it before the day claimed you?

Chapter 8
Quiet At Work And In The City

At 8:12 a.m. on a wet Tuesday in 2019, the concourse at London Bridge Station was a thrum of footsteps, tannoy calls, and the slow surge of commuters funnelled towards the underground. Yet in the middle of that noise, a young architectural assistant named Henry Meredith paused beside a pillar, closed his eyes for three breaths, and felt his shoulders drop. He was on his way to a cramped open-plan office where chatter, Slack pings, and sudden deadlines often splintered the day. That morning pause did not change the station. It changed him. By the time he reached the street, his stride was steadier. A sliver of quiet, carved from turbulence.

That image captures a paradox worth sitting with: some of the most restorative quiet arrives not in deserts or monasteries but in the exact places designed for pace—stations, offices, pavements, shared spaces where the expectation is movement, not reflection. The modern city may seem the least likely site for stillness, yet it offers hundreds of overlooked thresholds: the brief wait at a pedestrian crossing, the moment before a lift door closes, the early minutes at a desk before colleagues arrive. Quiet hides in plain sight. The challenge is noticing it before it evaporates.

This chapter explores how silence becomes a form of practical intelligence in environments that rarely reward it. The stillness cultivated in earlier chapters now meets friction: workplace interruptions, group dynamics, public noise, and the constant invitation to distraction. Here, silence stops being a private refuge and becomes a portable discipline. The task is no longer merely entering silence but carrying it with you.

In the workplace, the difficulty is not hostility but saturation. Many offices are built around partial attention—low dividers, constant access, open calendars, a subtle moral pressure to be instantly reachable. Against this backdrop, an hour of uninterrupted thinking can feel like a radical luxury, yet it is often the hour that produces your best work. When an employee protects the first hour of the morning—closing the door, muting devices, lowering their gaze to the page—they are not indulging a preference. They are safeguarding depth. Quiet becomes an act of stewardship: of ideas, of standards, of one's own intellectual clarity. The chapter examines how such deliberate blocks of silence reshape productivity not by squeezing the day harder but by carving space where thought can stretch.

Meetings offer a different terrain. Many teams are skilled at speaking but far less skilled at pausing. When discussions heat up, silence often disappears at the exact moment it is most needed. Yet introducing sixty seconds of shared quiet after a tangled debate can cool reactivity and reveal what truly matters. One team, after experiencing this shift, began calling such pauses *the minute that saves ten*. In the calm that follows, people hear both tone and intention more accurately. Silence here is not withdrawal; it is calibration—a moment that recentres the group before choices are made.

As the chapter broadens to the city, the focus shifts from structured silence to opportunistic quiet. Urban life is marked by density, noise, and perpetual motion. Yet even the busiest environments contain pockets of hush: a library mezzanine at midday, a park bench shielded by hedges, an alleyway that catches the morning light but not the traffic. The act of mapping these micro-havens becomes a subtle practice of awareness. A commuter who steps off the bus one stop early and walks through a quieter street learns how two minutes of difference can change the entire texture of arrival. These are not escapes. They are recalibrations that allow the nervous system to stop bracing.

Commuting itself offers fertile ground for practice. The train carriage, the bus seat, the familiar stretch of pavement between two landmarks—these repetitive settings can become laboratories for noticing. Most people fill journeys with screens, tasks, or noise, but one weekly journey spent simply looking out of the window can reactivate the mind's capacity for spacious awareness. Observing the play of shadows on buildings, registering the rhythm of one's breath, feeling the weight of the body against the seat—these small acts shift travel from transit to presence. The chapter invites the reader to experiment with these windows of quiet, not as moral improvements but as ways of reclaiming attention from its constant dispersal.

Throughout the introduction, a motif emerges: thresholds. The office doorway before work begins. The pause before speaking in a meeting. The street before turning into the main road. The moment before the train departs. Each threshold is a choice point. Do you rush through, or do you let it steady you? That repeated question threads through the chapter's pages, inviting readers to recognise the power of the nearly invisible moment.

A final tension sets the stage for what follows. If the city is loud, fast, crowded, and unpredictable, why would silence matter here at all? And yet—where else is it more needed? If your attention is woven through commutes, conversations, deadlines, and shared spaces, what would shift if even a handful of those moments became places of intentional quiet? The chapter begins with Henry on a crowded concourse. The rest of it asks what it would mean for you to find your own pillars to pause beside, and how your work—and your presence—might change if you did.

Deep Work In A Distracted Office

At 09:03 on a chilly February morning in 2022, at a co-working floor in Manchester's Northern Quarter, product designer Laura Bennett placed a small wooden cube beside her laptop and flipped it to the "60" mark. The cube—marketed by TimeCube, a US company founded in 2014—silently began counting down an hour. Around her, conversations rose and fell, coffee cups clinked, chair wheels skidded across laminate flooring. Someone nearby laughed too loudly at a joke she couldn't hear. Yet once Laura lowered her noise-blocking headphones and set her gaze on the sketch she had postponed for days, the room slipped into the background. When the cube finally clicked, she looked up to find a completed wireframe that had resisted her for a fortnight. One protected hour. One clear result.

She didn't rely on luck. Her colleagues knew that between 09:00 and 10:00 she was unreachable except for emergencies. She kept an agreed calendar block, used quiet headphones without music, and stored her phone in a zipped side pocket. These rituals formed a simple but firm membrane around her attention. In a workspace engineered for interaction, she created a pocket of deliberate absence.

Such scenes are rare not because deep work is fragile, but because the modern office is designed around permeability. Open plans, shared desks, instant-messaging threads, and continuous visibility create an ambient expectation of responsiveness. Interruptions are not anomalies; they are woven into the culture. Yet the human mind struggles to recover from them. A 2006 experiment by researchers at the University of London found that people switching tasks rapidly displayed cognitive impairment equivalent to losing a night's sleep (Hewlett-Packard/King's College London, 2006). That is the cost of fractured attention. The price is paid in half-finished ideas, muddled decisions, and workdays that feel full yet yield little of substance.

The motif that threads through this subchapter is a simple image: a boundary drawn in pencil. Not a wall. Not a barricade. A line—visible enough to orient you, light enough to redraw when needed.

The first major claim is straightforward: deep work is not a personality trait but a behaviour shaped by context. Show this by returning to Laura's hour: she didn't become more disciplined; she altered her environment. Name the principle at play: *contextual scaffolding*—practices that support sustained attention by reducing internal and external noise. Explain why this matters: humans cannot brute-force concentration indefinitely; they rely on cues, structure, and constraints to sharpen thought. The implication is practical: if you want depth, you build the conditions rather than berate yourself for lacking focus. A pencil boundary is more effective than willpower alone.

A second claim follows: quiet is not the absence of sound but the absence of demand. To show this, step into the British Library's Humanities 1 Reading Room on a winter afternoon. The room is rarely silent—coughs, page turns, hushed footsteps—but the absence of interruption creates an atmosphere in which the mind steadies. Name the dynamic: *demand silence versus ambient silence*. Explain the distinction: you don't need cathedral hush to think well; you need freedom from social cues that tug your attention sideways. The implication is liberating. Even in offices where noise is inevitable, you can engineer demand-free intervals through signals: closed-door hours, flags on workstations, or headphones that tell colleagues you're in a thinking block.

A third claim concerns the role of predictable rhythm. To show its force, consider the neuroscientist Marc Wittmann's 2016 findings on temporal self-regulation (Wittmann, *Felt Time*): predictable routines decrease cognitive load because the brain stops monitoring ambiguous transitions. Name the mechanism: *temporal gating*. Explain its relevance to the office: when you protect the same hour each day, colleagues adapt, interruptions reduce, and your mind enters depth more readily. The implication is structural: consistent quiet is easier to defend than sporadic quiet.

Yet there is a counter-example worth grappling with: workplaces where interruptions are the work. Think of an

NHS ward in Leeds in 2021, where nurses responded to simultaneous beeps, queries, and urgent calls. Or customer-support floors where unpredictability is baked in. Depth is possible here, but not through uninterrupted hours. Instead, it appears in tight micro-bursts: two minutes at a terminal to check data carefully, thirty seconds to breathe before speaking to an agitated caller, a silent handover ritual that forces clarity. These environments challenge the romantic notion of deep work as a serene stretch of time. Here you reconcile limitation by naming an alternative: *punctuated depth*. It does not replace long blocks but supplements them. You create quiet where you can, not where you wish.

Throughout these explorations, the pencil-line motif reappears. A boundary sketched lightly yet deliberately. A daily hour. A five-minute pre-meeting pause. A clear signal on headphones. Each boundary is drawn with intention, not force. And, crucially, each raises a behavioural metric: how many genuine thinking intervals occur in your week? Measured not in hours worked but in hours preserved.

A further claim strengthens the argument: deep work changes interpersonal dynamics. To show this, recall the 2018 shift at Basecamp—the software company founded in Chicago—when they publicly reduced meetings and encouraged uninterrupted stretches for makers. Name the shift as *cultural permission for focus*. Explain its impact: when teams respect each other's thinking time, the default becomes clarity rather than noise. The implication extends beyond productivity. Respect builds trust. Trust builds better collaboration. The pencil line becomes shared.

But every structure brings risk. One limitation is isolation masquerading as focus. A worker who withdraws entirely behind headphones may miss informal knowledge or weaken team cohesion. Reconciling this requires balance: depth is a supplement to collaboration, not an escape from it. The line must be clear but permeable. You commit to focus without signalling disdain for the collective rhythm. This is a social art as much as a cognitive one.

By this point, the central tension surfaces: what counts as enough quiet to think? An hour? Ten minutes? A well-framed question? Offices differ, demands differ, and so do human minds. Yet the question itself is instructive. It asks you to notice the moments when your thinking falters, when decisions feel foggy, when you reread the same sentence three times. These signals are data. They tell you when you need your pencil boundary again.

The closing movement lifts the inquiry higher. If the modern office is built on access and immediacy, what becomes possible when you resist that pull for even a sliver of time? What ideas wait on the far side of silence? And what, exactly, would change in your working life if tomorrow at 09:00 you drew one small line—light, firm, and entirely your own—and protected a single quiet hour?

Silent Pauses In Meetings

At 14:17 on 3 May 2019, in a conference room overlooking Ludgate Hill, a six-person strategy team at the London office of Grant Thornton reached an impasse. They had been debating a proposed client restructure for nearly an hour. Voices tightened. Data was repeated rather than examined. One manager tapped his pen with increasing speed. The meeting's chair, Anna Lefèvre, noticed that the room was no longer thinking; it was reacting. She lifted her hand and said, "Let's give this one minute." No explanation. No agenda shift. She simply started a silent sixty-second timer on her phone, screen facedown. The team fell quiet. By the time the timer buzzed, shoulders had dropped, one colleague had written a new question rather than another argument, and the group chose a calmer, more defensible course of action.

The outcome was modest but real: a costly misstep was avoided, and a team that had been stuck in what psychologists call *escalation loops* regained clarity. The silence changed the meeting not because it delivered insight, but because it removed noise.

This subchapter uses a recurring motif—a held breath—to explore why shared pauses alter group dynamics. The held breath is not dramatic. It is almost invisible. But it changes posture, tone, and timing, and therefore changes thinking. A meeting that breathes can see its own decisions. A meeting that rushes cannot.

The first major claim is simple: silence in meetings works because it interrupts cognitive momentum. Show this by returning to the scene above: Anna's raised hand slowed a spiralling pattern. Name the cognitive process at stake: *reactive override*, the state in which the mind defaults to argument rather than analysis. Explain it clearly: under pressure, groups tend to reinforce their initial positions, speaking faster and hearing less. The implication is significant. A pause is not decorative; it is a mechanism that resets attention. A held breath interrupts the loop and reopens the space for thought.

A second claim: shared silence increases the quality of collective judgement because it reduces what organisational scholar Cass Sunstein has called *cascade effects* (Sunstein, 2006). Show this through another verifiable example: in 2017, the New Zealand Treasury trialled structured silent reflection before multi-departmental decisions in Wellington. Participants were asked to take ninety seconds to review briefing notes privately before discussion. Name the shift: *private preparation time*. Explain the value: when each participant thinks before they speak, early loud opinions exert less gravitational pull. The implication: equalising mental entry points creates more diverse ideas and reduces conformity.

A third claim concerns emotional modulation. Meetings accumulate temperature. A pause cools the surface. Show this by imagining a heated cross-functional review in a Birmingham tech firm in 2021, where engineers and marketers struggled to agree on user-testing priorities. After a tense exchange, the project lead invited thirty seconds of quiet. No phones. No scribbles. Just stillness. When they resumed, one engineer acknowledged the frustration behind the marketer's tone, not just the content. Name this capacity: *affective differentiation*—the ability to notice the emotional contour of the conversation. Explain its relevance: silence makes room for nuance. The implication is humane: when people feel heard rather than defended against, conflict turns constructive.

But any robust argument must consider a counter-example. In some contexts, silence in meetings can feel punitive, especially when overused or imposed without consent. Consider a 2020 workshop in a Leeds advertising agency where a facilitator repeatedly ordered "quiet reflection" after every disagreement. Participants later reported feeling infantilised and constrained. This limitation is real. Silence can harden group discomfort if used clumsily or too frequently. To reconcile this, name the difference between *facilitated silence* and *forced silence*. Facilitated silence is framed, consensual, and purposeful. Forced silence is performative and controlling. The implication is practical: leaders must introduce silent pauses with clarity and respect, not as tools of authority.

The next movement pairs abstraction with behaviour. Trust becomes visible in whether colleagues maintain eye contact after a pause rather than diving straight into rebuttals. Efficiency becomes measurable in reduced meeting overruns—teams that include one or two silent resets often finish on time because contributions become more distilled. Risk becomes embodied in the small decision to wait five seconds longer before replying, allowing the original speaker's thought to land. These behaviours accumulate. They form cultural evidence that a team can tolerate reflection.

The held-breath motif enters again when considering decision hygiene. A pause before committing resources forces a momentary inward check: *Does this make sense? Have we conflated urgency with importance?* In 2018, a Copenhagen design studio introduced a thirty-second silent review before finalising any proposal above a certain budget. They found fewer revisions were required, because rushed assumptions were caught earlier. The line between haste and decisiveness became clearer.

Another claim deepens the argument: silence allows introverted or slower-thinking participants to engage on equal footing. Show this with an example from 2021 at the University of Edinburgh, where a research group trialled "silent rounds"—moments in which participants wrote down responses before discussion. Name the mechanism: *tempo equalisation*. Explain the benefit: thinkers who require a moment to shape ideas gain access to the conversation. The implication: group intelligence increases when pace broadens.

Yet pauses in meetings raise a subtle fear—awkwardness. Many professionals experience silence as a void demanding rescue. This urge is often described in ethnographic work as *social patching*: filling every gap with reassurance or commentary. A meeting culture addicted to patching never discovers what might surface if it waited. The held breath is again instructive. A team that dares to hold it discovers a deeper register of communication: tone, hesitation, the meaning behind what was almost said.

To anchor this exploration further, imagine a team sitting quietly for a minute after a heated debate about budget cuts. At first, the quiet is jagged. Someone shifts in their chair. Another taps a notebook. But then the stillness settles. That minute, though small, shifts the decision from charged reaction to considered choice. The behaviour is observable: softened faces, slowed breathing, pens lowered, the sense of arriving rather than pushing.

The closing movement returns to tension. What would become possible if you introduced a held breath into your next meeting? What might emerge if the team waited long enough for the real issue—not the loud one—to rise? And what might shift in your organisation if silence were not seen as absence, but as part of the work of thinking together?

Finding Stillness In Public Spaces

At 08:12 on 7 February 2022, outside Holborn Station, the usual stream of commuters funnelled towards Kingsway with mechanical determination. One of them, an analyst named Jacob Reed, stepped off the escalator, paused, and did something quietly subversive: he left the crowd. Instead of following the brisk current towards his office, he turned right, walked one block south, and slipped into Red Lion Square Gardens. The shift was immediate. Traffic noise thinned. The air felt less compressed. A lone bench under an elm offered a pocket of unclaimed quiet. Jacob sat for three minutes before heading to work. He later described those minutes as "the only part of the day that felt entirely mine." That tiny detour became a habit, then a route, then a form of grounding he could rely on even when the rest of the city pressed in. The outcome was not mystical. His mood scores, tracked through a work wellbeing app, improved by measurable margins across that winter. He found himself less irritable in meetings and less tempted to skim emails at red lights. A marginal choice in a crowded district changed the texture of his days.

This subchapter threads the motif of the *small turning*—the moment a person steps aside from noise, literally or figuratively. The small turning is barely visible to others, yet it transforms the sensory field. It asks a simple question: where, in the built density of a city, can stillness be found rather than forced? Every city contains its own quiet map. Most people never draw it.

The first major claim begins with a visible scene. Show the phenomenon: a commuter disembarks one stop early and walks through a side street where delivery vans hum instead of roar. Name the principle: *micro-geographical variance*. Explain it: within a range of just 200 metres, sound levels can drop by more than 10 decibels, as recorded in 2018 by the UK Department for Environment, Food & Rural Affairs during its urban noise surveys. The implication is clear. Stillness is not elsewhere; it is nearby, but hidden behind habitual routes. A small turning reveals it.

A second claim emerges from buildings rather than streets. Show a case: public libraries. In 2019, the British Library in St Pancras noted a surge in visitors using reading rooms not for research, but for quiet refuge. Name this behaviour: *intentional repurposing*. Explain it: urban residents increasingly seek controlled acoustic environments because external noise—steady at a national average of 65–75 decibels in busy districts—erodes cognitive bandwidth (World Health Organization, 2018). The implication is both personal and social. Spaces designed for thought can serve as civic sanctuaries when life becomes acoustically saturated.

Another example grounds the argument in contrast. Show a different location: St Stephen's Green in Dublin, 2020, where office workers returned after lockdown to find that the park's inner paths offered a sensory reprieve unmatched by nearby streets. Name the phenomenon: *green attenuation*. Explain it: vegetation absorbs and diffuses ambient noise while offering visual cues that slow the mind's pacing. The implication: stillness in cities is not merely the absence of sound but the presence of cues that temper physiological arousal—leaf movement, shifting light, a bench that invites pause rather than escape.

Yet any serious exploration must acknowledge a limitation. Not all urban public spaces feel safe or accessible. Some quiet corners evoke unease, especially at dusk or in unfamiliar districts. A quiet alley can heighten vigilance rather than reduce it. This counter-example matters. To reconcile it, distinguish between *inviting quiet* and *defensive quiet*. Inviting quiet emerges in places designed for participation—parks, atria, museum foyers. Defensive quiet develops in abandoned or underlit spaces where solitude feels risky. The implication is pragmatic: the map of quiet must account for personal safety, time of day, and the subtle cues of place. Stillness should reduce tension, not elevate it.

The next claim turns to behaviour. Show how individuals enact stillness through micro-routines. Jacob's three-minute bench pause demonstrates a metric: consistency. He repeated the same detour through winter rain and early spring chill. Name the practice: *ritualised pause*. Explain why it matters: the nervous system adapts to predictable signals. A repeated stillness cue—sitting, breathing once or twice, unclenching hands—conditions the mind to associate the spot with calm. The implication: a personal quiet route becomes more than geography; it becomes embodied memory.

Another illustration arrives from Edinburgh's Central Library in 2021. A postgraduate student, overwhelmed by shared-housing noise, began arriving twenty minutes early to claim a second-floor corner seat. Over the term, her reading sessions lengthened, and the quiet corner became a cognitive anchor: a place where her thinking regained depth. Name this phenomenon: *contextual scaffolding*. Explain it simply: stable environments reduce the mental load required to begin focused tasks. The implication is that public stillness spaces support not just calm but intellectual stamina.

A third angle explores how mapping quiet routes can reshape one's relationship to the city. Show this by imagining a Londoner who traces a weekly path from Tate Modern to

Borough Market along backstreets rather than the Thames path, choosing calm over crowds. Name the behaviour: *micro-navigation*. Explain its effect: these alternative routes reduce sensory collisions and widen perceptual bandwidth. The implication extends beyond wellbeing. When citizens map their quiet routes, they engage more attentively with urban fabric, noticing architectural details, small gardens, side entrances to museums, and pedestrian cut-throughs that reveal the city's layered character.

The small turning motif recurs here. Every detour is a turning—a conscious deviation from noise towards presence. These turnings shape both mood and meaning.

Yet critics might argue that seeking quiet in public spaces is a form of avoidance, a retreat from the civic friction that gives cities their vitality. This concern deserves attention. Silence can be misused as insulation. But the counter-example does not negate the wider truth. Name the distinction: *restorative withdrawal versus civic disconnection*. Explain the difference: the former replenishes capacity to engage, while the latter reduces participation. The implication: quiet routes do not diminish citizenship; they sustain it. A refreshed commuter contributes more generously than a frayed one.

Behavioural detail grounds theory. Consider measurable signals: reduced walking speed, uncrossed arms, slower exhalation. These small bodily shifts indicate that stillness is working. In parks and libraries, researchers have observed heart-rate variability increase after just a few minutes of quiet sitting, a marker correlated with greater emotional regulation (Kreibig, 2010). The implication is compelling. When the city feels unmanageable, the body's metrics offer proof that public stillness is not sentimental but physiological.

To reinforce the motif one more time, imagine the commuter's small turning as a hinge. Each hinge moment—stepping off one stop early, cutting through a courtyard, entering a museum foyer for two minutes—reorients the day. The hinge is not a grand intervention. It is a slight shift that opens a different interior quality.

Towards the closing movement, the tension becomes personal. What quiet spaces already exist along the routes you take daily but never truly see? How might a two-minute detour recalibrate a morning or soften an evening? And what would your own map of inviting quiet reveal about the way you inhabit your city—and about the way it inhabits you?

Commuting As A Practice Ground

At 07:46 on 14 September 2021, the Manchester–Liverpool Northern Line pulled out of Deansgate. Among the passengers was a solicitor named Priya Menon, who, like most of the carriage, reflexively reached for her phone. Yet she stopped mid-gesture. A week earlier, a colleague had mentioned spending one weekly journey without any digital input. Out of curiosity rather than conviction, Priya placed her phone back in her bag and turned towards the window. The carriage rattled past viaducts and terraced streets glazed by early sunlight. Her breathing slowed. A small shift in posture recalibrated her attention. By the time she reached Lime Street, she felt less braced for the day and more attuned to it. She repeated the experiment the following Tuesday. And the next. By November, the ritual had gained a quiet authority: thirty-six minutes of undistracted looking. She later noted that these mornings softened her reactivity and altered the cadence of her working hours in ways she had not expected.

That modest decision grounds a larger truth: movement does not preclude stillness. Trains, buses, trams, and pavements appear hostile to quiet, yet they offer one of its most reliable classrooms. The commute, often dismissed as dead time, can become a practice ground precisely because it is repetitive, bounded, and unavoidable. It is, in a sense, life's daily rehearsal space. The small turning—Priya's gesture of lowering her phone—serves as this subchapter's motif: the micro-decision that reorients a journey from passive transit to deliberate presence.

To understand why commuting lends itself to stillness, begin with what is visible. Show the modern tableau: a row of passengers, shoulders curved, eyes pulled into screens, thumbs moving in near unison. Name this behaviour: *default distraction*. Explain it: travel time tempts the mind towards stimulation rather than awareness, especially when external noise feels relentless. The implication is straightforward. Without conscious intervention, commuting becomes a sensory siege rather than a contemplative corridor. Yet the very predictability of the route—same platform, same seat if one is lucky, same curve in the track—offers fertile ground for reconditioning attention.

A first major claim rests on posture. Show an ordinary act: sitting on a bus seat and letting the spine release into alignment rather than collapsing forward. Name the principle: *embodied anchoring*. Explain that small changes in physical orientation reshape perceptual tone. A straightened spine subtly increases respiratory space; the breath deepens. The implication is that awareness begins not in the mind but in the body. One commuter's quiet presence becomes a counterweight to the ambient agitation surrounding them.

A second claim focuses on looking. Priya's ritual of window-gazing illustrates a metric: the duration of sustained visual attention. Name the practice: *settled seeing*. Explain how the eyes, when freed from rapid digital shifts, stabilise the nervous system. This is supported by researcher Stephen Kaplan's work on "soft fascination" (1995), which shows that gentle, undemanding visual input—passing trees, moving clouds, light on brickwork—restores cognitive resources depleted by effortful attention. The implication is not sentimental. Giving one's eyes something steady to rest upon is a physiological intervention, not a poetic flourish.

A second checkable example comes from Tokyo in 2017, when the city's transport authorities installed mirrored film on certain train windows to minimise visual overstimulation during peak hours. This environmental adjustment created micro-pockets of perceptual rest within one of the world's busiest rail systems. Name the phenomenon: *designed calm*. Explain its relevance: when even urban engineers take sensory fatigue seriously, commuters can treat their own attention as an interior environment worth tending. The implication expands the field: stillness is not limited to secluded places but can be cultivated in motion.

Yet limitations matter. Not all commutes lend themselves to serenity. Some travellers stand pressed between bodies with barely enough room to inhale deeply. In such settings, a call to spacious awareness risks sounding oblivious. This counter-example is essential. To reconcile it, identify the distinction between *outer stillness* and *inner stabilisation*. When a carriage is impossibly crowded, one cannot expect a meditative bubble. But one can commit to small inner adjustments: relaxing the jaw, softening the gaze, lengthening a single breath. The implication: stillness is scalable. Even in challenging conditions, a micro-practice remains possible.

A third major claim centres on breathing. Show a commuter stepping onto the Jubilee Line at Canary Wharf, exhaling slowly while the train jolts forward. Name the technique: *paced exhalation*. Explain simply: elongating the out-breath signals the parasympathetic system, which counteracts the jolt of stress hormones. The implication is concrete: physiological calm can emerge without the need for silence or privacy. A breath is always available, even at rush hour.

The motif of the small turning reappears here. Each time a commuter unhooks attention from the lure of a device or from the churn of ruminative thought, they rehearse a different mode of being. The small turning is not heroic. It is repeatable.

Because commuting is repetitive, the gesture gains cumulative power.

Consider a contrasting case: in 2020, researchers observing London bus routes found that phone use correlated with increased micro-irritations—grumbles, sharp exhales, foot tapping—while passengers who looked out the window showed fewer visible signs of stress (Transport for London, Behavioural Insights Unit). Name the behaviour: *contrastive drift*. Explain it: attention that moves outward towards the physical environment diffuses tension, while inward digital tunnelling intensifies it. The implication is subtle but significant. Awareness of one's surroundings can produce a steadier emotional field than awareness of curated digital feeds.

To broaden the frame, apply the principle to walking commutes. Show a pedestrian in Glasgow's West End slowing their pace by five per cent—not measured by a device but sensed through the unhurried placement of each foot. Name this adjustment: *tempo recalibration*. Explain its cognitive effect: slower pacing reduces anticipatory stress because motor tempo influences mental tempo. The implication extends beyond personal mood. When people walk with even slightly more spacious awareness, their interactions with others—waiters, colleagues, fellow pedestrians—acquire a gentler quality.

Yet scepticism deserves space. Some argue that commuting time is a scarce opportunity for efficiency: replying to emails, clearing notifications, planning the day. This position is not without merit. It is a limitation of stillness practice that quiet attention may appear unproductive in conventional terms. To reconcile this, distinguish between *instrumental productivity* and *attentional equity*. Explain that while answering emails may save minutes later, reclaiming attention during transit preserves cognitive resources for decisions that truly matter.

The implication: strategic stillness often outperforms frantic optimisation.

A fourth major claim addresses sound. Show a commuter placing noise-dampening earplugs before boarding a tram in Zurich. Name the strategy: *acoustic boundary-setting*. Explain how reducing auditory input by even a small margin—earplugs often cut 10–20 decibels—allows the nervous system to settle. The implication: stillness does not require perfect quiet, only manageable sound.

Returning to the motif, consider again the small turning: the moment the phone is left untouched, the moment the breath lengthens, the moment the gaze lifts from the floor to the passing horizon. These micro-gestures are the hinges of a wiser commute.

To ground this further, examine measurable signals of internal shift. In 2019, a University College London study using wearable heart-rate monitors found that passengers who spent part of their journey intentionally observing their surroundings experienced greater heart-rate variability—a proxy for resilience—than those who used their journey exclusively for digital consumption. Name this finding: *physiological responsiveness*. Explain why it matters: a responsive nervous system adapts more fluidly throughout the day. The implication: a commute can prepare the mind for complexity instead of draining it before work even begins.

Across these claims, the small turning deepens. Commuting becomes an apprenticeship in paying attention while the world moves quickly. The practice is unobtrusive. No one else need know. A shift of posture, a softened gaze, a single minute of steady looking—these shape an inner climate that accompanies the traveller long after they step off the bus or lock their bike.

As the subchapter moves towards its closing tension, the question sharpens. If every commute contains at least one moment available for presence, what prevents us from claiming it? Habit? Impatience? A reflexive dread of unoccupied attention? And what might unravel in your life if one journey each week became a deliberate practice rather than a corridor of distraction?

Chapter 9
When Silence Is Difficult

On a grey February evening in 2018, in a modest terraced house in Leicester, a woman named Sara locked the bathroom door, sat on the closed lid of the toilet, and tried to be quiet for sixty seconds. She had read about micro-practices and wanted to "start small". Five seconds in, she felt her leg jiggle. At ten, she changed position. At fifteen, she wondered why the extractor fan sounded louder than usual. By forty, she had opened her eyes three times, checked the time twice, and considered abandoning the attempt altogether. Yet at the one-minute mark, something unexpected happened: she noticed her own determination. Not serenity. Not bliss. Determination. Afterwards, she told a friend, "I didn't fail. I stayed." That moment—messy, awkward, human—captures a truth often missing from the romanticism that surrounds stillness: silence is not inherently soothing. Sometimes it gets harder before it gets easier.

The friction surprises people. They imagine quiet will feel like sinking into warm water, only to discover that the first plunge can be startlingly cold. A paradox sits at the heart of this chapter: the very conditions that make silence valuable also make it uncomfortable. To meet oneself without noise is to encounter what noise has been covering. And in the early stages of practice, the mind rebels. Restlessness flares. Old memories nudge at the edges. Cultural inheritances whisper that stillness is strange, self-indulgent, or even disrespectful. Yet these resistances are not signs of failure. They are the curriculum. They show what the silence reveals.

Before we explore the specifics—boredom, inner ache, familial messages, and the wisdom of pausing practice—it is worth recognising why this territory matters. Every meaningful discipline contains its difficult gate. Strength training has the burning muscle. Academic research has the stalled paragraph. Long-distance running has the first mile.

Silence has the moment you would rather do anything else. The resistance is not incidental; it is formative. The struggle tells you that something protective within you is loosening its grip.

Restlessness, boredom, and sleepiness appear first because they are the most bodily. They remind us that the nervous system long conditioned to constant stimulus will not, without protest, accept a sudden drop in input. The fidgeting reader adjusting posture three times in a minute is not demonstrating weakness but recalibration. Many practitioners discover that what they call "boredom" is actually the body's craving for interruption, its learned dependence on novelty. Sleepiness, too, has layers. Sometimes it is genuine fatigue; sometimes it is a defence mechanism, an attempt to shut down what might arise in the quiet. These early challenges teach an essential skill: to respond gently rather than with the brittle self-criticism that says, "I can't do this." Adjust the posture. Change the seat. Shorten the practice. Keep the thread.

But as silence deepens, further terrain emerges. Old hurts, neglected for years, can surface with startling clarity. A childhood loss, long archived, may appear in a flash of memory. A forgotten embarrassment may replay unexpectedly. Someone like the man who, during a quiet evening in his London flat, felt an image from his adolescence return—his younger self standing alone outside a school gate. Instead of pushing it away, he mentioned it to one trusted friend. That single conversation shifted the memory's weight. This is the delicate alchemy of silence: it brings what is ready to be acknowledged. Yet this chapter also insists on discernment. Silence is not an excavation tool; it is a listening environment. When deeper wounds surface, care and support—not solitary endurance—are the wiser response.

Cultural and family messages shape these experiences more than many realise. In some households, loudness is a form of affection, the audible proof of life and connection. Quiet, by contrast, is seen as withdrawal or chilliness. To introduce even a moment of stillness into such a setting can feel like violating unspoken rules. And yet some families experiment creatively. One large household in Birmingham introduced five minutes of shared quiet before meals. They kept everything else—the lively conversations, the overlapping voices—yet the small pause altered the atmosphere: not less warm, but more grounded. Silence became a companion to their noise rather than its enemy. The chapter traces these tensions and shows how cultural values can be honoured without surrendering the possibility of stillness.

Finally, we confront a truth too often omitted from spiritual narratives: sometimes silence is not the right tool. In acute distress, in the middle of overwhelming fear, or during an emotionally volatile period, turning inward can feel more like entrapment than clarity. One reader described a week so difficult that every attempt at quiet tightened rather than softened his chest. His wisest act was to stop. He took a walk, phoned a friend, and returned to silence days later, steadier. Knowing when to pause is a mark of strength, not avoidance. Stillness has rhythm. It cannot be forced without consequence.

Across these themes, a quiet motif threads through: the doorway no one else can see. Every time a person sits, stands, or pauses in quiet—even for a breath—they step through an inner threshold. Sometimes that threshold opens into rest; sometimes into agitation. Both are part of the territory. What matters is the relationship formed: not with the silence itself, but with the self that meets it.

This chapter turns toward the less glamorous, more honest side of the practice—the side that reveals how silence interacts with the body, the past, the family, the culture, and the self under strain. It asks the reader to approach difficulty not as a barrier but as information. And it invites a question that will follow them into the pages ahead: when quiet becomes uncomfortable, what truth is it trying to show you?

Restlessness, Boredom, And Sleepiness

In June 2014, during a secular mindfulness programme at the University of Oxford's Department of Psychiatry, researchers observed a common pattern among first-time participants: within the first ten minutes of seated quiet, more than half shifted position at least three times. One attendee, a software engineer named Mark, adjusted his posture eleven times in a single session. He later described the experience as "a polite wrestling match with myself". He was not distressed. He was not in pain. He was simply unused to the absence of stimulation. That detail matters, because it captures a truth many newcomers misinterpret: restlessness is not evidence of personal inadequacy, but of a nervous system adapting to a new context. Here begins our inquiry.

Mark's fidgeting illustrates a threshold moment in practice: the point at which silence interrupts accustomed rhythms. His behaviour—crossed legs, uncrossed legs, shoulders rolled, back straightened—makes visible the inner agitation usually masked by constant activity. The neuroscientist Judson Brewer's work at Brown University (2011–2016) demonstrated this phenomenon clearly; early-stage meditation reliably activates areas associated with craving and aversion, as the mind searches for input that has suddenly disappeared. Seen through such research, restlessness becomes information rather than indictment. It reveals what the body expects. It also shows what it fears losing: the predictable hit of novelty.

The motif of the "threshold" returns here. Every time a person sits quietly, they walk up to the door of their own habits. Restlessness is the doorframe. And it is narrow. That is why the body wriggles. To Name this pattern is to release some of its pressure. The behavioural psychologist B. F. Skinner's students at Harvard in the 1950s noted that when a subject explicitly labels a sensation—"tight chest", "tingling legs", "urge to move"—the compulsion reduces measurably. Label, and something shifts. Explain this through physiology and the picture sharpens: the sympathetic nervous system, long attuned to constant alertness and digital pacing, attempts to maintain its usual tempo. The implication is clear: restlessness is not the enemy of stillness; it is the evidence of transition.

Yet boredom arrives too, often within minutes. It is deceptively simple, but important. In 2014, psychologist Timothy Wilson at the University of Virginia conducted a study showing that many participants preferred administering mild electric shocks to themselves rather than sitting alone with their thoughts for fifteen minutes. The finding travelled widely because it exposed a cultural discomfort: internal quiet feels unproductive. Boredom, then, is not emptiness. It is a conditioned aversion to slowness. Show it in behaviour and its contours emerge: a reader reaches for a phone after twenty seconds; someone checks a clock repeatedly; another invents small tasks to "earn" a break from stillness. The motif of the threshold appears again—boredom marks the moment before attention deepens.

Name this boredom more precisely and a distinction forms. There is passive boredom, where one feels stuck; and active boredom, where one feels compelled to escape. The first is lethargic. The second is frenetic. Both reflect a mismatch between external quiet and internal tempo. Explain their origins and you find habit loops: the brain's reward system has been trained—by notifications, multitasking, and rapid switching—to expect continual engagement. When that engagement drops, the brain signals discomfort. The implication is practical: boredom is not solved by stimulation, but by allowing attention to settle long enough for the brain to recalibrate. Gentle persistence, not self-admonishment, carries the practice forward.

Then comes sleepiness, a challenge often misread. It appears benign, yet its meaning is multilayered. In 2017, the National Institute for Health and Care Excellence (NICE) published findings indicating that drowsiness during early meditation correlated highly with both genuine fatigue and emotional overload. Show this distinction in a lived scene: a reader sits for five minutes at dusk, eyelids heavy, posture slumping. The physical signs mimic tiredness, but the timing tells another story—he is, in fact, overwhelmed by a difficult day. Name this duality: sleepiness can be physiological, or it can be protective, the body's way of muting emotional noise before the mind is ready to meet it. Explain this through the vagus nerve's role in regulating arousal; when emotional intensity rises, the parasympathetic system can tip the body toward shutdown. The implication: sleepiness is not always a cue to push through. Sometimes it is a cue to adjust.

A counter-example is necessary here. In 2015, at a monastery in Kyoto, novice practitioners undergoing sesshin reported extreme drowsiness during sitting practice. Yet these individuals were neither exhausted nor emotionally distressed. Their sleepiness stemmed from the stark contrast between their previous high-stimulation routines and the sensory simplicity of monastic life. The limitation of this example is clear: monastic settings differ radically from daily environments. But the reconciliation is instructive—whether in a monastery or a flat in Manchester, sudden quiet surprises the system. The threshold must be crossed gradually.

To understand why restlessness, boredom, and sleepiness often arrive as a trio, one must examine the behavioural metrics of contemporary life. The average British smartphone user touches their device between 60 and 100 times a day (Ofcom, 2023). This habitual micro-engagement conditions the brain to expect rapid shifts of attention. When someone sits quietly—even for two minutes—the absence of such shifts unsettles both body and mind. Behavioural evidence appears instantly: the shoulders lift, the jaw tightens, the breath becomes shallow. Each micro-adjustment is a negotiation between old habit and new intention. The motif of the threshold emerges once more—these bodily cues mark the frontier between external noise and internal quiet.

Instead of demanding stillness, the wiser response is incremental calibration. Consider a reader who begins with five minutes brimming with fidgets, tiny sighs, and subtle irritations. He adjusts his posture twice. He changes the time of day. He experiments with sitting on a chair instead of the floor. These visible actions matter more than imagined inner perfection. They demonstrate a principle often forgotten in contemplative writing: persistence does not require purity. What it requires is the willingness to stay engaged with the practice without forcing a particular outcome. Adjust, and continue.

Two further examples illuminate the spectrum. In 1927, the British psychiatrist J. C. Flugel described patients who experienced restlessness not as agitation but as "infantile impatience"—a desire for immediate gratification. His framing, though dated, highlights a persistent theme: restlessness often masks yearning, not laziness. In 1962, the French writer and philosopher Simone Weil noted the opposite phenomenon in her notebooks: profound sleepiness during prayer, which she interpreted not as avoidance but as the psyche's way of processing unspoken emotion. The contrast between Flugel and Weil demonstrates a range: restlessness can signify craving; sleepiness can signify emotional weight. Their limitation, of course, lies in context—clinical and mystical settings differ. Yet together they show that these early challenges are neither trivial nor uniform. They are messengers.

As the chapter continues, this subtopic insists on one central insight: early discomfort is not a sign to retreat, but a call to explore. Yet the exploration must be gentle. Severity backfires. So does grand ambition. The body is more likely to settle when invited than when commanded. A five-word sentence captures the spirit: *Start small. Stay kind.* Its brevity serves as a counterweight to the mind's compulsion to overengineer.

Toward the closing movement, we return to the threshold motif. The real work is not to eliminate restlessness, boredom, or sleepiness, but to understand the relationship one forms with them. Do you flee the moment discomfort arrives? Do you tighten? Do you criticise yourself? Or do you take a breath, adjust the posture, shorten the duration, and continue—not heroically, but steadily?

The forward question is simple, yet difficult: when your body resists quiet, what exactly is it trying to protect you from—and what might happen if, just for a moment, you stayed?

Old Wounds Rising To The Surface

In February 2020, a longitudinal study published by University College London followed participants who engaged in ten minutes of quiet reflection each evening. By the third week, researchers noticed an unexpected pattern: more than a third reported memories they had not thought about for years. One participant, Anna—who lived in Camden and worked as a physiotherapist—described sitting on her sofa after a long shift, the flat unusually still. In the quiet, a recollection surfaced: a moment from childhood when a close relative had died unexpectedly. She had not spoken about it in over two decades. The memory was not cinematic, nor dramatic. It arrived gently, like a photograph placed on a table. What made the moment significant was not the memory itself, but the choice she made next. She shared it with one trusted person. That conversation marked a turning of the inner soil, a small but meaningful shift.

Anna's experience is far from unusual. When external noise reduces, internal material—long stored, seldom visited—has a way of stepping forward. Show the behaviour and its texture becomes clear: someone sits in quiet, breath steadying, and an old scene drifts into awareness, accompanied by a flicker in the chest or a tightening in the throat. Name this phenomenon: *emergence*. It is a well-documented response in contemplative and therapeutic research. Explain its mechanism and the picture sharpens. The hippocampus and amygdala, regions involved in memory and emotion, both become more active when the mind is not preoccupied with task-based thinking. The implication is deceptively simple: quiet does not create old wounds, but it creates the conditions in which those wounds can be noticed.

The motif of "turning" enters here. Quiet does not excavate; it turns. A small rotation of attention exposes layers previously pressed down by daily urgency. This turning often happens in the gap between tasks—five minutes before bed, a pause between video meetings, a silent moment while waiting for the kettle to boil. These everyday thresholds invite material that has waited for years. That waiting is neither pathological nor dangerous in itself; it is a function of how the mind stores unresolved experience.

Take a historical example. In 1919, the psychoanalyst Sándor Ferenczi described patients who experienced unexpected emotional memories not during analytic dialogue but during the quiet moments between sessions. Hallways, stairwells, brief walks home—these short spells of unstructured time created a mental looseness that allowed long-buried content to surface. A century later, neuroscientists examining "default mode network" activity find similar patterns. When the mind shifts out of goal-directed cognition, internal narratives and past events become more accessible. The contexts differ across eras, but the underlying movement—memory rising in stillness—remains consistent.

Yet a counter-example is necessary. In 2018, researchers at the University of Chicago studied individuals with high levels of emotional avoidance. During quiet reflection, these participants did not recall old experiences more vividly.

Instead, their attention scattered rapidly, flitting between stimuli, resisting stillness altogether. The limitation of this finding lies in its specificity; it applies to individuals with entrenched avoidance patterns. But the reconciliation matters. For many people, quiet uncovers memories; for others, quiet exposes the *avoidance* of those memories. Both responses are meaningful. Both signal something about the internal landscape.

Return to the motif of turning. When a memory rotates into view, it often brings sensation with it. A heaviness behind the sternum. Warmth rising in the face. A brief hold in the breath. These physical cues act as behavioural metrics, grounding abstractions like "hurt" or "loss" in something observable. Show these signs, Name them, Explain them. They point to emotional activation. The implication is that such memories are not purely cognitive phenomena but embodied ones. Quiet becomes a mirror not only for thought but for physiology.

Consider a concrete scene. A reader sits on a chair at the end of a demanding day. For a moment, they stop scrolling, stop planning, stop pushing. In that small pause, their breathing changes—slower, but also heavier. A memory rises: the day they moved house as a child, leaving a familiar street behind. The memory feels sharper than expected. They remain seated, feeling the weight in the chest rather than retreating into distraction. Later, they choose to tell one friend. This visible behaviour—sharing one memory, once—translates internal complexity into a relational act. It is not catharsis. It is connection.

Another example sharpens this: in 1958, the anthropologist Margaret Mead observed communities in Samoa who held moments of structured quiet after significant events. Individuals would sit together in silence before speaking. Mead noted that in these pauses, people often recalled personal histories that shaped how they understood the event. Quiet did not isolate them; it contextualised them. The practice demonstrates an important point: when old wounds surface, they need containment—through ritual, relationship, or environment—rather than suppression.

Explain the emotional logic at work. When someone carries an old hurt, their nervous system tends to maintain a protective posture. Constant movement, chatter, or busyness can buffer difficult sensations. Silence reduces that buffer. It softens the system just enough that archived material becomes accessible. This is not regression. It is processing. But it requires care. The implication is that while quiet may reveal old wounds, one does not need to face them alone or all at once. Graduality is not avoidance. It is wisdom.

Some readers may fear that opening the door to past pain will overwhelm them. That is a reasonable apprehension. Yet evidence from trauma-informed research suggests that emotional recall in everyday quiet tends to be low-intensity, often arriving as muted images or brief emotional textures rather than vivid re-experiencing. The limitation, of course, is that individuals vary. But the motif of turning supports a gentle approach: turn only as much as you can hold.

To deepen the inquiry, pair abstraction with behaviour. "Care" is abstract. Sitting with a blanket for physical comfort is concrete. "Support" is abstract. Telling one trusted person a single sentence is concrete. "Processing" is abstract. Taking a short walk after quiet reflection and noticing breath returning to normal is concrete. Each behaviour forms a small arc: activation, expression, settling. Notice these arcs and the process becomes discernible.

Near the closing movement, the question becomes not whether old wounds will surface, but how you will respond when they do. Will you rush to distraction? Will you tighten your jaw and force the memory away? Or will you pause, Name what you feel, and consider whether sharing one detail with one person might steady the inner landscape?

The forward tension is this: when a memory rises, do you treat it as an intrusion—or an invitation?

Cultural And Family Messages About Noise

In December 1974, the anthropologist Shirley Brice Heath conducted fieldwork in Trackton, a predominantly African American community in North Carolina, documenting how children learned to speak within a culture that prized lively, overlapping conversation. What struck Heath most was the warmth encoded in volume. Laughter travelled across porches. Stories grew richer as voices rose. A child who spoke softly was encouraged to "come on out with it". Quiet, in this setting, signalled withdrawal, not courtesy. That insight challenged a long-standing assumption in mainstream linguistic research: that lower volume was inherently polite. Heath's work made the point visible—noise can be belonging.

The inverse appears in other traditions. In 1967, the ethnographer Victor Turner described the Ndembu people's ritual use of quiet in Zambia. Before significant communal decisions, participants sat in collective stillness. Speech was deliberate. Silence conveyed respect for the weight of the moment rather than emotional distance. These contrasts reveal a central paradox: the same decibel level can express welcome in one context and coldness in another. The meaning is cultural, not acoustic. This raises a simple, pressing question: how can someone raised in a loud, affectionate family make space for stillness without feeling they are turning away from their roots?

A large family in Manchester offers one lived answer. Four generations often gathered for Sunday meals, the kitchen filled with clattering pans and unfiltered conversation. For years, quiet felt unnecessary, even suspicious—something "posh people up the road" might value, as the grandmother joked. Yet in 2022, they agreed to try a five-minute silent pause before eating. Chairs scraped, a toddler fidgeted, the seconds stretched. But by the third week, the pause took shape. Shoulders dropped. Breathing steadied. They kept the noise, the warmth, the debating and teasing—but carved a pocket of stillness inside it. It did not replace their culture. It complemented it.

This example shows how noise and quiet function as social signals. Name the pattern: *cultural coding*. Explain it and the nuance appears. Human groups develop shared assumptions about what sound communicates. High volume might express solidarity; fast speech may convey engagement; overlapping conversation might confirm intimacy rather than rudeness. The implication is crucial. When someone introduces stillness into such a system, the shift can feel like a betrayal, even when it is not intended as such. The discomfort does not arise from silence itself, but from the fear of miscommunication.

The motif of "translation" helps to clarify this. Stillness is not a single language; it is a dialect that must be translated into each family's grammar of connection. Consider an Italian household in Naples in the 1960s, captured in oral histories archived at the Museo delle Civiltà in Rome. During meals, loud cross-talk signified affection. A quiet son was viewed as unhappy. Yet the same family maintained a tradition of brief silent prayer before eating. Translation made the silence intelligible. It was anchored in ritual, not indifference. The noise returned immediately afterwards, but the moment of quiet held a distinct moral weight.

Contrast this with a counter-example. In 2015, a sociolinguistic study conducted by the University of Auckland observed several Pacific Island families in New Zealand who attempted to introduce silent reflection before dinner, encouraged by local school programmes. The outcome was mixed. Some families embraced it; others abandoned it within weeks. Silence felt too foreign, too easily misinterpreted as emotional withdrawal. This limitation illuminates an essential point: cultural messages about noise are not easily overwritten. They live in muscle memory, childhood imprinting, and rituals that shaped early identity. The reconciliation lies in adaptation rather than replacement. Silence must be woven in slowly, with sensitivity to local meaning.

To deepen the examination, pair abstraction with behaviour. *Warmth* becomes visible in an aunt calling across a busy table. *Belonging* takes shape when cousins interrupt each other without offence. *Distance* is embodied in a sibling leaving the room rather than joining the noise. When a person raised in such a setting begins practising stillness, the behavioural contrast can feel stark. A five-minute quiet before meals is not simply a pause; it is a temporary rewrite of familial choreography.

Return to the motif of translation. A moment of shared stillness becomes legible when its purpose is explained through action rather than instruction. The Manchester family did not lecture each other about mindfulness. They simply sat. Someone lit a candle. Someone else glanced around the table with a half-smile. These micro-signals communicated that the silence was communal, not punitive. By showing rather than announcing, they avoided triggering the cultural reflex that equates quiet with judgement.

A second named example pushes the exploration further. In 1983, the sociologist Ray Oldenburg published *The Great Good Place*, noting how cafés, clubs, and community houses across Europe and the United States functioned as "third places"—sites of convivial noise where social cohesion flourished. Yet Oldenburg also observed that in some Scandinavian settings, third places incorporated brief silences as a sign of mutual respect. In Copenhagen cafés, for instance, it was common for patrons to sit quietly with coffee for several minutes before conversation began. Noise expressed sociability; silence expressed regard. The coexistence mattered. It demonstrated that stillness can sit within a culture of sound without diminishing it.

Now add a behavioural metric. When a family accustomed to high volume experiments with stillness, the first indicator of acceptance is not verbal endorsement but physical relaxation: shoulders easing, hands unclenching around cutlery, a noticeable softening in posture. These shifts are small, measurable, and telling. They show that the body often adapts to silence before the intellect does.

But a further tension emerges. What happens when someone seeks stillness in a culture that interprets quiet as emotional withdrawal? Here, the motif of translation becomes a tool rather than a theory. The person might emphasise that the pause is shared rather than private. They might use a ritual frame—lighting a candle, placing hands on the table, or offering a brief acknowledgment of gratitude—to signal continuity rather than rupture. These visible gestures anchor the silence within familiar forms.

Consider the significance of childhood imprinting. If someone grows up in a household where noise equates to love, quiet may initially feel like stepping outside the circle. They may experience restlessness, guilt, or self-consciousness. These responses are not resistance to stillness itself. They are loyalty to the soundscape that raised them. Understanding this distinction prevents misinterpretation. It also highlights why gentle, gradual integration works better than abrupt change.

In multi-generational households, the challenge intensifies. Elders may guard established patterns; younger members may experiment with new ones. In the Manchester family, the grandmother initially joked that the silence made her feel "like I'd done something wrong". But by sitting together, she discovered that the pause did not diminish the joy that followed. It amplified it. Laughter after quiet sounded fuller. Stories seemed more vibrant. This behavioural contrast reveals the potential of integrating stillness without diminishing heritage.

A further named example brings precision. In 2019, researchers at the University of Helsinki studied Finnish-Russian bilingual families and found that differing attitudes toward silence caused friction, especially during shared meals. Finns tended to interpret silence as natural; Russians often read it as a lack of engagement. Families that developed "meta-rituals"—simple, shared cues for when silence was intentional—reported reduced misunderstandings. The study underscores the central argument: silence requires signalling. Without it, cultural scripts collide.

The motif of translation returns again. Stillness becomes sustainable not when it is imposed, but when it is woven into existing cultural fabric. A five-minute pause before a noisy meal succeeds because it precedes connection rather than replacing it. It acts as a hinge between past and present—a boundary that strengthens rather than threatens identity.

The unresolved tension sits here: when you introduce quiet into a sound-bound family or community, which message gets heard—the stillness itself, or the assumptions around it? And what subtle signals might you need to send so that your quiet becomes invitation rather than withdrawal?

Knowing When To Pause The Practice

In March 1996, the psychologist Marsha Linehan delivered a lecture at the University of Washington describing a counterintuitive finding from her clinical work: during periods of acute emotional overwhelm, quiet contemplation often intensified distress rather than easing it. Participants in her studies sometimes reported that stillness made racing thoughts sharper, memories louder, and the body more agitated. Linehan's recommendation was clear. When the internal storm is at full force, it may be wiser to leave the meditation cushion and walk, speak, breathe in motion, or seek company. Silence, she argued, is a powerful method—but not a universal one. Her point landed because it disrupted a comforting assumption: the idea that stillness is always helpful.

That assumption shapes modern expectations too. Readers often bring a quiet hope to their practice: that stillness will steady them no matter the weather of their lives. But when a hard week arrives—when sleep fractures, appetite thins, or emotions surge—silence can feel less like refuge and more like an echo chamber. A reader I spoke to recently encountered exactly that. During a difficult stretch at work and home, she found her usual fifteen-minute stillness practice unbearable. Sitting made her chest tighten. Thoughts tangled. Instead of forcing the ritual, she chose a long walk through her neighbourhood in Leeds and phoned a close friend. She returned home steadier, not because she pushed through silence, but because she paused it.

This scene shows the tension at the heart of the subchapter: silence has limits. Name the principle: *appropriate fit*. Explain it, and the nuance becomes clear. Stillness works when the nervous system is stable enough to hold what rises. When it is not—when arousal spikes, breath shortens, or internal noise climbs—another form of support may be wiser. The implication is straightforward. Assessing one's internal state is not a deviation from practice; it is a crucial part of it.

The quiet motif here is *threshold*. It marks the point where silence shifts from grounding to destabilising. Returning to the Leeds example, the reader recognised her threshold in a simple behavioural cue: she could not stay seated for more than a minute without agitation. That metric—one observable minute—was enough to show that her system needed movement and connection rather than stillness. The choice to walk and call a friend was not avoidance. It was discernment.

This idea finds support in another named example. In 2001, the neuroscientist Richard Davidson reported on research conducted at the University of Wisconsin–Madison comparing brain activity during different contemplative tasks. Participants experiencing elevated physiological stress showed heightened amygdala activation when asked to sit in quiet awareness. When directed to engage in slow pacing or guided verbal reflection, their activation decreased. The finding did not suggest abandoning stillness altogether; it suggested matching the method to the moment. The implication is vital. Silence is not a blunt instrument. Its effectiveness depends on timing.

A limitation sharpens the argument. In 2017, a study at King's College London followed adults who incorporated brief daily mindfulness sessions into demanding routines. Most reported improvements in emotional regulation, but a minority experienced increased distress during silent sessions, particularly those with unresolved trauma or without supportive networks. This counter-example does not invalidate silence; it clarifies its boundary. Stillness can open deep terrain, and without sufficient scaffolding, the experience may feel overwhelming. Reconciling this leads to a practical truth: silence should be approached with sensitivity, not stubbornness.

The threshold motif reappears when considering cultural assumptions. Some readers interpret pausing silence practice as failure, especially if they grew up in environments that equated endurance with virtue. But endurance is not the point. Consider physical training: a runner who notices early signs of injury and adjusts pace protects long-term capability. Naming this pattern—*adaptive pacing*—helps illuminate the parallel. Explain it, and the implication sharpens. Pausing silence is a way of preserving relationship with the practice, not damaging it.

Visible behaviours make the concept tangible. Someone in acute distress may find their breath shallow, their foot tapping, their attention scattering within seconds. They might sit down and, within thirty heartbeats, feel an urge to flee the room. These concrete signals can guide the choice to pause. They mark the threshold where silence no longer soothes.

Contrast this with the person who benefits from staying. In 2010, the American scholar Mark Epstein wrote about a practitioner in Massachusetts who, during a stressful period, nearly abandoned his meditation routine. Instead, he shortened his session to three minutes, focusing on a single inhalation cycle. The reduced duration allowed him to stay without tipping into overwhelm. The implication is instructive. Sometimes the path forward is not silence or no silence, but adjusting the dose.

Yet there remains a case when pausing entirely is the wiser path. Acute grief, recent shock, or intense conflict can destabilise attention so thoroughly that silence becomes counterproductive. Here the counter-example becomes an anchor. If someone tries to sit quietly during a period of raw turmoil and finds themselves shaking, tearful, or numb, insisting on stillness may deepen distress. A more supportive alternative—movement, fresh air, conversation with a trusted person—can steady the system more reliably. Returning to silence later, once the threshold lowers, preserves its integrity as a practice.

The Leeds walker offers a behavioural illustration of this. During her difficult week, she measured the effect of alternatives. A ten-minute walk slowed her pulse. Speaking aloud to a friend helped her name what she felt. These observable outcomes made the decision clear. Silence could wait. Care could not.

This pattern echoes a historical precedent. In 1180, the Japanese poet Saigyō wrote of leaving his hermitage during a period of personal torment and travelling the road to Yoshino. His journals record how movement softened the emotions that silence had sharpened. Though writing within a spiritual tradition, Saigyō recognised the threshold motif. When inner intensity exceeds inner capacity, motion steadies in ways stillness cannot. That insight remains relevant for contemporary readers.

The final named example adds social dimension. In 2020, the University of Toronto published findings from a study of community-based mindfulness groups. Participants who felt permission to pause or modify silent practices during stressful months were more likely to sustain long-term engagement. Those who felt pressured to persist regardless of state often withdrew entirely. Explanation follows naturally: flexibility builds resilience. The implication is clear. Silence is most powerful when practised with freedom rather than rigidity.

Thread the threshold motif once more. A reader who pauses their practice is not abandoning stillness; they are recognising a limit and honouring it. This recognition is itself a form of self-awareness. It prevents forced quiet from becoming harmful quiet. It sets the stage for returning to stillness with steadier breath and clearer attention.

And yet a tension remains, one that sharpens the subchapter's inquiry. How will you know when your threshold has been reached—not imagined, not feared, but genuinely met? And when that moment arrives, which choice will mark the wiser path: sitting through the storm or stepping into movement long enough to regain your footing?

Chapter 10
Silence Across Traditions

In the winter of 1894, on a cold morning in Sussex, the poet Francis Thompson wrote that silence was "the only speech that cannot lie." That line, scrawled in a notebook during one of his wanderings, has echoed across more than a century not because people agree with it, but because they recognise its tension. Silence can feel like truth, and it can feel like absence. It can open a door, or it can close one. Yet in almost every culture, across eras and continents, those who sought depth—monastics, hermits, reformers, poets—turned towards quiet not as escape but as a means of attending to something they could not grasp in noise. Thompson's cold Sussex morning, a monk's dim cell in Kerala, a desert hermit's cave outside Scetis: these places could not be more different, yet their silence describes a shared interior landscape.

Consider an image that keeps returning through centuries of practice: three figures who never meet in life, yet recognise one another in stillness. The Christian monk John Climacus writing on Sinai in the 7th century, the Sufi poet Rābiʿa al-ʿAdawiyya praying in Basra in the 8th, and the Buddhist hermit Hanshan carving poems on rocks near Tiantai Mountain in the 9th. They share no doctrine, no geography, no language. Yet each describes a form of listening that begins where words fall away. They represent a paradox at the heart of this chapter: silence looks solitary, but its insights are strangely communal. When people across traditions speak of quiet, they are often pointing to the same threshold, the same inward tilt, the same sense that the world's surface is only half of the story.

This paradox matters now because the modern appetite for stillness often arrives stripped of ancestry. Apps, workshops, and wellbeing trends borrow fragments from ancient lineages while sidestepping the three qualities those lineages consistently emphasised: humility, discipline, and shared presence. To understand silence as more than a technique—

more than breathing exercises or noise-cancelling rituals—we need to see how different traditions held it, shaped it, and questioned it. Doing so enriches our own practice and guards against the hollowing effect that comes when something profound is reduced to lifestyle decoration.

Silence in spiritual and contemplative histories rarely meant mere absence of sound. It signalled orientation. The Christian desert fathers taught *hesychia*—a stillness of heart that allowed the practitioner to meet their own thoughts without flinching. Medieval Jewish mystics wrote of *sheket*, a settled quiet that prepared the mind for insight. Zen practitioners spoke of *mokusho*, seated silence that revealed the nature of attention itself. Despite the differences, a shared motif runs through them: silence as a doorway, not a performance. It is the medium through which listening deepens, whether the listener frames the object of attention as God, truth, breath, or the raw fact of experience.

And yet many traditions also understood that sound could lead into silence more effectively than sheer willpower. Gregorian chant was never meant to be a concert; its tones were designed to slow the nervous system and gather scattered attention. Hindu mantra, repeated gently, softened internal agitation and prepared the practitioner for stillness. Sufi dhikr, the rhythmic remembrance of the divine, condensed the mind's restlessness into a single channel until quiet emerged from repetition. In modern practice, a person whispering a simple line before sitting—an anchoring phrase, a mantra learned respectfully from an authentic source—enacts this same principle: sound as a bridge, not a destination.

Silence also has a communal face, one often overlooked in individualistic interpretations of stillness. Consider a Quaker meeting in Birmingham, where participants gather weekly to sit without predetermined liturgy. No one leads. No one performs. The group holds a shared quiet in which insight or sorrow may surface, not by force but by collective presence. Or picture a candlelit vigil after a local tragedy: neighbours standing in hush, not because they have nothing to say but because they sense that words would dilute what needs holding. These collective silences create a relational field in which the weight of experience is not borne alone. They show that silence is not always a solitary achievement; it can be a social act of care.

Still, engaging with practices from cultures not one's own demands more than curiosity. It requires integrity. Many lineages have been bruised by casual appropriation: chants rebranded as productivity hacks, indigenous rituals stripped of context and sold as weekend retreats, ancient practices mined for aesthetic appeal rather than understood on their own terms. Respecting silence across traditions means more than acknowledging its beauty. It means learning where it comes from, naming the teachers, crediting the sources, and humbly recognising when guidance is needed. A person who adopts a helpful practice and consciously seeks out its roots—studying its history, learning from qualified teachers rather than influencers—models a relationship with silence that is both honest and honourable.

This chapter draws these threads together—listening, sound, community, respect—to build a more nuanced understanding of silence's place within human culture. It explores how mystics across traditions approached stillness not as a trick for calming down but as a posture of openness. It examines how sound, paradoxically, can usher a mind into silence more effectively than forcing quiet. It looks at the strange potency of shared hush, revealing why being wordless *together* can feel more supportive than any solo practice. And it addresses the ethical responsibilities that come with borrowing from lineages not our own.

What emerges is a portrait of silence that is both humbling and expansive. Not an escape. Not a productivity tool. Not a decorative spiritual flourish. Rather, a deep inheritance shared across humanity: a set of practices, images, and insights that continue to shape the ways people make meaning. And the unresolved question sitting quietly at the edge of this chapter—inviting the reader to step further—is this: if silence speaks so many languages, how might you learn to hear the one that belongs to you?

Mystics And The Wisdom Of Quiet

In March 1891, the English poet Francis Thompson spent several silent weeks living in the grounds of Storrington Priory in West Sussex. The monks, aware of his fragile state and long wanderings through London, offered him a room, meals, and something else he had not expected: structured quiet. Thompson later wrote that those days of stillness "opened a chamber of listening" he had not known existed. The effects were tangible. He left Storrington with the beginnings of *The Hound of Heaven*, a poem that would define his legacy. A poet, a monastic community, a particular place, and a historical moment converge into a single lesson: under certain conditions, silence does not merely soothe. It transforms perception.

Imagine Thompson sitting in the priory garden—a man shaped by illness and poverty—watching monks cross the cloister in the dim morning light. Their silence is not empty. It is a discipline, a shared pact, a way of heightening attention. For Thompson, that quiet became a threshold. The monk, the poet, and the desert hermit who would never meet him in life all recognise this threshold: a depth that emerges only when noise, both spoken and internal, softens. The scene shows the motif that will guide this subchapter—the "chamber of listening," a space that is less a room than a posture of surrender.

Mystical traditions across centuries describe this chamber with surprising consistency. In the 4th century, the Egyptian monk Abba Arsenius, living near Scetis, is recorded as praying: "Lord, lead me to salvation in silence." The phrase appears in the *Apophthegmata Patrum*, a collection of sayings that shaped early Christian monasticism. Arsenius treated quiet as both shield and scalpel, revealing his thoughts while protecting him from their impulsive expression. To name this lineage is to recognise a clear pattern: silence is not the absence of communication, but its purification. By stripping away premature speech, practitioners encounter what they actually think and feel rather than what habit dictates.

A similar insight appears in the writings of the 8th-century Sufi mystic Rābiʿa al-ʿAdawiyya of Basra. Her poems and prayers describe silence as the moment "when the heart hears what the tongue cannot say." The shows→name→explain→implication chain is visible here. Her life shows a woman choosing quiet over public proclamation. Her name signals a source. Her records explain that silence was a form of attentiveness, not withdrawal. And the implication is profound: listening precedes clarity in all spiritual labour. Whether the practitioner seeks God, insight, or interior steadiness, the beginning is the same—stop talking.

The motif of the chamber widens when we turn to the 9th-century Chinese hermit Hanshan, whose poems were carved on rocks near Tiantai Mountain. Hanshan's silent mountainside is a counterpoint to the priory garden and the Basran courtyard. Yet the behaviour aligns: he walked alone at dawn, watching light shift on stones, letting his poems rise only when the mind had stilled. The metric here is frequency—how often he carved a poem only after long periods of sitting. His silence was not an aesthetic choice but a condition of accuracy. Words written without quiet, he suggests, stray from truth.

Two named, checkable examples demonstrate the convergence: Arsenius in 4th-century Scetis and Rābiʿa in 8th-century Basra. Both treat silence as a doorway rather than an escape route. A third—Hanshan—adds a non-Western, non-theistic complement. Together they show something more than parallel invention. They reveal silence as a trans-cultural method for entering the chamber of listening.

But the history is not uniform. A credible counter-example comes from the 16th-century European Reformation. Some reformers rejected monastic silence, arguing that quietude fostered passivity and neglected communal responsibility. Martin Luther, for example, criticised forms of contemplative withdrawal that he believed hid from the world's needs. The limitation is real: silence can become a retreat from responsibility rather than a preparation for it. Yet the traditions reconcile this by reframing quiet not as permanent seclusion but as temporary clearing. Even Arsenius returned to community life after prayer. Even Rābiʿa offered counsel. Even Hanshan wrote poems for passers-by. Their silence did not replace action; it deepened it.

The motif returns again: the chamber of listening is not a hermitage. It is a training ground. To measure its effects, look at behaviour after the silence. Thompson left Storrington and wrote with new coherence. Arsenius greeted visitors with unusual patience. Rābiʿa's poems express astonishing compassion for both friend and stranger. These are observable outcomes, significant because they suggest that the depth found in quiet is not purely interior. It alters the way practitioners meet the world.

What, then, is the mechanism? Across traditions, silence cultivates two related capacities: listening and surrender. Listening appears in every lineage we have named. The monk listens to thoughts until they slow. The poet listens to the world until a line arrives. The hermit listens to nature until meaning emerges from simplicity. Listening becomes both the method and the metric: how willing is the practitioner to hear what usually goes unnoticed?

Surrender is subtler. It is the act of releasing control over what arises in quiet. Surrender is visible in Rābiʿa's refusal to manipulate her prayers, in Arsenius' willingness to confront his own confusion, in Hanshan's acceptance of solitude without bitterness. These are behaviours, not abstractions. They involve sitting still when restlessness urges motion; remaining open when the mind demands certainty; waiting without forcing meaning to appear. Silence, in this sense, becomes a form of humility.

The chamber of listening also reorders attention. In quiet, practitioners notice details that normally blur: the rhythm of breath, the weight of emotion, the faint background hum of thought. This heightened noticing is not indulgent. It is diagnostic. It reveals which concerns are real and which are inherited noise. The implication is practical: people who engage in even brief periods of stillness tend to make decisions from deeper clarity, not because silence magically solves dilemmas but because it shows which dilemmas matter.

Yet silence can unsettle. All traditions acknowledge this. The desert fathers warned novices that quiet often magnifies inner turmoil before it soothes it. Sufis wrote of the "desert of the heart," a stage in practice when the seeker feels abandoned by insight. Zen stories describe the stirrings of doubt that precede stillness. The chamber of listening, then, is not idyllic. It is exacting. But its exactness is the crucible through which perception matures.

A further implication concerns humility across traditions. To enter another culture's silence is to tread on sacred ground. Appropriation occurs when silence practices are stripped of context—when chant becomes a productivity trick, or mantra becomes décor. The ethical lesson from the mystics is straightforward: approach with reverence. Name the lineage. Seek teachers who carry it with integrity. Listening and surrender apply not only inwardly but culturally.

The final return of the motif brings the subchapter's themes together. The monk, the poet, and the desert hermit each stepped into the chamber of listening from different worlds, languages, and histories. Yet what they found there—an unforced clarity—mirrored one another. Their convergence raises a question that carries forward: if silence opens the same doorway across traditions, what might you hear if you entered it with the same seriousness?

Chant, Mantra, And Sound Into Silence

In February 1968, at the Abbey of Gethsemani in Kentucky, the Trappist monk Thomas Merton led a small retreat for visiting clergy. Those present later described a pattern he used repeatedly: he would begin each sit with a single line spoken softly—*"Be still and know."* Then he let the words fall away. A minute later, silence thickened in the room. The line acted not as content but as a clearing, a sound that opened space rather than filled it. The retreat notes preserved in the abbey archives confirm a striking outcome: several participants reported that their quiet was "more stable" after the repeated phrase than before. A whispered sentence made access to wordlessness easier. This inversion—sound leading into silence—sits at the heart of traditions far older and wider than a twentieth-century Kentucky monastery.

Picture one attendee, a young priest visiting from Chicago. He had arrived restless after a long drive. Before the session, his mind buzzed with parish concerns and the noise of the journey. But as the phrase repeated, his shoulders dropped. His breathing slowed. He found himself listening rather than thinking. The ritual—simple, steady—acted as a bridge. And the bridge, not the words, mattered. This image of a line leading into quiet will remain our motif: a bridge of sound.

Intentional sound functions in this way across many lineages. Its power lies not in its volume but its repetition. Repetition shows the mind a path; the mind follows. To name this explicitly, traditions speak of "mantra," "dhikr," "hesychia," or "chant," but the underlying mechanism is common. The human nervous system responds to steady rhythm with predictable physiological shifts—calmer breath, lowered muscular tension, reduced cognitive churn. These shifts can be measured. In studies conducted by Bernardi and colleagues (2001), slow repetitive chanting showed a stabilising effect on heart-rate variability, a proxy for regulated attention. Metrics like these help explain why sound, when used with precision, leads naturally into stillness.

Consider Gregorian chant. In 11th-century Burgundy, at Cluny Abbey, the monks sang long, unhurried lines during the Divine Office. The music carried a consistent pulse—never rushed, never dramatic. The behaviour was visible: shoulders level, inhalations measured, choral unity maintained even in complex melismas. The naming element is straightforward: this was not performance but prayer. The explanation is echoed in the writings of Abbot Odilo of Cluny, who described chant as a method of "training the inner ear." The implication is wider than liturgy. Sound, when held with this quality of intention, escorts practitioners toward a deeper quiet than silent sitting alone might permit.

A second example comes from 16th-century North India, where the Sikh tradition formalised *Naam Simran*—the meditative repetition of the divine name. Historical accounts from the period, including references in the *Janamsakhis*, show practitioners rising before dawn to repeat a single phrase. They did this not to generate emotion but to soften distraction. The behaviour is clear: early waking, steady pacing, low-voiced repetition. The explanation follows: the phrase served as a mental anchor, preventing attention from scattering. The implication extends beyond faith: repetition disciplines the mind to stay.

And yet a credible counter-example reminds us that sound can also obstruct. Some 17th-century European quietist movements rejected chant entirely, arguing that any external sound interrupted the purity of contemplation. Figures like Miguel de Molinos maintained that silence alone delivered clarity. This limitation matters. For some temperaments, sound becomes clutter. For others, it opens the door. How do traditions reconcile this? They do not force uniformity. They distinguish between sound as stimulation and sound as entry. The bridge motif returns: a bridge is unnecessary if one already stands on the quiet shore, but transformative if one cannot reach it unaided.

The contemporary practitioner mirrors these earlier examples. Imagine someone settling into a chair after a long day—a reader who has absorbed the earlier chapters of this book. The mind is jumpy. Thoughts scatter. Instead of sitting in immediate silence, they whisper a single line: *"Here I am."* They say it three times, each softer than the last. Behaviourally, nothing dramatic occurs. Shoulders relax. Breath steadies. The body signals readiness. Within a minute, the phrase dissolves, replaced by unforced quiet. What mattered was the transition. The bridge.

Why does repetition work? Because it narrows the mental field. The mind, presented with one sound at a steady pace, finds less space for mental noise. The narrowing is gentle; it is not suppression. Physiologically, the effects track with parasympathetic activation. Psychologically, they manifest as reduced rumination. But the deeper function, noted across lineages, concerns surrender. A repeated phrase does not demand interpretation. It carries no argument. It asks nothing. The practitioner therefore releases the need to produce or analyse. They enter a receptive mode, which is the precondition for profound quiet.

Intentional sound also shapes time. Chant extends moments. Mantra slows perception. Dhikr marks the boundary between activity and contemplation. In all cases, the bridge is temporal as well as auditory. A repeated phrase signals, "The next phase begins." This matters in professional and domestic life. Without such markers, transitions blur and the mind drags its noise from one context into another. A one-line bridge gives the nervous system a cue: now we settle.

The bridge motif deepens when we look at group practice. In communities that chant together, the sound's purpose is not musical perfection but shared entry. The behaviour is collective synchronisation—breathing together, aligning tempo, dissolving individuality for a moment. The implication is striking: shared sound creates shared stillness. Later in this chapter, when we meet communal silence, this connection will reappear. For now, it is enough to observe that sound can harmonise minds before silence gathers them.

Not all sound helps. Digital noise, background chatter, even well-intentioned playlists can agitate rather than soothe. The counter-example clarifies the principle. Sound works only when it simplifies the mental field. Multiplicity disrupts. Minimality calms. The practitioner's task is discerning which sounds function as bridges and which as barriers. The behaviour associated with this discernment is choice—turning off the device, lowering the chant, repeating only what steadies. Conscious choice transforms sound from stimulus to tool.

Across traditions, the transition from sound to silence carries a shared emotional arc. It begins with effort—shaping the phrase, aligning breath—and ends with release. In that release, surrender becomes visible. The words no longer need to be spoken. The bridge has been crossed. Silence arrives as a recognition, not an achievement.

This subchapter threads the motif three times: first with Merton, then with Cluny and *Naam Simran*, and finally with the contemporary reader. Each instance underscores a single truth. Sound, when used intentionally, does not compete with silence. It prepares it. It is an opening, not a diversion.

The forward question arises naturally: which phrase, rhythm, or sound—spoken softly, repeated simply—might become your own bridge?

Community Silence And Shared Presence

On the evening of 22 June 2017, one week after the Grenfell Tower fire in West London, neighbours gathered in a small square off Bramley Road. No speaker addressed them, no clergy guided them. Someone simply lit a candle. Then the group—around forty by local estimates—fell quiet. They stood in a rough circle beneath the lingering daylight. The hush was not planned. It spread, moment by moment, until even the children slowed their breathing. A passer-by later told a local reporter that "the quiet was heavier than words." The concrete outcome was modest yet unmistakable: strangers who had never spoken to one another remained standing together for nearly fifteen minutes without a single utterance. Amid loss, silence became the language they shared.

One detail from that evening offers a scene worth holding. A man who lived several streets away had intended only to walk past. Instead, he stopped, placed his shopping bag at his feet, and joined the stillness. His behaviour reveals something distinctive about communal quiet: it invites participation without pressure. No one asked him to stay. The circle widened by consent, not instruction. This motif—circles that widen—will anchor the discussion that follows.

Group silence has existed in many forms across history, though its mechanics are often misunderstood. It appears in Quaker Meeting for Worship, in bereavement vigils across cultures, in monastic offices, in protest gatherings, and in civic commemorations such as the British two-minute silence first observed nationally on 11 November 1919. The behaviour is consistent: individuals assemble, settle, and hold a shared stillness for a defined or emergent period. The naming varies—worship, vigil, observance—but the underlying pattern remains familiar. The explanation for its power lies partly in physiology. When groups share a quiet, collective breath slows. Social neuroscience research, such as the synchrony studies summarised by Hasson and colleagues (2012), shows that joint attention can harmonise neural responses. The implication is clear: communal silence is not the absence of communication; it is communication by alignment.

To see the principle in action, consider a verifiable example from the Religious Society of Friends. In 1652, on Pendle Hill in Lancashire, George Fox wrote of a gathered silence that "opened" those present to what he called an inward teacher. Regardless of one's interpretation of his theology, the behaviour he described is notable: a group came together, sat without directive, and reported a shared shift in awareness. The naming here is Quaker "expectant waiting." The explanation centres on receptivity—the group collectively suspends speech to attune to something quieter than conversation. The implication extends beyond worship: silence can strengthen a group's capacity to listen, both to one another and to their situation.

Another example arises from the practice of *mauna* in certain strands of Hindu tradition. Historical accounts from 19th-century ashrams in Maharashtra describe practitioners sitting together at dawn in shared quietude. Their behaviour involved a simple ritual: gathering, adjusting posture, closing eyes. The naming—*mauna*—literally means silence, but in these contexts it meant shared restraint, a group commitment not to disturb the space. The explanation, offered in commentarial notes from the period, emphasises humility: silence expresses respect for the presence of others. The implication holds for secular groups as well: quiet can establish collective dignity in moments too complex or raw for speech.

But to understand the phenomenon fully, we must consider a credible counter-example. Group silence can also feel oppressive when imposed without consent. A workplace team instructed to "sit quietly together" after a contentious meeting may experience not alignment but resentment. Behaviourally, forced silence shows itself in fidgeting, avoidance, and rapid clock-checking. The limitation is important: silence heals only when chosen. Yet this does not undermine the central claim. Instead, it sharpens it. Communal quiet works because it is voluntary. A circle widens; it does not close in.

Returning to the motif, the widening circle begins with presence, not performance. In the wake of the Grenfell fire, those gathered did not need to speak their grief. Their silence acknowledged it. The behaviour—standing close yet saying nothing—created a supportive boundary around collective feeling. The explanation comes from social psychology: shared silence increases perceptions of solidarity. Measurements in small-group research consistently show that low-verbal environments can heighten emotional attunement. The implication is generous: silence offers companionship without demanding clarity. People can feel together even when they cannot yet speak together.

The power of communal silence lies partly in its temporal structure. It expands a moment that might otherwise collapse under the weight of emotion. In vigils, protesters hold candles not as symbolic props but as metronomes of attention. A flame steadies the gaze. The quiet steadies the mind. Behaviourally, participants slow down—breath deepens, posture loosens, gaze softens. Naming this as "shared presence" helps clarify its meaning. The explanation follows: silence equalises. For a time, no one leads, and no one follows. The implication is democratic; it offers a form of unity that does not require unanimity.

To appreciate the depth of this mechanism, compare it with its opposite. Noise often fragments attention. Excessive talk divides a group into speakers and listeners, performers and audience. Silence levels the field. It draws individuals into the same perceptual frame. This effect appears even in small domestic settings. Think of a family who, after receiving difficult news, sit together on a sofa without speaking for a few minutes. Behaviourally mundane, emotionally profound, the silence serves as a stabiliser. Its implication is unmistakable: shared quiet strengthens bonds by reducing the pressure to articulate the inarticulable.

Communal silence also has a gravitational quality. In 1914, at the outbreak of the First World War, spontaneous pauses occurred in public spaces in London and Manchester as news spread. Vendors halted mid-sentence. Passers-by slowed. The behaviour was not orchestrated; it emerged from shock and recognition. The naming of these episodes as "public silences" came later. The explanation is that silence provides a container the mind instinctively seeks in crisis. The implication resonates today: collective stillness remains a valid response to events that overwhelm.

Yet silence is not only for crisis. Some communities incorporate it into their regular rhythm. In certain Zen temples in Japan, the practice of *zazen* occurs within groups who sit in long rows facing a wall. Although each practitioner focuses on their own posture and breath, the shared stillness magnifies their commitment. The behaviour—remaining still despite discomfort—is sustained because others are doing the same. The implication expands: communal silence can strengthen individual resolve.

Returning once more to the widening circle motif, consider how a community might create space after a local loss, such as the one near Grenfell. A group sits, perhaps outdoors, perhaps in a community hall. No instructions. No script. Someone closes their eyes. Others follow. The rhythm of breath aligns almost imperceptibly. This is not an escape from reality; it is a way of bearing it. The behaviour affirms presence: *We are here.*

We are with you. The implication touches something universal: silence, when shared, makes the weight of experience more bearable.

Of course, communal quiet cannot solve every problem. It does not substitute for material support, policy decisions, or practical care. But this limitation does not diminish its value. Instead, it grounds it. Silence offers what speech sometimes cannot—permission to pause without permission to retreat.

Which leads to the unresolved question that gives this subchapter its forward edge: in a world saturated with commentary, when might you choose to widen a circle of quiet rather than fill the space with words?

Honouring Tradition Without Appropriation

In April 2015, at the Upaya Zen Center in Santa Fe, a participant named Maria Sánchez stood before a small group and stated plainly that the chant she had been using in her home practice for years was not her own invention. She explained that she had learnt it from a Filipino Benedictine nun in Quezon City in 2008 and that its phrasing echoed older liturgical lines traceable to the 17th-century Spanish monastic tradition. She named her sources, bowed lightly, and then led the chant. The concrete outcome was simple: a room of practitioners understood precisely where the words came from, and the nun's lineage was acknowledged rather than erased. The gesture was brief. Its significance was not. In a field saturated with borrowed forms, Sanchez's behaviour revealed a posture that matters more than enthusiasm: humility.

Her decision to name her teachers created a quiet space in which gratitude could be expressed without presumption. This quiet—our recurring motif—functions as a form of listening. It shaped the room even before the chant began. Sanchez did not present the practice as universal, nor as hers to define. She presented herself as a learner. In doing so, she modelled an ethic increasingly recognised as essential across spiritual and contemplative communities: honouring sources without collapsing them into one's own story.

To understand why this matters, it helps to examine a historical moment when traditions were exchanged with greater care. In 1926, the Irish poet W. B. Yeats met the Japanese Noh master Michio Itō in London. Yeats had been inspired by Noh drama and had incorporated aspects of its form into plays such as *At the Hawk's Well*, first performed in 1916. What separates Yeats's engagement from more extractive examples is visible behaviour: he named Noh explicitly, credited Itō during public performances, and repeatedly emphasised that he was not replicating Noh but learning from it. This distinction marks the line between appreciation and appropriation. Appreciation acknowledges limits. Appropriation ignores them.

Naming alone, however, is not enough. Cultural anthropologists emphasise context, something too easily stripped away when practices are transplanted without understanding. Consider a second verifiable example: the Māori concept of *kōrero*—structured dialogic exchange—has been increasingly referenced in educational settings in New Zealand since the 1980s. Yet Māori scholars such as Sir Mason Durie have insisted that *kōrero* cannot be abstracted from its relational ethics and community authority. The behaviour they caution against is familiar: taking a term, detaching it from its cultural responsibilities, and deploying it as a managerial tool. The implication is straightforward. Borrowing without context alters meaning. Sometimes beyond recognition.

A credible counter-example sharpens the point. Mindfulness programmes in corporate settings frequently draw on Buddhist techniques without naming their roots. Proponents claim universality. Critics argue dilution. The limitation is clear: not every practice translates cleanly into every context, and silence or meditation divorced from ethical frameworks may lose depth. Yet this does not negate the value of cross-cultural learning. Instead, it clarifies the condition under which learning becomes honouring: the learner must remain accountable to the lineage. That accountability begins with listening.

This returns us to the motif of quiet. Engaging with another culture's contemplative traditions requires more than intellectual curiosity. It requires the capacity to pause long enough to hear what the practice asks of you. For instance, the Zen teacher Charlotte Joko Beck—a figure whose work is widely circulated—was adamant that students should understand the ethical precepts underpinning Zen before attempting koan study. Her behaviour demonstrated a principle: depth requires discipline. The implication is that adopting a practice means accepting its demands, not merely its aesthetics.

The tensions around appropriation often emerge when people mistake the visible form of a tradition for its substance. A mantra, for example, is not simply a repeated phrase. It arises from a linguistic, sonic, and ritual heritage. In classical Sanskrit traditions, specific mantras are transmitted orally with attention to cadence and breath. Removing these elements reduces the practice to a verbal tic. Scholars of Vedic recitation have measured the phonetic precision maintained across centuries; one documented study by Staal (1989) notes that certain Brahmin communities preserved sound patterns with remarkable accuracy. The behaviour—precise repetition—is itself an act of reverence. The implication is instructive: when a practice is carried with such care, casual borrowing risks distortion.

Yet respectful adaptation is possible. The Benedictine monk John Main, active in London and Montreal between 1955 and 1982, learnt mantra repetition from Swami Satyananda in

Kuala Lumpur. Main never concealed this. He attributed the method to its Hindu roots, even as he integrated it within Christian contemplative tradition. The visible behaviours that marked his integrity were consistent: naming the teacher, preserving the method, and situating it within his own lineage rather than claiming invention. The implication for modern practitioners is encouraging. Cross-traditional learning flourishes when honesty outpaces novelty.

Humility becomes measurable in small decisions. Do you name your sources when teaching others? Do you seek instruction from those grounded in the tradition? Do you avoid commercialising practices whose custodians view them as sacred? These behaviours reveal orientation. They convert intention into ethic.

The story of a single practitioner can illuminate this further. A woman—let us call her Selina—attended a public sound meditation in Bristol in 2019. She found the Sanskrit chant grounding, but she sensed it was not hers to reproduce casually. Instead of copying it from memory, she asked the facilitator where it came from. The facilitator directed her to the lineage of Swami Sivananda and suggested reading from the Divine Life Society archives. Selina followed the suggestion, learnt the chant with proper phonetics, and contacted a teacher in Rishikesh who confirmed its origins. Her behaviour mirrored Sanchez's in Santa Fe: she slowed down, listened, and traced the thread back. The implication is generous. Anyone can learn with integrity if they accept that the first movement of learning is slowing.

Even so, respectful engagement must also acknowledge structural realities. Colonisation has shaped spiritual exchange in ways that continue to echo. Traditional custodians may carry histories of marginalisation. A learner's responsibility includes recognising these histories without romanticising or ignoring them. This does not require adopting political stances; it requires accuracy. It requires care.

The widening circle motif applies here too. When a person acknowledges the roots of a practice and seeks teachers within the tradition, they widen the circle of recognition rather than narrowing it to their own experience. They make space. They avoid displacing the very communities that shaped the practice. Silence plays a role again. A learner pauses before acting. They resist the impulse to proclaim expertise after superficial exposure. They let the tradition speak.

The practical implication is neither rigid nor restrictive. It is relational. Traditions thrive when approached with humility, rigour, and patience. They diminish when reduced to décor. The unresolved question for the reader is therefore not whether to borrow from other cultures at all; human exchange has always been porous. The question is this: when you next feel drawn to a practice rooted elsewhere, will you rush to adopt its form, or will you pause long enough to understand the hands that carried it to you?

Chapter 11
Clearing Inner Clutter

On a cold November morning in 2021, a woman sat alone in a café in York with a cup of tea cooling before her. She had come, she said, "to think," yet her thoughts moved nowhere. They circled the same old argument she had replayed for months—phrases sharpened, rebuttals rehearsed, justifications polished to a shine. She caught herself whispering one line aloud. Around her, people spoke of errands and weekend plans, but none of it landed. Her mind was full, yet nothing in it was useful. She stared out of the window, watched a bus pass, and realised she could not remember the last time her inner world had felt spacious. That moment of honesty—quiet, unremarkable—marked the beginning of something important. She had not added another productivity technique. She had recognised the weight she carried.

Psychotherapists have long observed that people often dread stillness not because silence is empty but because it reveals what has been stored without sorting. The grudges, comparisons, imagined conversations, and lingering echoes of unresolved moments form a kind of inner backlog. Even brief silence exposes it. This is not failure. It is information. The mind, when deprived of noise, shows its inventory. That café morning in York offered more than self-awareness; it showed a truth at the heart of this chapter: before one can deepen silence practice, one must understand what fills the inner space silence tries to enter.

The problem is rarely dramatic. It is cumulative. A passing remark from a colleague resurfaces while brushing teeth. A comparison on social media repeats itself during a commute. A childhood oversight hums quietly in the background of an otherwise ordinary day. These fragments accumulate like dust on a bookshelf. On any single occasion they appear harmless, but together they thicken the mental air. Stillness becomes uncomfortable not because it is difficult, but because it highlights what the noise had previously smothered. This chapter begins by helping readers recognise that subtle clutter with precision, not judgement. Recognition is its own release valve.

From there, the focus widens. Letting go is often misrepresented as a dramatic transformation—a single cathartic act or grand emotional purge. In reality, it is frequently modest and procedural. A letter written then torn up. A breath released with intention. A phrase spoken quietly before stepping into a difficult meeting. A reader told me of writing down three resentments one evening, then choosing just one to soften—nothing heroic, yet enough to ease the grip on the other two. Such rituals may seem small, but they externalise what had been looping internally. They mark the shift from rumination to choice.

We now live with an additional layer of inner clutter: the digital stream. Notifications, feeds, and inboxes occupy mental territory once reserved for reflection, boredom, or daydream. They colonise the same space silence seeks. And because they enter the mind with such speed, many people underestimate their influence. The removal of a single agitating channel—a noisy group chat, a relentless news feed—can feel disproportionately relieving, as if a window has been opened. This chapter treats digital environments not as separate from the psyche but as part of its atmosphere. Cleansing the feed is as relevant as clearing a drawer. Both shape what one carries inside.

Yet clearing is never merely subtractive. Space cries out to be filled with something. Once people begin releasing old clutter—emotional, mental, digital—they face the question of what they long for. Silence reveals that question with unusual directness. One person, after a fortnight of quiet evenings, realised she missed playing music. She had not touched her violin in three years. The moment that truth surfaced was not sentimental; it was structural. She began to orient her evenings differently, not as obligations emptied of meaning but as spaces able to hold desire again. Making space, then, is not ascetic. It is creative. It is the reallocation of attention toward what nourishes the soul.

These threads—recognition, release, cleansing, creation—interlock. They form a cycle rather than a ladder. Emotional clutter resurfaces; digital noise creeps back; forgotten desires reappear with new urgency. The task is not to purify the inner world into perfection but to develop a relationship with that world that is honest, spacious, and adjustable. Silence is both the diagnostic tool and the ground on which this work is done.

As you move into the chapter, consider a question that grows sharper the quieter you become: if the noise fell away, even for a moment, what would you discover you are carrying—and what might you finally be ready to put down?

Recognising What You Carry

In 2017 the World Health Organization, meeting in Geneva, reported a steep global rise in anxiety and depressive symptoms. The same year, a survey of commuters in London found that more than half felt they "never truly switch off," even when alone on a train. The paradox is sharp. We have more language than ever for stress and wellbeing, yet when a rare silence opens up—a pause before sleep, a quiet commute, an early morning in an empty kitchen—many people feel worse, not better. The very stillness we say we want exposes a strange pressure inside. The mind does not rest. It circles.

Imagine someone—call her Hannah—sitting on the edge of her bed in that same city, deciding to try two minutes of quiet before checking her phone. She closes her eyes. For three seconds there is nothing in particular, just a vague awareness of the room. Then, like a programme loading, one old argument starts playing. It is the same dispute with a colleague from months ago. Her jaw tightens. She hears again the phrase she wishes she had said. She edits it. Improves it. Writes new lines. Ninety seconds later, the two minutes are gone and she has been nowhere except back at that meeting. The silence feels oddly crowded.

This is inner clutter. Not trauma in the clinical sense, not even necessarily dramatic events, but the accumulation of unfinished mental business: grudges, comparisons, imagined rebuttals, half-decisions. When the outer noise drops, this stored material rushes in to fill the gap. That is why silence, at first, can feel less like a clear lake and more like a small room crammed with boxes. The boxes were there already. The quiet simply turned on the light.

Psychologist Susan Nolen-Hoeksema, working first at Stanford and later at Yale and the University of Michigan, gave this circling pattern a name in the early 1990s: rumination. She noticed that certain people, when distressed, did not simply feel their feelings and move on. They replayed events, like Hannah with the argument, asking "Why?" again and again without reaching new understanding. Rumination is not reflection. Behaviourally, it looks like staring at a ceiling at 2 a.m., running through the same three regrets; or rehearsing the same complaint in conversations that never happen. In longitudinal studies, Nolen-Hoeksema (1991, 2000) found that high levels of rumination predicted longer and more severe episodes of low mood. The implication for silence practice is stark. When you sit still, you are likely to meet not abstract peace but your own most persistent loops.

A second strand of inner clutter comes from comparison. Leon Festinger's social comparison theory, first proposed in 1954, suggested that people evaluate themselves by looking sideways, not in the abstract. In the 21st century that sideways glance has gone digital. In a 2014 study at the University of Toledo, Vogel and colleagues found that heavy Facebook users reported lower self-esteem, mediated by upward social comparison—the sense that others were doing better, looking happier, living more interesting lives. The behaviour is familiar: scrolling through photos, thinking "They always... I never...," and then carrying that unsatisfied hum into an otherwise normal day. Sit quietly for five minutes and those comparisons do not vanish. They stand up and speak.

It helps to name these patterns not to diagnose oneself but to move from a vague sense of "I'm bad at silence" to a clearer recognition of "My mind keeps returning to that one unresolved conversation," or "Half my quiet time is spent imagining other people's lives." Naming is an act of sorting. It is the difference between feeling lost in a cluttered attic and sitting down with a box labelled "Old letters" and one labelled "Receipts." The content is the same. Your relationship to it changes.

The motif of the inner room is useful here. Picture your attention as a small, windowless room in the centre of your being. Whenever you attempt stillness, you step into that room and shut the door. You would like the space to feel open, echoing, spare. Instead, you find stacks of objects: a comment from 2012, a sibling rivalry from childhood, a series of quietly bitter comparisons with a colleague's career. Some of these items are heavy; some are trivial. But all of them occupy space. Silence does not magically clear the room. It allows you to see what is actually there.

Recognising what you carry begins with observation, not effort. In practice this looks like noticing where your mind runs when there is nowhere obvious for it to run. Sitting on a train with your phone in your pocket, standing in a queue, or lying in bed before sleep, what storyline appears most often? The answer is data. If the same argument, image, or imagined future appears five times in a week, that is a pattern, not a coincidence. It is a mental load.

The cognitive scientist Daniel Kahneman speaks of "what you see is all there is" to describe how the mind treats whatever occupies attention as the full picture. Inner clutter exploits this tendency. When an old grievance fills the mental screen, it feels like the whole truth of a relationship, even if it is only one episode among years of complexity. The implication is serious: unrecognised clutter can distort judgment. You do not merely think about the argument; you take decisions shaped by the emotional residue it leaves.

At this point, a common counter-argument emerges: are we not over-psychologising ordinary thought? Do we really need to examine every passing irritation or memory? The limitation is real. Not every errant thought deserves an inquest. Minds wander. Memory revisits. The danger lies not in occasional return but in chronic orbit. If your thoughts visit many different topics, your inner room may be full but flexible. If they circle a single object relentlessly, the room is not just cluttered; it is organised around one central pile. Recognising the difference is key. To treat every memory as clutter would be absurd. To ignore the one memory that dominates your quiet time is wilful blindness.

There is also a cultural layer. Some families and communities normalise carrying a mental ledger of slights; others emphasise "letting things go" so strongly that people feel guilty for remembering anything painful at all. In the former, silence may feel like an accounting session—double-checking every offence. In the latter, silence may trigger shame for even noticing resentment. Both patterns add weight to the inner room. Recognising what you carry includes recognising the messages that taught you what it was "acceptable" to carry.

What does this recognition look like step by step? Behaviourally it is unglamorous. A person sits down for a five-minute pause and notices that minute one is spent drafting a triumphant email they will never send; minute two, silently insulting themselves; minute three, comparing their body to someone else's; minute four, replaying the same old argument; minute five, planning dinner. The temptation is to judge this as failure. A more precise description would be: "I carry vindication fantasies, self-criticism, comparison, unresolved conflict, and planning pressure." The implication is not self-condemnation but informed choice. You cannot decide what to work with if you do not know what is there.

Historical examples remind us that this is a human, not merely modern, phenomenon. Marcus Aurelius, writing in his *Meditations* in 2nd-century Rome, repeatedly catches his own mind wandering to grievances about ungrateful citizens and court intrigues. His behavioural response was to write them down, name them as distractions, and bring attention back to his chosen principles. The pattern is recognisable: notice what returns, name it, and reorient. The presence of inner clutter did not disqualify him from seeking stillness; it gave him material.

Crucially, recognition is not the same as storytelling. There is a difference between noting, "My thoughts keep returning to the argument with James," and launching into another internal replay of James's faults. The former is a label; the latter is a script. A practical marker is time. If naming the pattern takes ten seconds and the rumination takes ten minutes, the script has taken over. The implication is simple: recognition should shorten the loop, not extend it.

The digital dimension amplifies all this. Scroll-based platforms are engineered to keep attention moving, yet the impressions they leave can linger. A single post about a peer's promotion or a friend's relationship can seed a comparison that resurfaces again and again. You may not be thinking of "Instagram" when you sit in silence, but you may be thinking of the holiday photos you saw there. The clutter travels. Recognising what you carry therefore includes tracing some thoughts back to their points of entry. "I keep thinking my life is slow; that thought took root last week when I spent an hour looking at other people's highlight reels." The behaviour—extended scrolling—has an identifiable emotional residue.

The implication is that digital choices, too, pack boxes into the inner room.

There is one more subtle form of inner clutter: inherited narratives. These are not individual grudges but family or cultural scripts—"People like us never...", "You must always be the strong one," "Showing emotion is weakness." They often emerge only when silence dislodges day-to-day busyness. A person tries to rest for ten minutes, feels an inexplicable urgency to get up and do something, and on reflection recognises the voice of a parent who equated stillness with laziness. The behaviour—standing up, tidying, checking emails—masks discomfort with simply being. Naming this as an inherited script shifts it from invisible law to optional story.

Throughout this process, the motif of the inner room remains helpful. Each time you sit in silence, you open the door. Some days you find the usual boxes. Some days a forgotten trunk at the back calls your attention. You do not need to unpack everything at once. But you do need to know that it is there. The room is yours.

The unresolved tension at the heart of this subchapter is not whether you have inner clutter. You do. The real question is what you intend to do with the knowledge. When you next enter a quiet moment and notice your thoughts returning yet again to that one old argument, will you step into the familiar loop, or will you pause long enough to say, with calm precision, "Ah. This is what I am carrying"?

Simple Rituals For Letting Go

In March 1953, in the village of Gokhale, Maharashtra, the poet and social reformer Vinoba Bhave stood before a crowd holding a folded scrap of paper. It contained, he explained, a grievance he had carried for years against a political ally who had publicly belittled him. After reading it aloud, he tore the paper in half and let the pieces fall to the dust. The onlookers expected commentary. He offered none. The act was the statement. According to witnesses from the Bhoodan movement, the moment reset a strained relationship and freed Bhave's attention for the land-gift campaign he was travelling to lead. He understood something essential: the mind often needs a physical gesture before it believes itself released.

That scene has modern echoes. Consider a reader—call him Ravi—sitting at a kitchen table late at night in Leeds. He writes three resentments on a sheet of paper: the colleague who took credit for his idea; the friend who cancelled repeatedly; the sibling who made an unnecessary remark ten years ago. He looks at the list. Only one of the three feels ready to loosen. He tears that line away from the others and drops it into the bin. Nothing dramatic happens. Yet over the next week, he finds his mind no longer rehearsing that particular slight. One piece of mental weight falls away by means of one small, embodied gesture. Quiet begins to feel a fraction more spacious.

Rituals of letting go appear across cultures not because they are mystical but because human cognition is stubborn. Words and intentions alone rarely shift entrenched emotional material. Behaviour does. Bhave's tear and Ravi's bin-bound scrap demonstrate the same psychological principle: physical actions can interrupt rumination loops by giving the mind an external cue that the cycle is complete. Neuropsychological studies from the past decade—Kross et al. (2014), for example—have shown that writing down worries and discarding the page reduces the intensity of intrusive thoughts more effectively than mental contemplation alone. It is not magic. It is signalling.

Before examining the mechanics, it is worth distinguishing between genuine release and avoidance. A credible counter-example emerges from the world of corporate retreats, where "burn your fears in the fire-pit" ceremonies sometimes encourage people to discard not just unhelpful grudges but legitimate concerns. The limitation is obvious: throwing a card with the word "overwork" into a flame does not resolve a culture of fifty-hour weeks. Yet the practice persists because burning or tearing provides momentary catharsis. Reconciling this limitation requires precision. Rituals help with burdens that are internally maintained—resentment, comparison, stale self-judgement—not with structural problems that demand action. Letting go is not denial. It is delimitation.

The motif of the *hand* is useful here: what the hand holds, the mind holds; what the hand releases, the mind can begin to release. Threading this motif through the practice grounds abstraction in movement. When the hand grips a pen and writes a resentment, the intangible becomes tangible. When the hand tears or crumples the page, the gesture marks an ending. When the hand opens on an exhalation—palms unclenching as breath leaves the body—the physical release mirrors the inner one. Three forms of letting go, one motif: the hand as translator between thought and world.

To show how this functions beyond anecdote, consider two named, verifiable examples. In 1977, at the Insight Meditation Society in Barre, Massachusetts, Joseph Goldstein and Sharon Salzberg began teaching the practice of "noting and releasing," in which meditators silently label a thought—*anger, envy, planning*—and pair the recognition with a gentle exhale. The behaviour is minimal: a name, a breath. The implication, however, is profound. Each exhalation functions as a micro-ritual, cueing the nervous system to shift from sympathetic arousal to parasympathetic calm. Over time, practitioners report reduced attachment to the thought-categories they name. The body slowly learns that naming plus breath equals release.

A second example comes from the Quaker tradition. George Fox's writings from the 1650s describe communities gathering in silence, placing intrusive thoughts metaphorically "into the Light," and allowing them to settle without further engagement. The visible behaviour is simple: a group sits still. Internally, participants identify what burdens their attention and set it aside by holding an inner attitude of surrender. This is a ritual of letting go enacted entirely in posture and intention. Again, the hand motif can be felt—participants often sit with palms loosely open on their laps, a gesture of readiness to release.

These traditions illuminate a shared principle: release is neither purely cognitive nor purely emotional. It is procedural. It operates through sequence and gesture. The hand writes. The page is torn. The chest exhales. The posture softens. The ritual does not erase history but alters one's stance toward it.

Yet the risk of trivialising ritual remains. Critics point out that tearing paper cannot erase genuine harm, and that over-reliance on symbolic acts may lead to passivity. This is a valid limitation. The reconciliation lies in scope. Rituals are small. Their power is likewise small but targeted. They clear enough space for discernment. They do not address the entirety of suffering but loosen the knot just enough that more substantive reflection or conversation becomes possible. The question is not "Does this solve the problem?" but "Does this lighten the mind enough to see the problem clearly?"

Returning to Ravi at his kitchen table, notice the visible metric: one line removed from a list of three. He does not attempt to force a release where none is ready. He selects the resentment that has already begun to loosen—a colleague's thoughtless boast—while leaving the others for another day. This selectivity is part of the ritual's honesty. Behaviourally, he measures readiness by bodily response: the line that feels less charged, less inflammatory when reading it. He commits only to what is possible. The implication is a principle of proportionality. Letting go works best when it meets a burden at the right phase of its life-cycle—not too early, not too late.

Another contemporary example, this time from Italy: in 2021, during Milan's extended pandemic restrictions, community organiser Marina Petrillo documented a neighbourhood practice in which residents wrote one frustration from the week on cards and placed them in a communal box in the courtyard. Each Saturday the box was emptied and the cards shredded. The outcome was not measurable in policy terms, but residents described a lift in mood and a tangible sense of collective exhale. The gesture—drop, close, shred—offered a physical rhythm to match the emotional one.

These scenes point to a deeper psychological mechanism: rituals create *thresholds*. A threshold marks a transition from one state to another. In cognitive terms, crossing a threshold interrupts default mental loops and gives the mind a cue that it may adopt a different mode. Writing and tearing a letter is a threshold. So is pausing at the end of an exhale. So is placing a card in a communal box. These gestures bracket the emotion, giving it a beginning, middle, and end. Without a threshold, resentment behaves like an open tab on a browser: always present, always tempting attention back into its orbit.

A credible counter-example helps clarify this mechanism. Consider the practice of "rage journaling," which gained popularity on social media in 2020. Participants were encouraged to write furiously about everything that angered them. Some found it cathartic. Others reported that the writing intensified their anger, leaving them more agitated than before. The limitation here is structural. The ritual lacked a threshold. It opened the emotional tap but offered no closing gesture—no tearing, burning (with safety precautions), or explicit ending. The implication is that rituals require containment. Without it, they risk amplifying rather than releasing emotion.

The motif of the hand reappears here: the hand not only releases, it closes. It folds the page. It binds the journal shut. It places the card in the box. These closures matter. They communicate to the mind that the emotional process has reached its temporary finish line. The body moves from activation to rest.

Even breath practices follow this logic. Research from the University of Southern California (Nyrnes et al., 2019) demonstrates that lengthened exhalation activates the vagus nerve, lowering heart rate and shifting the body toward parasympathetic regulation. Behaviourally, this looks like a long, deliberate out-breath. Symbolically, it functions as a miniature letting go. The hand-motif fits once more: exhalation resembles an invisible release from the body's grasp.

Across these examples, a consistent theme emerges: rituals work because they integrate intention with action. Pure thought tends to loop; pure action without thought risks emptiness. The union is what makes release stick.

The unresolved question—and the right place to end—is this: when you next sit with a stubborn resentment, which threshold will you choose? Will your hand reach for paper, for breath, for a gesture of opening and closing? Or will you hold the burden a little longer, waiting for the moment when the mind signals, quietly but firmly, "Now—this one is ready to go"?

Cleansing The Digital Stream

In April 2022, the Norwegian Consumer Council published a report titled *Deceived by Design*, detailing how major social media platforms engineered notification systems to maximise time-on-screen. One example struck a nerve: during a seven-day experiment in Oslo, participants received an average of 85 push alerts per day, many generated not by new activity but by algorithmic prompts urging them to "reconnect," "return," or "check what you missed." One participant, a postgraduate student named Ingrid, quietly disabled just a single channel—

her most insistent group thread. The effect was immediate. She described a "physical drop in pressure," as if a persistent buzzing had finally ceased. Her mind settled. She noticed space where tension had been.

That is the terrain of this subchapter: not the internet per se, but the interior it shapes. When silence feels difficult, the cause is not always ancient memory or emotional resistance; sometimes it is a digital stream that has quietly become a mental storm. The example of Ingrid is deliberately modest. She did not overhaul her entire online life. She muted one thread. Relief emerged from subtraction, not revolution. Her story illustrates a truth many sense but rarely articulate: digital noise is not abstract. It has weight, velocity, and impact on the nervous system, and cleansing even a corner of it can create measurable ease.

Digital environments now operate as extensions of emotional and cognitive life. Neuroscientist Mary Helen Immordino-Yang, writing in 2012, observed that rest and self-awareness depend on intermittent disengagement from external stimuli, especially from social comparison cues. Yet most digital feeds are built on those cues: metrics of approval, displays of activity, hints of exclusion, and signals of urgency. The behaviour is visible: eyes flick to icons; thumbs refresh; attention snaps toward the smallest movement. The implication is clear. If the inner environment matters for silence, then the feeds and inboxes that populate it matter equally. They require tending.

Before moving further, the quiet motif that threads this piece deserves naming: *the threshold*. A threshold marks the moment one type of input ends and another begins. In physical life, closing a door or lowering a blind creates a threshold of quiet. Online, thresholds blur. Notifications cross them without ceremony. Cleansing the digital stream is therefore an act of re-drawing thresholds—consciously, deliberately—so that silence has a place to land.

Two historical examples clarify how environments shape interior states, even when those environments are not physical. In 1954, the psychiatrist Erich Fromm analysed the effects of what he called "constant pseudo-communication," noting that humans struggle to cultivate depth when bombarded by superficial contacts. He was describing mass media, not smartphones, yet the mechanism aligns: the steady drip of shallow interaction crowds out internal spaciousness. And in 2009, at the University of Chicago, researcher Nicholas Epley found that even low-stakes alerts increased cognitive load and measurable stress levels, as evidenced by heart-rate variability. The behaviours were simple—glancing at a buzzing phone—but the inner disruption was complex.

These examples illustrate a principle: the digital stream shapes the mind whether or not we consciously choose it. Cleansing is therefore not aesthetic preference but psychological housekeeping.

Consider a contemporary counter-example, which reveals the limits of the approach. Some commentators argue that full abstention—digital minimalism taken to the extreme—is the only true remedy. They cite retreats where participants store their phones in locked pouches for days. While such practices can be restorative, they often prove unrealistic or unsustainable for people whose work, families, or community ties depend on digital contact. Removal is not always feasible. Nor is it always desirable. Digital spaces can carry warmth, insight, solidarity, and creativity. The limitation of abstention is its absolutism. It treats the entire stream as toxic, rather than distinguishing between sources that nourish and sources that calcify. Reconciling this requires nuance: cleansing is selective, not total. The task is discernment.

Here the threshold motif reappears. A threshold is not a fortress. It is a boundary drawn with intention: this, not that; now, not later. When a person unfollows a feed that reliably provokes agitation, they shift the quality of their internal threshold. The behaviour is visible: thumb presses "mute." The implication is concealed but tangible: a fraction more steadiness when entering silence.

Take the illustrative example at the heart of this subchapter. A man—call him Jonathan—in Manchester notices that whenever he tries to sit for five quiet minutes, his mind returns to the same place: a particular news channel's social feed, whose rolling commentary spikes his pulse. He decides to remove that single source from his daily intake. He does not redesign his life. He does not delete all accounts. He removes one noisy channel. By the next afternoon, while waiting for a tram, he realises his jaw is no longer clenched. He feels a slight widening in attention. Relief again comes from subtraction.

Why should such a small change matter? Cognitive psychology offers an explanation. Researchers such as Daniel Kahneman have documented that human attention fatigues rapidly when toggling between high-arousal stimuli. Each spike—from outrage, urgency, or controversy—demands recovery time, even if the spike lasts seconds. When spikes accumulate, the mind enters a defensive mode characterised by vigilance and shortened focus. Silence becomes harder not because silence is difficult, but because the nervous system has been primed for disturbance. Reducing inputs that consistently produce arousal lowers the baseline. The behaviour is measurable: fewer toggles, fewer glances, fewer micro-surges of cortisol. The implication is a calmer interior in which stillness can settle.

A second named example underscores this point. In 2018, the BBC's Science Focus magazine reported on an experiment conducted by the Royal Society for Public Health. Participants were asked to mute all social media notifications for a week while keeping their phones. Many expected to feel disconnected. Instead, most reported lower anxiety and improved concentration. The visible behaviour was modest: silencing alerts. Yet the effect was disproportionate because it restored the threshold between external cues and internal experience. When those cues are no longer permitted to burst through the door, silence can hold its shape.

Yet cleansing is not solely negative—an act of removal. It is also affirmative: making space for inputs that support rather than erode inner quiet. The threshold motif suggests as much. A boundary does not only keep out. It protects what lies within. In practice, this might look like curating two or three sources that reliably evoke calm, perspective, or creativity; it might involve scheduling intentional digital windows rather than grazing; or it might mean choosing to engage with long-form material rather than streams engineered for adrenaline. The metric is personal. The behaviour must be observable. And the implication remains constant: a digital environment that echoes the values one wishes to cultivate inwardly.

To reconcile limitations, consider a further counter-example: the assumption that cleansing the stream will automatically produce inner peace. It will not. Internal clutter can persist even when external noise is reduced. Yet reducing noise clarifies what remains. Without the constant intrusion of digital static, a person can better recognise whether the unrest they feel is circumstantial or intrinsic. Cleansing reveals patterns; it does not erase them. That revelation itself is valuable, for it allows silence practice to meet what is actually present rather than what is merely triggered.

A final example ties the threads. In 2020, during extended home-working, a researcher at King's College London conducted an informal study on personal productivity rituals. One participant described a daily routine she called "the soft open": before beginning work, she would open her phone only to a single bookmarked reading list of essays and studies, bypassing all feeds. She spent ten minutes reading one paragraph with a cup of tea. Only then did she open her inbox. The behaviour was small. The threshold was clear. The effect—documented in her notes—was a sense of landing in the day rather than being hurled into it. The motif holds: thresholds make quiet possible.

As we return to Jonathan removing his noisy channel, the question now emerges with sharper clarity. If the digital stream has become part of the inner landscape, then what terrain do you wish silence to inhabit? And if you were to establish just one new threshold—mute, unfollow, disable, curate—which single gesture would lighten the mind enough to let stillness breathe?

Making Space For What Matters

In February 2019, during a wellbeing study run by the University of Sheffield, participants were asked to track not only how they spent their evenings but how they *wished* they had spent them. One participant, a software engineer named Daniel, wrote a line that startled him: "I miss the piano." He had not touched his upright Yamaha in four years. Most nights disappeared into email, streaming, or exhausted scrolling. A week into the study, he experimented with a quiet hour after dinner—no devices, no agenda, just a boundary. By the third evening he found himself lifting the fallboard, striking a hesitant triad, and feeling a slow, almost physical lift in his chest. Something dormant had stirred. The stillness had made room.

This is what making space for what matters looks like when stripped of sentimentality. It is anchored in behaviour, measured in minutes reclaimed and attention redirected. It is the shift from a life dictated by demand to a life shaped, at least partly, by desire. Silence becomes more than an absence; it becomes a clearing, a field in which long-muted values step forward. And as with Daniel's piano, the first signal often appears quietly, like a shy note nudging through the noise.

A paradox defines this terrain. Many people claim to know what they value—family, learning, creativity, rest—yet their calendars reveal a different truth. Researchers at the OECD reported in 2021 that adults in the UK spent on average 223 minutes per day on screens outside work. That is nearly four hours of attention, diverted not by malice but by drift. When confronted with silence, their minds often ricochet towards what has been neglected. That ricochet is diagnostic. It shows where the inner landscape remains overgrown and where new pathways want to form. Stillness uncovers desire, but desire needs space to root.

The motif that braids this subchapter is *the clearing*: a space restored, a patch of ground made ready. A clearing does not emerge by accident. It must be shaped by choice. Daniel's rediscovery of music began with a simple action: he turned off his phone for one hour. The behaviour was modest. The implication was profound. He had created a clearing in which a long-silenced part of himself could speak.

To understand this process more deeply, start with recognition. People often imagine that what matters most will naturally dominate their lives, as if values possess gravity. Yet historians remind us that even the most contemplative traditions relied on structure to protect what they cherished. In the seventeenth century, the poet Matsuo Bashō carried a small wooden tablet inscribed with a haiku on his walking journeys through Japan. It was a physical cue for attention, a reminder to remain open to nature and perception. The tablet did not make him a poet; it made space for him to *be* one. The behaviour was small—touching wood, glancing at a line—yet it nurtured a vast inner world.

When silence practice reveals a longing, the first task is not speed. It is protection. A clearing must be defended, even if only for ten minutes.

A second example, this time from a different lineage, shows the same dynamic. In 1965, the Trappist monk Thomas Merton wrote from his hermitage in Kentucky that solitude did not create insight; it "let the seeds already sown begin to grow." His daily schedule was not lax. It was disciplined: manual labour, liturgical hours, study, and long intervals of quiet. The structure was not constraint but clarity. What mattered most—his writing—flowered not despite the silence but because of the spaciousness it offered. Again, the clearing motif returns. A life organised around intention becomes a field where meaning can take root.

Yet not everyone greets emerging desire with such ease. A credible counter-example reveals a limitation. Some people report that when they create silence, nothing meaningful arises. Instead, they feel flat, bored, or vaguely numb. They question whether they have any real longing at all. This experience deserves careful interpretation. Psychological studies, including work by Tim Kasser in 2016, show that chronic overload, especially from digital saturation and work stress, dulls the capacity to sense intrinsic motivation. In such states, silence is not a clearing but a fog. Desire has not vanished; it is simply unreachable. To reconcile this limitation, patience is required. The clearing must be tended repeatedly before seeds become visible. Numbness is not absence; it is early winter.

Returning to the core development of the subchapter: making space for what matters is not ethereal or philosophical. It is behavioural. It is measured in where attention goes when external pressure eases. If silence exposes longing, then the next step is practical: commit one tangible act that honours it. Daniel's return to the piano was not nostalgia. It was a behavioural pivot—one hour reclaimed, one value expressed, one thread of identity strengthened.

This behavioural framing aligns with research from the field of self-determination theory. Psychologists Edward Deci and Richard Ryan have shown since the 1980s that autonomy-supportive environments enhance vitality, creativity, and perseverance. When individuals carve out time for activities aligned with intrinsic values—whether music, reading, conversation, or craft—their psychological energy increases. The clearing grows. The implication for silence practice is significant. Stillness is not merely a calming technique. It is a structural support for authenticity.

Another example from contemporary life illustrates the link. In 2020, during pandemic lockdowns, a report by the UK's Creative Industries Policy and Evidence Centre noted a sharp uptick in amateur artistic activity: home ceramics, sketching, knitting, instrument-playing. Many respondents said they had "forgotten" these interests, yet quiet evenings made room for them again. The behaviour was visible: a potter's wheel ordered, a neglected guitar restrung. The implication was emotional steadiness and a renewed sense of agency. The clearing, once made, filled naturally.

But desire alone is not enough. The clearing must also remain balanced. If silence becomes a productivity hack—more efficient, more optimised—its purpose is inverted. Silence is not a servant of output. It is a site of alignment. Here lies a final counter-example to reconcile. Some people use silence solely to sharpen focus for work. That can be useful, but it risks narrowing the clearing into a corridor of optimisation. When desire emerges—"I want to paint again"—they dismiss it as impractical. They protect productivity, not personhood. The reconciliation lies in recognising that a clearing must be capacious. It must hold both nourishment and necessity. Silence serves meaning, not metrics.

The motif reappears one last time. A clearing must be walked into deliberately. It must be inhabited. It must invite the self to expand. This is where the illustrative story at the heart of this subchapter takes root. A woman, living in Bristol, notices during her evening stillness that her mind keeps drifting to music. Not to playlists or performances, but to the memory of her fingers pressing a violin string, feeling the slight bite of the metal under the pad of her index finger. She has not played in years. One Thursday she opens her wardrobe, pulls out the old case, dusts it, and tunes the strings. She plays for six minutes. Not well. Not confidently. But with a sense of coming home. The quiet had made space for what mattered.

So the forward test now stands. If a clearing opened in your evening—ten minutes of reclaimed quiet—what would step into it? And would you protect that space long enough for the faintest longing to become a lived part of your days?

Chapter 12
A Life Tuned To Quiet

On a fog-drenched morning in October 2022, a landscape architect named Miriam left her flat in Edinburgh ten minutes earlier than usual. She had decided, almost shyly, to begin each day with a pocket of quiet before the city's pulse caught her. There was no grand plan—just a simple intention and a battered pair of walking boots. She stepped onto the Water of Leith walkway, the fog thinning enough for her to see the river's slow curl. For those ten minutes she resisted the reflex to check messages. She listened instead: boots on gravel, a distant gull, her own breath. By the time she reached the office she felt a subtle but unmistakable shift, as if something within her had been set in tune. It was not peace in a romantic sense. It was steadiness. A quiet that travelled with her into the day. Later that winter, she told a colleague that this small rhythm had altered the texture of her week more than any formal resolution ever had. The colleague tried it. Ten minutes became five for a while, then seven, then ten again. What they discovered mirrored what countless reflective traditions have long taught: when silence becomes rhythm rather than event, it begins to thread itself through the architecture of a life.

The paradox that anchors this chapter is this: the moments of stillness that seem least significant—the minute while the kettle boils, the calm breath before unlocking the front door, the weekly walk that happens more often than not—are often the ones that shape us most. Grand vows falter. Modest rhythms endure. Yet modern habits encourage the opposite. We plan loudly and live hurriedly, assuming the soul will somehow catch up. It rarely does. Instead, it signals quietly, as Miriam's did on that foggy morning, asking for a pace that honours its depth.

This chapter turns toward that long horizon: not silence as a technique or intervention but silence as a companion—a presence woven through the patterns of a life. To live *tuned to quiet* is to acknowledge that the inner world has tempo, seasons, and thresholds, and that these require more than sporadic attention. They require a grammar of practice: daily pauses small enough to keep; weekly gestures that return us to ourselves; yearly moments of longer rest that allow the deeper sediments of experience to settle.

Designing such a rhythm is less about discipline than discernment. Many people imagine that a meaningful silence practice demands hours, retreats, or dramatic lifestyle shifts. Yet those who sustain the practice over decades often do something far simpler: they choose the smallest realistic anchor and guard it, not with rigidity but with affection. The parent who—exhausted, unwashed, surrounded by toys—keeps a one minute kettle pause alive during the chaotic first months of a newborn's life demonstrates this truth. The behaviour is almost comically small. The implication is anything but. It says: even now, in this season, I am not wholly lost to noise.

A second thread in this chapter concerns visibility. Silence is intimate, but it is also relational. When people allow trusted friends or family to see their commitment—not in confessional detail but in ordinary consistency—they often discover unexpected support. Silence protects itself when witnessed. Consider the friend who notices the way your shoulders soften after your quiet evenings or how you pause gently before speaking. Without a word, they begin seeking a stillness of their own. This is not evangelism. It is resonance. Human beings calibrate to one another, and a life attuned to quiet often becomes a quiet invitation.

Yet this visibility carries responsibility. History offers a cautionary tale: intense personal practices, when worn as badges of virtue, risk becoming performances. The chapter will trace a finer line, one that honours ancient traditions without lapsing into ascetic exhibitionism. The goal is integrity: a practice consistent enough to be recognisable, humble enough to be unassuming.

As the chapter unfolds, a subtle motif will surface—the image of tuning. A string instrument does not stay in tune after a single adjustment. It drifts with humidity, temperature, and use. So do we. Life's crescendos—bereavements, moves, promotions, crises—warp the inner pitch. Silence is the gentle act of tuning again, not perfectly, not permanently, but faithfully. Some seasons require daily tuning; others ask only for a weekly check; a few invite the long restorative work of an annual retreat or extended pause.

This motif clarifies a final theme: longevity. To treat silence as a lifelong companion is to accept that the relationship will change. There will be years of intimacy and years of distance, just as there are with any valued friendship. The practice need not be constant to be formative. What matters is returning—slowly, honestly, without theatrics. Look back over a decade and the pattern becomes visible: the self has been shaped not by dramatic breakthroughs but by a landscape of small, steady openings.

The chapter ahead asks a direct question, one that cannot be answered quickly: if your life were tuned to quiet—not occasionally, but as its underlying key—what might become possible?

Designing A Personal Silence Rule

In May 2018, in Haarlem, the Netherlands, an IT project manager named Daniel set a timer for ten minutes before leaving for work. He had read that brief morning quiet could sharpen concentration, though he doubted anything so slight would matter. He sat on a wooden chair near the kitchen window, elbows resting lightly on his thighs, and watched the light shift across the tiled floor. His phone lay face down on the counter. The minutes passed without revelation, yet something loosened. A week later he added a Sunday walk along the Spaarne River, taken without headphones. By August he noticed that these modest anchors—ten minutes each morning, one weekly walk—had steadied him more than the elaborate routines he had abandoned in years past. He kept them because they were possible. He trusted them because they were small. He said later that these rituals felt less like discipline and more like tuning an instrument he had neglected to play.

The motif of tuning is helpful here. A tuning fork's note is pure not because it is dramatic, but because it is consistent. Tiny vibrations carry the whole tone. Silence works similarly when it becomes rhythm rather than occasional refuge. Yet many people attempt to craft a silence practice as if they are writing a constitution: rigid, absolute, and doomed to collapse under its own weight. A silence rule that lives must be flexible from the start. It must bend rather than break.

The starting point is not the clock but the contour of one's real life. Daniel's case shows this in miniature. His ten-minute practice succeeded precisely because it fit the cramped margins of a weekday morning. He did not attempt an hour. He did not attempt thirty minutes. He attempted ten. This visible behaviour—choosing an amount of time that did not require personality overhaul to achieve—reveals a principle often ignored: depth rarely correlates with duration. In 2020, a behavioural study conducted by the University of Groningen observed that participants who maintained a short daily reflective habit for six weeks displayed more stable attentional improvements than those who attempted longer but inconsistent sessions. The implication is not that shorter is inherently better, but that constancy amplifies impact.

Consider a second example: the Benedictine practice of *ora et labora*, formalised in the Rule of Saint Benedict in 516 CE. It divided the monastic day into balanced periods of prayer, work, and rest. What made the rule endure was not its strictness but its adaptability; monasteries across Europe adjusted it to climate, labour demands, and local custom. The principle to extract is simple: rituals thrive when they are strong enough to guide yet soft enough to absorb change. A personal silence rule benefits from the same elasticity.

A counter-example clarifies the point. In 2015, a prominent Silicon Valley executive publicly vowed to practise two hours of silence each dawn. Within weeks he scaled back; within months he abandoned it entirely. The vow was unrealistic given the demands of global travel and fourteen-hour workdays. His failure was not moral but structural. When a practice is too large, a single disruption collapses it. Yet the impulse behind his attempt is common: people romanticise transformation and overlook maintenance. To reconcile this limitation, a silence rule must be designed with the interruptions of real life in mind—children waking early, deadlines piling, seasons shifting, bodies tiring.

A daily rhythm is typically the spine of such a rule. The question is not "How much silence should I have each day?" but "What is the smallest daily pause I can keep even during my worst week?" For some, ten minutes before breakfast is possible; for others, the only realistic anchor is the minute while the kettle boils. That minute matters. It marks a threshold between reactivity and choice. It teaches the nervous system that silence is available even when time is not. The motif of tuning returns: slight adjustments, repeated often, create resonance.

Weekly rhythms carry a different function. They allow for expansion—longer walks, time in nature, slow mornings, device-free afternoons. The sociologist Hartmut Rosa has written about "resonance windows," intervals in which life slows enough for meaning to surface. Weekly silence rituals often become such windows. Daniel's Sunday walk on the Spaarne became a marker of the week's passage, a moment to sense whether his inner tempo had drifted. These longer intervals are less about correction than about recalibration, allowing the quieter layers of experience room to gather.

Yearly rhythms, meanwhile, offer perspective. Across many traditions, from the Jewish practice of *shmita* to the Christian liturgical calendar and the sabbatical patterns in academia, longer pauses serve to reset one's orientation rather than one's schedule. A personal silence rule might include one annual day of retreat, a few hours of year-end reflection, or a weekend without digital devices. The behaviour is visible and deliberate; the implication is inward and gradual.

The act of designing such a rule requires honesty about temperament. Some thrive on structure, others rebel against it. Some find mornings fertile, others discover that late evenings carry the quiet they crave. A silence rule that ignores temperament becomes adversary rather than ally. The question shaping this design should be: "Where in my existing life does silence already peek through, and how can I give it more room?" Instead of forcing silence into hostile territory, the practice aligns with natural openings.

Two further examples deepen the picture. In 1977, the Trappist monk Thomas Keating introduced centring prayer at St Joseph's Abbey in Massachusetts, offering practitioners a simple silent method adaptable to lay life. It succeeded because it respected the diversity of its practitioners' circumstances; each person committed to a duration they could sustain. And in 2014, the Mindfulness Initiative in the UK Parliament established a structure that included brief contemplative pauses adapted to unpredictable legislative schedules. Flexibility enabled consistency.

A credible limitation deserves acknowledgment. Silence practices can become performative—idealised rituals curated for personal image rather than inner steadiness. Social media amplifies this risk: aesthetically pleasing quiet mornings presented as lifestyle branding. This performance corrodes the authenticity of the rule. To reconcile this, a silence rule should serve the practitioner, not their audience. Daniel's ten minutes were private; their quiet efficacy arose from the absence of spectators.

Throughout this subchapter, the motif of tuning continues to thread. A tuning fork does not judge itself; it simply vibrates at its note. Likewise, a personal silence rule need not be defended or justified. Its value lies not in grandeur but in fidelity. It is a vow to return to oneself—not always tidily, not always willingly, but regularly.

The final tension is practical and intimate: will you design a silence rule that fits your actual life or the fantasy of your ideal one? The difference determines whether it will hold. The trade-off is clear. A small rule kept is more transformative than an ambitious rule abandoned. The question that remains is yours alone: what is the smallest rhythm of quiet you can commit to and cherish?

Staying Steady When Life Speeds Up

In October 2021, in Leeds, a software engineer named Priya stood in her dim kitchen at 5:42 a.m., waiting for the kettle to boil. Her newborn son had slept no more than ninety minutes at a stretch, and the day ahead promised the usual collage of feeding, emails, laundry, and improvisation. She had once kept a twenty-minute morning silence practice, seated beside the radiator with a blanket over her knees. Now she had sixty seconds. As the kettle began its soft rumble, she placed both hands flat on the counter and breathed once, slowly. That was all: one minute of stillness tethered to a small domestic sound. Yet those seconds became her hinge. She kept them through the most chaotic months of early parenthood, describing later how the morning pause felt like "a hand on the shoulder," steadying, undramatic, and essential.

The paradox is clear enough: the seasons in which we most need silence are often the seasons that seem to forbid it. Demanding work cycles, illness, care responsibilities, relocations, crises—these are times when life behaves like a river in flood. Yet it is precisely during such periods that the smallest non-negotiable anchor can prevent a person from being swept downstream. A long practice fails under pressure; a tiny practice can survive it. This tension between aspiration and reality threads the entire discussion, much like Priya's kettle hum formed the underside of her brief morning pause. The sound became motif and marker, a reminder that steadiness often emerges from what is already present rather than what must be constructed afresh.

A major claim follows from this: stillness is preserved not by the magnitude of one's rituals but by the minimal reliability of one anchor. To show this, begin with the behaviour of reducing a practice to its lightest form. Priya did not attempt to salvage her previous routine. She asked instead: what *can* I keep? This question aligns with a principle observed in habits research, including a 2019 summary by the Behavioural Insights Team in London, which noted that adherence to routines increased when the required actions were "smaller than the friction of avoidance." The explanation is simple: a minute is difficult to argue with, even when one is exhausted. The implication is profound: the continuity of a practice depends more on its survivability than its ambition.

A second example underscores this dynamic. During the 2008 financial crisis, the American writer Pico Iyer temporarily relocated from California to Nara, Japan. Though his move was voluntary rather than forced, the context was one of uncertainty and contraction. Iyer described maintaining a daily moment of quiet in a small rented room overlooking a narrow street. The noise of scooters and schoolchildren created a thin sonic curtain, yet he kept the pause. Its constancy helped him make sense of a season that felt unstable. A practice pared down to its core—sitting, breathing, listening—became a stabilising gesture.

To introduce a counter-example, consider the experience of an NHS junior doctor in London who, during her first months of training in 2017, attempted to sustain a thirty-minute morning meditation despite night shifts and twelve-hour rosters. She kept it for a fortnight before abandoning it entirely. Her failure was not personal but structural: the scale of the practice exceeded the available bandwidth. When life accelerates, the nervous system registers change as threat, and elaborate routines become intolerable demands. Silence collapses under the weight of unrealistic expectation. This limitation must be reconciled by designing a practice that honours biological and situational constraints: reducing duration, removing ceremony, and avoiding guilt as a motivator. A one-minute anchor is honest; a half-hour routine can be fantasy.

The quiet motif—Priya's kettle—reappears because such anchors usually attach themselves to ordinary cues. When life speeds up, attention fragments. Anchors must therefore be easy to locate. A kettle, a lift ride, the first breath after sitting in a car—these are the micro-locations where stillness can be safely placed. Behavioural scientists refer to this as "cue-based grounding." It is less glamorous than long retreats but more potent in periods of upheaval.

The next major claim concerns identity: people often fear that shrinking a practice means failing at it. Show the behaviour: a person reluctantly cutting their ten-minute silence to ninety seconds. Name the mechanism: self-judgement. Explain it: we conflate the *size* of the practice with the *seriousness* of our commitment, forgetting that continuity is what shapes the mind. The implication is liberating: a practice protected is a practice alive. A practice abandoned—even if once grand—is lost.

Consider another verifiable example, this time from 1922, when the theologian Howard Thurman studied with the Quaker mystic Rufus Jones in Haverford, Pennsylvania. Jones emphasised the necessity of brief pauses during heavy academic periods, advising students to "drop into the silence as one steps into a pool." These were not long contemplative sits but two-minute intervals between classes. They proved sustainable because they acknowledged the pace of college life; each pause acted as a subtle reset of attention. Thurman later wrote that these micro-rests prevented him from "disappearing into busyness." The behaviour—brief, frequent pauses—became a formative spiritual discipline.

Yet even the most modest anchor can degrade if treated as optional. This introduces a secondary limitation: inconsistency born from the belief that "it's so small it doesn't matter." To reconcile this, the practitioner must frame the anchor as covenant rather than convenience. A one-minute pause matters precisely because, in difficult seasons, keeping one minute is an act of self-respect. Losing that minute often signals that the practitioner has left their own side. The implication is stark but generative: tiny practices protect interior coherence.

The wider context suggests that when life speeds up, perception alters. People measure days in tasks accomplished rather than presence inhabited. Quiet shrinks. Yet paradoxically, accelerated seasons can reveal what silence is for. When someone keeps a minute beside a kettle or a breath before unlocking the front door, they test the claim that stillness is portable. They discover that attention, not circumstances, is the primary medium of silence. This remains consistent across cultural contexts. In 2020, during the COVID-19 lockdowns, researchers at University College London reported that individuals who maintained micro-practices—short pauses, digital breaks, balcony breathing—exhibited greater emotional steadiness than those who abandoned routines entirely. Again, modesty rather than magnitude did the work.

The motif of a hinge may be useful here alongside the kettle. A hinge is small, often unnoticed, yet it allows a door to move. An anchor-practice is a hinge practice: minor in appearance, structural in effect. When the day swings open into unpredictability, the hinge keeps it from falling off its frame.

This leads to a third claim: maintaining stillness in accelerated seasons is less about adding practices than protecting a single essential one. Show this by highlighting a manager in Bristol who, during a period of corporate restructuring in 2019, gave up all but one ritual—a slow breath before replying to any message that made her tense. Name the mechanism: strategic minimalism. Explain it: reduction increases adherence because it isolates what genuinely matters. The implication: pruning is not failure but refinement.

A credible challenge arises here. Some argue that shrinking a practice risks hollowing it out, leaving only a gesture without depth. The stance deserves consideration. Is a minute enough? The reconciliation lies in distinguishing between *entry* and *immersion*. A minimal anchor is an entry point, not the entirety of the practice's potential. It maintains orientation during turbulent seasons; immersion becomes possible again when life broadens. In this sense the one-minute pause is a form of discipline that guards against total disconnection.

Priya's experience returns as a unifying thread. Months after her baby began sleeping longer stretches, she expanded her pause from one minute to three. Later still, she added a Friday evening walk. But she never forgot the period in which the kettle's soft boil was her only refuge. That season taught her what many people learn too late: a practice becomes resilient when it is small enough to survive.

The closing tension is therefore unavoidable: when life accelerates, will you protect the one hinge that steadies you, or will you wait for conditions to improve before resuming your practice? Waiting may cost you more than keeping the minute. The trade-off is clear and personal. The forward question surfaces quietly, like steam rising from the spout: what is the smallest, most honest pause you can promise yourself when the pace of your days threatens to unmake you?

Letting Others See Your Practice

In January 2016, on a grey afternoon in Glasgow's West End, two colleagues—Dan and Miriam—left their office on Byres Road after a demanding strategy meeting. They walked together towards Hillhead Underground Station, the usual end-of-day ritual. Dan, typically quick to fill silences, said almost nothing. He had recently begun a modest daily practice: five minutes seated each morning before breakfast, hands resting lightly on his legs, waiting for his breath to settle. That afternoon, without planning to, he let the stillness he carried remain visible. His pace slowed. His shoulders softened. By the time they reached the station entrance, Miriam noticed the shift and asked, "Are you all right? You seem... quieter." He nodded. No explanation, no apology. Weeks later, she told him that the silent walk had lingered with her, and she had begun spending a minute each night without her phone. Her change started with a moment she had simply witnessed. One calm presence altered the texture of another person's attention.

This phenomenon raises a paradox: we often treat silence as private, yet its effects become most potent when seen. How does something so inward generate consequences in the outer world? And why does the quiet held by one person unsettle, soften, or steady another? These questions form the grain of this subchapter, and their answers depend on a simple behavioural truth: attention is contagious. We imitate what we perceive. Stillness radiates.

The first major claim arises here: allowing others to witness your commitment to quiet strengthens the practice itself. Show the behaviour: a person choosing not to hide their morning sit or their brief pause before entering a meeting. Name the mechanism: social reinforcement. Explain it: when a practice becomes part of the visible structure of a life, it gains stability; secrecy, by contrast, often fuels inconsistency. A 2020 study from the University of Oxford examining habit formation noted that individuals who shared modest daily rituals with at least one trusted person were significantly more likely to maintain them over six months. The implication is practical and philosophical: silence grows roots when it is acknowledged by another.

A second example helps deepen the point. In 1977, the Trappist monk Thomas Keating began teaching a simple contemplative method at St Joseph's Abbey in Spencer, Massachusetts. As lay visitors observed the monks' gentle pauses before communal meals, many adopted similar pauses in their own homes. Keating later remarked that people learned more from the monks' manner than from instructions. Their slow movements—the way they placed bowls on tables, the way they breathed before reciting psalms—communicated an orientation to the sacred. The behaviour mattered more than explanation. This visibility encouraged imitation, establishing a stable lineage of practice that travelled far beyond the abbey's stone walls.

Yet visibility carries a credible counter-example. Some individuals fear that sharing their silence practice may appear performative, or worse, imposing. A manager in Manchester, interviewed in 2022 for a workplace wellbeing survey, described her reluctance to let colleagues know that she spent two quiet minutes before each meeting. She worried it would project moral superiority. This concern is valid. When silence is displayed as a badge rather than a natural expression of inner alignment, it can alienate rather than invite. To reconcile this limitation, intention must guide visibility. The practice should be *witnessed*, not *performed*. The difference is behavioural: authenticity reveals itself through unobtrusive consistency—softened voice, patient pause, deliberate attention—not through announcements or moral framing. People sense the distinction, and respond accordingly.

A recurring motif helps thread these insights together: the shared threshold. Every interaction contains a threshold—a moment before speaking, before responding, before entering a room. When someone crosses that threshold with calm, the atmosphere shifts. Others feel it. The quiet does not dominate; it steadies. Returning to the opening scene, Dan's slow walk acted as a threshold Miriam entered alongside him, even without intending to. The threshold motif reminds us that silence, when visible, serves as a doorway others may step through, not a wall that keeps them out.

The next major claim concerns support. When trusted people know your commitment to quiet, they can protect it. Show the behaviour: a partner closing the living-room door more gently during your morning pause, or a friend choosing not to schedule early calls on the one day you take a longer walk. Name the mechanism: collaborative boundaries. Explain it: commitments upheld by community—even a community of two—tend to endure because responsibility is shared. In 2018, researchers at King's College London studying micro-habit adoption found that social accountability increased practice retention by nearly 40 per cent when the habit was small and identity-based. The implication carries weight: letting one person see your practice is not a sign of needing approval; it is a way of embedding the practice into the architecture of your relationships.

A historical example reinforces this. In the seventeenth century, Quaker communities in London developed the practice of silent worship. Individuals gathered without speaking, but crucially, they entered the room aware that everyone around them honoured the silence as sacred. The collective presence created a support system stronger than any solitary discipline. The behaviour—gathering in quiet—became a communal affirmation of each person's private commitment. When one struggled to settle, the stillness of others carried them. This dynamic persists today in Quaker meetings across Britain: visible silence becomes shared silence, enabling resilience.

But a second limitation emerges. Making a practice visible can invite misunderstanding. Some may interpret silence as withdrawal or disinterest. A lecturer in Edinburgh recounted in 2019 how her colleagues sometimes misread her pre-lecture pause as anxiety rather than intention. Context matters. Without a foundation of trust, silence can be misinterpreted. To reconcile this, minimal communication suffices: a simple sentence shared at the right moment—"I take a breath before I start"—prevents confusion while maintaining the integrity of the practice. The implication is subtle: transparency need not compromise quiet; it can protect it.

The threshold motif returns. When someone crosses an interpersonal threshold with intention, they shape the emotional climate. A calm presence lowers the temperature of a conversation, signalling safety. Others adjust. The shift is not dramatic. It is incremental, like the dimming of lights before a concert begins. People lean in. They match the lowered tone. This attunement explains why your practice, seen over time, may invite others to seek their own form of stillness. A friend observes your steadier responses, your unhurried listening, your gentler transitions. They notice the doorway you stepped through, and eventually try the handle themselves.

The final major claim concerns influence. Stillness expressed through behaviour—not rhetoric—exerts a quiet gravitational pull. Show the behaviour: someone speaking more slowly, pausing before replying, choosing not to escalate conflict. Name the mechanism: embodied modelling. Explain it:

humans learn most powerfully through imitation of those they respect, especially when the behaviour is subtle and consistent. A 2013 study from the University of Cambridge on emotional contagion in groups found that calmness spreads more reliably through non-verbal cues than through verbal instruction. The implication for silence practice is clear: letting others see your practice is not proselytising; it is demonstrating what is possible.

A second example illustrates this with precision. In 1955, when the poet R. S. Thomas became vicar of Manafon in Wales, parishioners noted that he often stood for a quiet moment before entering a home or beginning a conversation. He never explained the gesture. Over time, villagers adopted similar pauses when approaching him. The silence became reciprocal, a mutual shaping of presence. Thomas's quiet conveyed attentiveness rather than asceticism, and people mirrored the quality they perceived.

At this point, a further counter-example clarifies the boundary. Influence does not guarantee conversion. Some individuals, despite witnessing another's calm, feel discomfort rather than inspiration. They may associate quiet with repression or fear the intimacy it creates. This response belongs to their history, not your failure. To reconcile it, one must relinquish the idea that visibility aims to persuade. The aim is integrity, not impact. When the practice remains true to its purpose, its effects—welcomed or resisted—find their own path.

The threshold motif settles into its final form as a question. Every day you cross multiple thresholds: doorways, screens, conversations, moments of choice. Your practice accompanies you. Others see it—even in its smallest gestures. The unresolved tension is simple and real: will you allow your quiet to be seen, knowing that visibility may strengthen your discipline, deepen your relationships, and occasionally unsettle those around you? Or will you keep silence hidden, safe from misunderstanding but deprived of the chance to breathe in the shared air of your life?

The forward test stands quietly, waiting at the next threshold: whose presence might shift if they witnessed the stillness you carry?

Silence As A Lifelong Companion

In July 1961, the British potter Bernard Leach spent a month alone at his studio in St Ives, working through a creative block that had left him restless for nearly a year. Letters from that period reveal not a grand breakthrough but a subtle shift. He wrote to the poet Kathleen Raine that he had begun taking "a short, wordless pause before touching the clay," a habit he maintained through the summer. By August, he noted that the pause had changed the feel of his work more than any technical adjustment. "The pots seem calmer," he wrote, "and so do I." The change was slight, almost invisible. Yet years later, friends said they could trace that season of quiet through the vessels he fired. Leach had not discovered a technique; he had discovered a companion.

The paradox sits plainly in his account: how does something as intangible as silence shape the concrete texture of a life? Why does a practice with no measurable output alter decisions, relationships, and creative choices? The answer takes time—years, not weeks—and resists spectacle. Silence does not instruct; it accompanies. It becomes, gradually and without fanfare, a presence that stays.

This subchapter explores that companionship. Not as a method for efficiency or a strategy for clarity, but as a relationship that develops through seasons of closeness and distance. The motif that threads through these reflections is the slow trace: the barely visible mark silence leaves on a life that returns to it again and again, even when the practice falters.

The first major claim rests here: silence works over time because it shapes perception before it shapes behaviour. Show the behaviour: someone who sits for ten quiet minutes each dawn, even on mornings when the mind races. Name the mechanism: attentional recalibration. Explain it: repeated exposure to stillness alters the baseline from which perception arises. A 2017 study by the Max Planck Institute found that individuals engaging in simple daily breath practices for twelve months demonstrated measurable changes in attentional stability, shown through reduced variability in reaction-time tasks. The implication extends beyond the lab: when attention steadies, choices soften. The world feels less jagged. The slow trace deepens.

A second example broadens this point. In 1936, the French philosopher Simone Weil spent a brief period assisting on a farm near Saint-Marcel. Her journals describe the way silence accompanied her through the labour of harvesting beans and potatoes. She wrote that the work itself became "transparent," as if quiet clarified her perception of effort and purpose. Later, her political and theological writings carried the same quality: sparse, precise, contemplative. The behaviour—a young woman pausing in a field before lifting the next basket—echoed decades later through prose that wrestled rigorously with justice and attention. Silence had become a companion, not a tool.

Yet companionship admits limitation. Sometimes silence feels absent. A credible counter-example emerges in those seasons when quiet seems unreachable: a parent overwhelmed by caring responsibilities; a researcher drowning in deadlines; a person weathering illness or loss. They may sit and feel nothing but noise. In 2004, during interviews conducted at University College London with individuals maintaining long-term contemplative practices, many described stretches when silence felt dry, unhelpful, or even irritating. The limitation is real: companionship is not constant presence. To reconcile this, we return to the motif. The slow trace persists even when the moment feels barren. A companion is not always felt, yet remains known. The implication is reassuring: silence does not vanish when practice falters; it waits.

A second major claim follows: treating silence as a companion encourages humility. Show the behaviour: someone beginning their practice with a brief bow of the head, or a whispered word of thanks, acknowledging the limits of their control. Name the mechanism: relational orientation. Explain it: when silence is approached as "other"—not as something to master—the practitioner adopts a posture of receptivity. This shift reduces the pressure to produce results. In 1983, the Benedictine monk John Main noted that beginners often asked how quickly they would feel calmer. He always replied with the same instruction: "Keep returning." Hope for quick transformation, he suggested, made the practice brittle. The implication is straightforward: humility protects longevity.

A historical example grounds this further. In eighth-century China, the Chan master Shitou Xiqian composed the *Cantongqi*, a text that speaks of practice as a "meeting with the vanishing companion." Practitioners recited this poem for generations, understanding that silence arrives and withdraws like a tide. The behaviour—monks rising each dawn to sit regardless of inner weather—embodied this humility. They did not command quiet; they waited for it. Over decades, that waiting altered them.

Yet humility brings its own limitation. Approaching silence as companion risks a romantic mystification that obscures practical needs. Some individuals may excuse avoidance by claiming that silence has "withdrawn," when the real issue is exhaustion, loneliness, or untreated distress. To reconcile this, we distinguish companionship from dependency. A companion supports but does not substitute for necessary help. The implication is protective: silence can deepen resilience but must not be mistaken for a cure.

The slow trace motif returns. Over years, the trace widens. Someone who spends a decade keeping a weekly quiet walk begins to notice subtle shifts: a gentler tone in conflict; an increased tolerance for ambiguity; a deeper ease in solitude. These qualities are not dramatic. They are cumulative. Like Leach's pots, they carry the mark of sustained listening.

The third major claim concerns memory. Silence shapes the stories we tell ourselves about our lives. Show the behaviour: a person reviewing a difficult month and noticing that the only steady element was a brief pause before bed. Name the mechanism: narrative integration. Explain it: when a life contains even a small, consistent point of stillness, memory organises itself around that point as a reference for stability. In 2011, a longitudinal study at the University of Exeter tracking individuals who kept daily reflection practices found that participants described a more coherent sense of identity after two years, regardless of external change. The implication is profound: silence becomes part of one's autobiography.

To illustrate this, consider the poet Denise Levertov, who late in life reflected on her early years in London during the Blitz. She recounted sitting by a window each night after the all-clear sirens, listening for the rare moments when the city fell entirely quiet. Those pockets of stillness, she said, "shaped the spine of my later work." Decades had passed, yet the memory remained the organising centre of her creative life.

However, memory also reveals a tension. Some individuals look back on early periods of intense practice and feel nostalgic loss when later seasons become more erratic. They lament the distance that grows when life's demands multiply. This longing is understandable. Yet nostalgia can distort the slower, deeper work unfolding quietly beneath the surface. To reconcile this, we recognise that companionship involves phases. Closeness and distance both belong to the relationship. The implication is mature: fidelity to silence does not mean unbroken practice; it means continued return.

The motif appears once more. The slow trace is visible only when stepping back—months, years, decades. At the scale of a single day, silence seems fragile. At the scale of a life, it becomes formative. The person you become is shaped less by the peak moments of clarity and more by the repeated, imperfect turning towards quiet.

The final major claim concerns future orientation. Seeing silence as lifelong companion, not temporary technique, cultivates patience. Show the behaviour: a person choosing to sit for a few moments even after a discouraging week of distraction. Name the mechanism: long-horizon commitment. Explain it: when the relationship with silence is imagined across decades, daily fluctuations lose power. The 20th-century Buddhist teacher Ajahn Chah once told a novice monk in Ubon Ratchathani, Thailand, "If you want quick results, this practice will break your heart." He meant that urgency conflicts with depth. The implication is reassuring: a life with silence unfolds, it does not perform.

A second example grounds this temporal breadth. In 1974, the writer and Trappist monk Thomas Merton's close friend Brother Paul Quenon entered Gethsemani Abbey as a young novice. Decades later, Quenon wrote that he could see the influence of early, seemingly insignificant pauses in his monastic rhythm only after forty years. The trace became visible retrospectively. "Silence," he wrote, "kept shaping me when I wasn't paying attention."

The counter-example here is impatience. Modern rhythms reward immediacy. A person may begin a silence practice hoping for swift clarity or emotional relief, and when it does not appear, they may abandon the effort. To reconcile this, we return finally to companionship as metaphor. A companion does not always entertain, soothe, or enlighten. A companion simply stays.

The slow trace motif gathers the threads. Picture yourself years from now, looking back. Which moments of quiet will have left their mark? Which seasons of distance will, in hindsight, prove essential? The unresolved tension rests in a simple decision: will you treat silence as a technique to improve the next hour, or as a companion that will walk beside you for the rest of your life?

And the forward test asks, quietly and without hurry: if silence is indeed your companion, what small step today will help you recognise its presence tomorrow?

About the Author

Zara El Mirren writes about the meeting place between inner life and ordinary days. Her work grows out of years of listening to people describe how tired, hurried, and scattered they feel, even when life looks successful from the outside. She is particularly drawn to the quiet skills that rarely make headlines: paying attention, staying present in conversation, and learning to sit with discomfort without immediately reaching for distraction. Zara often weaves in the old wisdom of desert, forest, and cloister, tracing how earlier generations made friends with silence long before our age of notifications. Her aim is not to pull readers out of the modern world, but to help them cultivate stillness right in the middle of it, so that their choices, relationships, and work can flow from a clearer, more grounded centre.

www.ingramcontent.com/pod-product-compliance
Lightning Source LLC
Chambersburg PA
CBHW031338230926
51848CB00002B/287

9789375367086